RETROSPECTIVE MISCUE ANALYSIS

RETROSPECTIVE MISCUE ANALYSIS
Revaluing Readers and Reading

Yetta M. Goodman
Ann M. Marek

with contributions by Joel Brown, Sarah Costello, Alan Flurkey,
Debra Goodman, Kenneth S. Goodman, Sharon Hoge,
Dorothy Watson, David W. Weatherill, and Chris Worsnop

Richard C. Owen Publishers, Inc.
Katonah, New York

Library of Congress Cataloging-in-Publication Data

Goodman, Yetta M., 1931–
    Retrospective miscue analysis : revaluing readers and reading /
Yetta M. Goodman, Ann M. Marek, with contributions by Joel Brown . . .
[et al.].
        p.   cm.
    Includes bibliographical references and index.
    ISBN 1-878450-85-9 (pbk.)
    1. Miscue analysis.   2. Reading.   I. Marek, Ann M.   II. Title.
LB1050.33.G667   1996
372.4′14—dc20   95-23805
                                                 CIP

Photographs on the front and back cover are © 1995 by Joel Brown.

Every effort has been made to include complete bibliographic information on the texts
used in the retrospective miscue analysis sessions. Please excuse any omissions, and
please send any additional reference information to the publisher.

Portions from *The Reading Detective Club* by Debra Goodman are reprinted in Chapter 15
by permission of The Wright Group, 19201 120th Avenue NE, Bothell, WA 98011.
206/486-8011.

RICHARD C. OWEN PUBLISHERS, INC.
PO Box 585
Katonah, New York   10536

PRINTED IN THE UNITED STATES OF AMERICA

9 8 7 6 5 4 3 2 1

CONTENTS

Acknowledgments and Dedication / vii
Preface / ix

Part I   **Foundations for Revaluing** / 1

1   Profiles of Readers / 3
        Ann M. Marek and Yetta M. Goodman
2   Principles of Revaluing / 13
        Kenneth S. Goodman
3   Understanding the Reading Process / 21
        Ann M. Marek and Yetta M. Goodman
4   Retrospective Miscue Analysis / 39
        Yetta M. Goodman and Ann M. Marek

Part II   **Research in Revaluing** / 49

5   An Accomplished Professional: A Reader in Trouble / 51
        Ann M. Marek
6   Surviving Reading Instruction / 71
        Ann M. Marek
7   Retrospective Miscue Analysis in Middle School / 87
        Yetta M. Goodman and Alan Flurkey
8   Revaluing and Revelations / 107
        Alan Flurkey
9   Strategies and Metaphors / 119
        Joel Brown
10   Building Confidence in a Proficient Reader / 131
        Sarah Costello
11   Revealing Strategies for a Good Reader / 143
        David W. Weatherill

Part III   **Instructional Strategies for Revaluing** / 149

12   The Beginnings of Retrospective Miscue Analysis / 151
        Chris Worsnop
13   Reader-Selected Miscues / 157
        Dorothy Watson and Sharon Hoge
14   A Teacher/Researcher Uses RMA / 165
        Sarah Costello

15   The Reading Detective Club / 177
        Debra Goodman
16   At the Critical Moment: RMA in Classrooms / 189
        Yetta M. Goodman
17   Revaluing Readers and Reading / 203
        Ann M. Marek and Yetta M. Goodman

Appendices

A   Reading Interview / 209
B   RMA Session Organizer / 211
C   RMA Response Form / 212
D   Burke Interview Modified for Older Readers (BIMOR) / 213
E   Closing Interview / 215
F   Miscue Analysis Procedure I Coding Form / 216

References / 219
References for Stories Used by Readers / 221
Index / 223

ACKNOWLEDGMENTS AND DEDICATION

THIS BOOK IS THE CULMINATION of years of interactions with teachers and students who helped us to question our work, to challenge our thinking, and to maintain an inquiry stance toward understanding readers and the reading process. We must especially acknowledge the children, adolescents, and adults who came to us with views of themselves as learning disabled, dyslexic, bad readers, or nonreaders. They helped us revalue readers and the reading process as they revalued themselves as literate members of a democratic society. They have informed our work more than anyone else.

There are many people who have been instrumental in the development of retrospective miscue analysis over the years. Rather than mentioning individual names, we commend the process of collaboration through which we have learned to share research, experiences, and knowledge about the nature of reading with members of the teaching profession.

We thank Amy Haggblom and Richard Owen, who have provided consistent encouragement throughout the publication of this book. The National Council of Teachers of English Research Foundation furthered the development of retrospective miscue analysis with a research grant in 1989. We thank them for their support.

PREFACE

TWENTIETH-CENTURY SOCIETY HAS FOCUSED a great deal of attention on readers in trouble. Politicians assert that low levels of literacy contribute to poverty, crime, and unemployment. Bureaucrats and business leaders relate inadequate reading ability with low productivity in the workplace and assert that the former causes the latter. These negative misperceptions place a heavy burden on those for whom becoming literate has not been easy, and an equal burden on their teachers. Unfortunately, readers in trouble too often readily accept total responsibility for their so-called failure to learn and, in so doing, "they have become their own worst enemies" (K. Goodman, Chapter 2, this volume).

The number of persons in the United States who do not read as well as they or someone else would like has been difficult to estimate, but there is no doubt that many children, youth, and adults perceive themselves to be readers in trouble. They believe there are three kinds of readers in the world—good readers, bad readers, and nonreaders. To the good readers they ascribe unrealistic qualities: good readers know all the words they encounter; they never make mistakes; and they remember everything they read. Measured against this mythical good reader, many find themselves lacking. Because readers in trouble are consciously aware of their inadequacies, many become immobilized in their attempts to grow as readers.

This is a book about teachers and students revaluing the reading process and, at the same time, revaluing readers themselves. It is about the struggle faced by many who want to become better readers and about the challenges for teachers who want to help them. Throughout the volume, you will hear the voices of readers and their teachers as they work together to restore readers' confidence in their abilities as language learners. Specifically, you will learn how to use retrospective miscue analysis and similar instructional strategies for helping readers revalue their reading.

Retrospective miscue analysis (RMA) is a strategy that engages readers in reflecting upon and evaluating the reading process through analyzing their oral reading miscues. The term *miscue* is used to define those instances in oral reading when someone reads a text in a way that another person listening would not expect. Miscues, then, are observed responses that differ from expected responses, acknowledging that what someone expects to hear is influenced by his or her own perceptions about the way we use language to describe and interpret the world. Central to our work is an understanding that miscues are not simple deviations from text, each equally detrimental to comprehension. Nor do we believe that reading instruction should aim to eliminate miscues, since very proficient readers also make them. Rather, we believe that miscues provide a wealth of information about the reading process in action and about individual readers' strengths and weaknesses. We also believe that this knowledge can be made accessible to readers themselves and that it can help them come to revalue themselves as readers. Through analyzing their own reading, readers discover for themselves that reading is a process of predicting, inferring, sampling, confirming, and correcting, terms that Kenneth Goodman uses in his model of the reading process (K. Goodman 1984, 1994). Readers become aware that graphophonic, syntactic, and semantic cueing systems in language provide information as readers construct meaning from print. Most important, they dismantle the notion that good reading is represented by error-free reproductions of text. The research we refer to shows that, as their models of the reading process shift from text reproduction to meaning construction, their reading strategies (analyzed through miscue analysis or through less formal observations) reflect an increase in miscues that are syntactically and semantically acceptable and do not disrupt meaning.

Retrospective miscue analysis, in short, is a strategy that has been effectively used to demonstrate to readers what we know about the reading process (Marek 1987; Costello 1992; Worsnop 1980). This demonstration actually occurs as a result of self-reflection and self-study, as readers become engaged in analyzing their own miscues. Much in the same way that researchers learned about the reading process using miscue analysis, readers analyze their own miscues to discover the reading process for themselves. In a typical retrospective miscue analysis session, readers listen to a previous tape recording of themselves reading a text. Then, one by one, they analyze several miscues, asking questions like: Did the miscue make sense? Was it corrected? Should it have been? Why was the miscue made? Did it affect my understanding of the text? Possibilities for adaptations are discussed throughout.

This strategy can result in readers shifting from a skills-based, text-reproduction model of the reading process to one that is holistic and that acknowledges the importance of the reader's expectations and interpretations in transactions with text. Retrospective miscue analysis is most effectively used by teachers and researchers who understand miscue analysis and sociopsycholinguistic transactional reading theory. It also provides a view of the reading process that allows oral reading phenomena to inform teachers and researchers and to help them raise questions and inquire into the reading process. With these theoretical foundations, educators will be able to explore adaptations of the procedures based on their knowledge about language and about their students as language learners. But we also invite others to join us in revaluing readers and the reading process, even those who may not know miscue analysis or consider themselves well versed in theory, but who, through their work with students, have come to appreciate the importance of self-esteem and risk-taking as critical to the development of reading proficiency.

The work is organized in three parts. In Part I, Foundations for Revaluing, we set the stage for the concept of revaluing through a discussion of its philosophical roots in sociopsycholinguistic transactional reading theory and its research roots in miscue analysis. The authors of these chapters have long been involved in miscue analysis research and have popularized retrospective miscue analysis.

Ann M. Marek is an education consultant for the Nevada Department of Education. She began working with miscue analysis in 1979 as part of her master's degree program at the University of Arizona, and she used retrospective miscue analysis in her doctoral dissertation, completed in 1987.

Yetta M. Goodman is regents professor of education at the University of Arizona, College of Education, Department of Language, Reading, and Culture. Yetta has been exploring research in retrospective miscue analysis and its instructional implications since 1980.

Kenneth Goodman is professor of education at the University of Arizona, College of Education, Department of Language, Reading, and Culture. Ken pioneered the use of miscue analysis as a research tool in his search for understanding the reading process.

In Part II, Research in Revaluing, we share some of the research that supports the use of retrospective miscue analysis as an instructional strategy to support readers' development. The reading, retellings, and voices of teachers, researchers, and students tell powerful stories of the revaluing process. Students range from middle school through adult readers. The contributors for these chapters, in addition to Ann Marek and Yetta Goodman, all have studied retrospective miscue analysis as a research tool.

Alan Flurkey was a special education teacher for several years and has taught primary grades in the Phoenix area. He is currently a research assistant at the University of Arizona, exploring retrospective miscue analysis for greater insights into the reading process.

Joel Brown taught on the Navajo Reservation in Arizona. His doctoral research at the University of Arizona is concerned with trends and influences in miscue analysis research. He participated in a retrospective miscue analysis study with adolescent students.

Sarah Costello has taught primary through middle school students for many years. She uses retrospective miscue analysis in her seventh- and eighth-grade language arts classes. Her doctoral research involved the phenomenon of collaborative retrospective miscue analysis in her own classroom.

David Weatherill is a school administrator in Melbourne, Australia. He uses retrospective miscue analysis to help teachers understand reading and to help children develop positive views about themselves as readers.

Part III, Instructional Strategies for Revaluing, contains chapters by teachers and researchers who use retrospective miscue analysis or similar techniques to help readers revalue reading within the classroom setting, although retrospective miscue analysis is certainly not the only strategy teachers have used to encourage readers in self-discovery. Their instructional strategies are the focus of these chapters. The authors of these chapters who have not been introduced above include the following:

Chris Worsnop is a Canadian educator who has taught secondary school students and has worked with teachers as a resource consultant. In addition to literacy development, Chris also has interests in popular culture and the media.

Dorothy Watson developed Reader-Selected Miscues as an instructional strategy influenced by her miscue analysis research with teachers. She is professor and department chair in Curriculum and Instruction in the College of Education at the University of Missouri, Columbia.

Sharon Hoge is a coordinator for K–12 Reading and K–6 Language Arts for the Columbia, Missouri public schools. She has taught reading at the junior high level and is currently investigating commercial reading materials. She works extensively with parents and with teachers in their classrooms.

Debra Goodman is on leave as a teacher at the Dewey Center in the Detroit Public Schools. She has used retrospective miscue analysis in her elementary classrooms and as a reading specialist. She is presently pursuing her doctorate at Michigan State University in the English Department.

We believe that teachers who are knowledgeable about language, reading, learners, and teaching have invented revaluing strategies in their classrooms and tutoring sessions for a long time. We also believe that effective revaluing strategies are those that demystify the reading process and place students in charge of their own learning. What we hope to accomplish in this volume is to place those strategies within a theoretical context of revaluing as opposed to remediating; to share research-based conclusions about the benefits of revaluing; and to add to teachers' already useful strategies one or two that may be new.

Yetta M. Goodman
Ann M. Marek

Part I

FOUNDATIONS FOR REVALUING

TEACHERS KNOWLEDGEABLE ABOUT THE READING PROCESS and about readers wonder how to share their growing understanding with their students. Because they respect their students, many teachers discuss the reading process with them. We have had wonderful conversations with teachers about how their students need to know about the potential of miscues as they involve their students with cross-age tutoring or in multi-age programs. Kids need to know how to respond to their peers' miscues when they read. Based on discussions with these teachers and their experiences working with students of all ages, we became increasingly convinced that strategies designed to help readers understand the reading process have enormous potential. Our work has been especially influenced by teachers who hold a sociopsycholinguistic transactional view of the reading process. Teachers in tune with their students have found many ways to engage them in wondering about how reading works in general and for them in particular. In order to understand the ways in which teachers use retrospective miscue analysis with their students, it is necessary to consider the theory and research that support miscue analysis and to be aware of the procedures that teachers and researchers use to engage students in retrospective miscue analysis.

In Part I, Ann Marek and Yetta Goodman provide the theoretical and research foundations of miscue analysis to enforce the concept of revaluing as discussed by Kenneth Goodman. The chapters provide the philosophical roots of revaluing in sociopsycholinguistic transactional reading theory developed from research in miscue analysis. Ann, Yetta, and Ken have been involved in miscue analysis research and theory building and have popularized miscue analysis and retrospective miscue analysis (RMA) for use with readers.

Ann and Yetta introduce several people who have helped them explore the power of retrospective miscue analysis as a tool in helping readers revalue themselves as readers. You will meet these readers in other chapters, and their experiences will be shared throughout the volume. This chapter establishes the urgency for the use and understanding of RMA by teachers and researchers.

**CHAPTER 1:
PROFILES OF READERS**

Ken's chapter "Revaluing Readers and Reading" establishes the philosophical underpinnings of this volume by drawing distinctions between typical remedial approaches to helping readers in trouble and the "revaluing" approaches we recommend. This chapter is based on an article written a number of years ago to help reading professionals consider that readers build definitions of themselves as readers and that the attitudes of teachers and parents are often reflected in the way readers perceive their own abilities.

**CHAPTER 2:
PRINCIPLES OF
REVALUING**

CHAPTER 3:
UNDERSTANDING THE
READING PROCESS

Ann and Yetta then move to a basic discussion of miscue analysis to demonstrate how analyzing a reader's miscues has led to the building of a sociopsycholinguistic transactional model of the reading process. Since miscue analysis procedures are basic to RMA, this chapter provides an important overview.

CHAPTER 4:
RETROSPECTIVE
MISCUE ANALYSIS

Ann and Yetta present the retrospective miscue analysis strategy for both research and instructional purposes. Readers are given an opportunity to build the same insights into the reading process that teachers and researchers have built using miscue analysis.

1

Profiles of Readers

Ann M. Marek
Yetta M. Goodman

WE WOULD LIKE TO INTRODUCE you to several people with whom we have worked as we developed the use of retrospective miscue analysis over the last several years. These people have shared their understandings about language, learning, and teaching in ways that helped us see how an understanding of language processes affects the use of those processes. In major part, this book is an attempt to tell their stories to other teachers who may work with similar readers. We invite you to meet Carla, Gina, Marlene, Rolando, Kari, and Bernice. We invite you to discover whether they are in some ways like the so-called remedial readers you know. And we invite you to consider whether the insights we have gained through our research may be applied to your work with readers who struggle to make meaning in the texts they read.

Three major research projects served as the basis for collecting and analyzing the data we will reference throughout this volume. During a two-year period, Ann Marek worked with three adult women who sought assistance with their reading difficulties at their local university and community college. In a second project, Yetta Goodman headed a team of researchers who worked for eighteen months with middle school students identified by their standardized test scores and by their teachers as either "good" or "poor" readers. Finally, in her dissertation, Sarah Costello explored the use of retrospective miscue analysis as a collaborative technique in her seventh-grade classroom.

What we suggest in the pages to follow is that, although these readers were in many ways unique, they each needed to revalue both the reading process and their accomplishments as readers. Retrospective miscue analysis (RMA) as an instructional technique provided a vehicle for helping them revalue reading, and in Chapter 4 we describe in detail the use of that technique. This, then, is a book about readers revaluing reading and about teachers revaluing readers. But before we proceed, we want you to meet some of the readers who collaborated with us.

When we first met her, Carla was a young mother in her early twenties living in Tucson, Arizona, with her husband and eighteen-month-old son. One day, she took what may be an unusual step for a woman who is probably included in estimates of adult illiterates in this nation: she telephoned the Program in Language and Literacy at the University of Arizona and announced, "I only read at the fourth-grade level. Can you help me?" Yetta answered that telephone call and invited Carla to become part of a course Yetta was teaching at that time. The course was called "Psycholinguistics and Reading," and for one semester Carla became a class

CARLA—TUCSON, ARIZONA

project for the students who were taking the course. Among other things, Carla helped us pilot our first attempts at using retrospective miscue analysis (RMA) as a technique for helping readers revalue the reading process.

Carla was not working when we knew her; her primary motivation for wanting to improve her reading was related to her young son ("I want to be able to read to him") and to her envy of her friends who, in her words, "read beautiful books."

You may be wondering whether she was accurate in her representation of her reading ability as being at a fourth-grade level. Research has already documented the fallacy of assessments that attempt to pinpoint a grade-level reading achievement for any reader. Those kinds of tests cannot account for readers' interests, motivations, or genre preferences, and they fail to acknowledge that linguistic complexity is related to more aspects of language than word and sentence length. But was she having difficulty with reading? Yes. Was she aware of those difficulties? Most definitely. And, very important from our point of view, she was willing to try what to her were rather novel approaches to helping her with her reading.

GINA—RENO, NEVADA

Not unlike some other adults who describe themselves as illiterate, Gina had an extremely successful career—so successful that she had been able to employ others to handle most of the literacy requirements in her profession. She had dropped out of the British school system in her mid-teens and launched a career as an ice skater. She skated professionally for a number of years, eventually opening her own skating school in Australia. When physical limitations forced her to sell her business and leave skating, she found herself in her early forties, unemployed, and living with an airline pilot in Reno, Nevada. She had children of her own (now adults themselves), and she always thought she would enjoy working with young children. When Ann met her, she was living in Reno's finest neighborhood, toying with the idea of returning to school to become a teacher's aide. Her dream of spending hours reading to children was compromised by her inability to read well, and that explained her motivation to focus her attention on improving her reading.

Gina described herself as a "cheater" who had managed to hide the fact that she was a nonreader by avoiding situations where she would be revealed or discovered. It is easy to imagine how she was able to run a business and fit in to a variety of social circles—Gina was very bright, beautiful, and accomplished. Ann had cause to wonder on more than one occasion whether Gina's boyfriend was satisfied with the ornamentation she provided in his life and therefore somewhat reluctant to see her change. Perhaps literacy would provide for Gina the kind of liberation that could threaten the balance of their relationship. It is doubtful, however, that either of them consciously understood this potential.

Gina was convinced that she was dyslexic and that her problems in reading stemmed from the fact that teachers "in her day" didn't understand dyslexia, nor did they practice teaching methods that would lead to its cure. She held these teachers blameless—never in her reflections on schooling did she reveal any bitterness or resentment for the failure of schools to help her become a reader.

MARLENE—SPARKS, NEVADA

While Gina held no rancor for the schooling system, 21-year-old Marlene bitterly resented what had been her experiences in school. When Ann met her, she was living with her parents and brothers in Sparks, Nevada, a residential community bordering Reno. While she and Ann worked together, she was working as a dishwasher at a nursing home. More than once, she looked at Ann and asked, "But what if I want more out of life?"

Marlene had a long history of remediation—she was labeled "learning disabled" and became a special education student in third grade in one of Nevada's rural school districts. She spent the years until high school graduation in special education classes. She said when she was very young, doctors told her parents to institutionalize her—that she would never be able to learn. What would have prompted such a recommendation is very unclear—Marlene was an intelligent young woman, and it is doubtful that her intelligence was the result of years spent in special education. But what is important is the fact that Marlene *believed* these things: that she could not learn; that she would never have a good job or a place of her own. She had spent some time working with a teacher at the local community college who had tried various techniques, including tracing and other kinesthetic methods, to help Marlene with her reading. When Ann met her, Marlene also suspected that no one, including Ann, would be able to help her. With the chip on her shoulder almost visible, she dared Ann to try.

ROLANDO—TUCSON, ARIZONA

Rolando was a seventh grader who participated in our study funded by the National Council of Teachers of English (NCTE). Yetta, Ann, and a team of doctoral students at the University of Arizona examined the use of retrospective miscue analysis with a group of seventh-grade readers. Alan Flurkey, one of the researchers, worked extensively with Rolando, a student who was a puzzle from the start. He was a bilingual, Mexican-American twelve-year-old whose home language was Spanish and school language was English. As a student, he did poorly on district and state standardized tests, yet he was an avid reader of Civil War history and science fiction who always had two or three novels cached in his backpack for out-of-school reading. His memories of school were uniformly distasteful, but he remembered with affection one teacher who listened to him and valued him as a thinker. He was frequently put on in-school detention for fighting; as a student, however, he knew how to collaborate with others and provide striking insights. As a philosopher, he questioned the relevance of school but unequivocally valued the pursuit of knowledge. Perhaps most remarkable was Rolando's buoyancy. Here was a young person who, in spite of his school difficulties, believed in himself. In an unguarded moment he said quietly, confidently, "You know, I think I'm going to make it. I think I'm going to be a success in life." It was as if he had already decided that being a success in life would not depend on his experiences in school.

Rolando contributed to the study of retrospective miscue analysis through illuminating the fallacy of time-honored notions about good and poor readers. He allowed us to see how unwise the conventional wisdom was about good and poor readers and their relative abilities to reflect thoughtfully on how they go about making meaning. Rolando knew himself to be a good reader, but to an untrained ear his oral reading sounded labored, filled with partial sentences, and uncorrected, nonmeaningful errors and omissions. On the surface this might suggest a reader who painstakingly and unsuccessfully was trying to produce a copy of the written text. But his responses to our interviews suggest that he viewed reading as a meaning-centered process. He valued reading for its own sake and believed that the only way to improve was to do more reading. Isn't this the profile of a "good reader?" This apparent dichotomy is further explored in Alan Flurkey's case study of Rolando.

KARI—TUCSON, ARIZONA

Kari, at twelve, may have seemed shy when she showed up for her first reading session in our study of retrospective miscue analysis with seventh graders. She was comfortable with the idea of not having to be "in class," not because she didn't like classes but because she had differences with some of the other students. P.E. was her favorite class to miss. A surgical operation when she had been very young and the continuing medication for epilepsy often left her feeling apart from the group. Her sensitivity was exceptionally well expressed for a student of her age. She spoke often of friends from Tucson and Tennessee, where she had lived for a time before her father and mother divorced. She would worry about something she had said in a letter, about whether it caused her friend any trouble if her friend's mother had read it—and she hadn't seen this friend in the last six of her twelve years. She even felt sorry for teachers who disagreed with a curriculum that they had to teach because, if they didn't teach it, they'd "lose their job!"

Her mother had supported her in ways she recognized and appreciated. When it came to tests, she felt that taking her time and doing the best she could was how her mother measured her success, not by the scores. She liked to think and to write. Poetry had been a major problem for her until a teacher had told her that a "poem was just a thought." Her thoughts have helped us immeasurably in exploring the concept of revaluing.

BERNICE—TUCSON, ARIZONA

Bernice is another student we worked with in the NCTE-funded study of seventh-grade readers. For the purpose of the study, the readers were grouped according to whether they were good readers or poor readers, which was determined by standardized test scores and their previous teachers' assessments of their abilities. What we confirmed, among other things in this small study, is that distinctions between good readers and poor readers are not easy to draw. Bernice was one of the so-called good readers—her scores on standardized reading tests placed her at the seventh stanine. Her sixth-grade teachers confirmed that she was a good reader, and she consistently attained Honor Society status throughout the school year. Bernice had not always been a good reader, however. In her primary years in school, she had been targeted for remedial training, and she spoke about having learned principles of syllabication and other remedial techniques. She believed these techniques had been very helpful.

At the beginning of the study, Bernice described her mother as a good reader who "never stumbles on a long word and she knows how to pronounce it and everything." Bernice may have had attitudes held by many good readers, perhaps especially held by those who have been exposed to skills training. She valued error-free reading and believed that looking words up in the dictionary is a useful strategy when you come to something you don't know. Not once during her first interview did she mention reading for meaning or for understanding the story. The interviewer was a teacher, after all, and maybe Bernice was telling us what she thought we wanted to hear. Only in subsequent sessions were we able to confirm that she believed reading was essentially a decoding task.

CHARACTERISTICS OF ALL READERS

What do readers like these and others we will mention, so very different in age, socioeconomic status, linguistic backgrounds, and cultural experiences, have in common? We suggest that they are similar in a number of respects.

1. Each reader brings to the reading process a wealth of knowledge about language and about the world.

Their knowledge about the world and their expectations about people and events have been shaped by the social and cultural contexts in which they have lived. Clearly, 41-year-old Gina, who had traveled around the world, owned her own business, and raised a family, had an incredible fund of knowledge from which to draw as she read. Her experience with British and Australian dialects of English influenced her expectations about both oral and written language, and she had in mind a very clear purpose for wanting to improve her reading.

Carla had been born in Mexico, and Spanish was her first language. She recalled having begun to read in Spanish as a young child, prior to moving to the

United States in second grade and attempting to learn to read in English. From her perspective, it was this linguistic barrier that had inhibited her early progress in becoming a proficient reader. At age twenty-one, however, she had lived in two countries and brought an adult's knowledge about the world to her interactions with print. Though Gina's interest in improving her reading was related to some career choices, Carla shared somewhat more personal reasons—a desire to read to her young son and to enjoy for herself the beautiful love stories her friends talked about.

Zack, a fourth grader who was referred to us because of his "reading problem," read *The Magic School Bus at the Waterworks* (Coles 1986), a book we used because of its humor and high interest. This is a complex science narrative of Ms. Frizzle, who takes her class on a fantasy trip. The narrative is represented by usual print, but many fonts are used on charts and signs in the innovative classroom and imaginary bus ride. Zack showed his knowledge of how text cohesion works. He read the usual print at the bottom across a two-page spread. He then returned to the upper part of the right-hand page to read "water fact #3." He completed this informational genre before he read the language in the speech balloons representing the kids' humorous commentary on their adventure in the bus going up into a cloud. His response to this complex text revealed his knowledge of the worlds of kids, of imagination, of water vapor, and of how written texts are organized.

2. Each reader has misconceptions about the reading process.

As these readers reflected on the reading process, they demonstrated that they had bought into a skills and subskills approach to reading. They rarely indicated that reading is for the purpose of enjoyment, constructing meaning from the text, or gathering information to answer questions that interest them. They stated that to become better readers they needed to perfect their use of skills: to sound out words, look up words in dictionaries, and never skip words. Often they suggested that they didn't do such things because they were careless or lazy. Marlene told Ann that her mother was a good reader who looked up words in the dictionary when she came to something she didn't know. When Ann asked Marlene whether she ever did that, Marlene answered, "Not really, because I can never find the words." Carla went so far as to say that her brothers (good readers, according to Carla) "never come to something they don't know. They're very smart."

In our study of seventh graders, Rudy was designated as a "poor" reader. He tenaciously held to the belief that good reading was an act in which the most important feature was the ability to "pronounce [words] right." Even highly articulate Rolando, who seldom used "sounding-out" as a strategy and who had a decidedly holistic view of the reading process, cited this rule during his final interview with Alan, the researcher:

Alan: Let's just talk about your reading and your vision of it. When you are reading and you come to something you don't know, what do you do?
Rolando: Try to sound it out and see if I can read it, or just skip it.
Alan: Do you ever do anything else?
Rolando: No.

These misconceptions about reading are often reflected in the ways in which such students read. They read slowly and carefully, they make few omissions and insertions of function words, and they are willing to sound out words and produce nonword substitutions rather than take the risks necessary to make a good guess and produce a high-quality miscue that makes sense within the context of the material they are reading. They strongly believe that reading is attending to each word and to every punctuation mark. In other words, the surface features of the text control what and how they read rather than their own abilities to select only the features necessary to construct meaning.

These readers often share contradictions as they talk about their reading. For example, although most of these readers state that they will become better readers when they read faster, in response to why they made a particular insertion or omission of an article or some other function word, they usually respond that they were reading too fast and being careless. From their point of view, good readers read slowly and carefully, they remember everything that they have read, and they know every word. José in Sarah Costello's study said that good readers read perfectly: "Reading perfect means reading loudly, pause when there is a period, know all the words, that's it."

3. Each reader has misconceptions about his or her proficiency as a reader.

As we document through quotations from the readers we introduced at the beginning of this chapter, these readers easily buy into the labels designed to describe what they *cannot* do. They are learning disabled or dyslexic, and some teacher either did not diagnose it properly or did not know what to do when they were diagnosed. Although the labels seem to be comforting, these readers blame themselves. It is as if they believe that they could learn to read if they could only find the right button to press. They tend to blame themselves (their habits or their intelligence) with unfortunate and far-reaching ramifications. Gina told us she believed she was dyslexic as a young girl, but that her teachers weren't able to diagnose her since she "had always appeared to be intelligent."

Alfredo (designated as a "poor" reader in the seventh-grade study) expressed the belief that he was a slow reader, even though his pattern of strategy use revealed that he was frequently an efficient as well as an effective reader.

Alan: What would you like to do better as a reader?
Alfredo: I would like to read faster. I think I read too slow. It don't sound good.

Rudy expressed a similar desire.

Alan: What would you like to do better as a reader?
Rudy: Read quicker—read faster and know the words better.

Such misconceptions were apparent in the so-called good readers as well. Even though Bernice was an efficient and effective reader, she initially attributed her substitutions and omissions to laziness as opposed to mature control over the reading process.

Sarah: And what did you do when your miscues didn't make sense?
Bernice: Half of the time I went back.
Sarah: No. More than half. Over 80 percent of the time you went back.
Bernice: Some of them I just didn't go back. Lazy.

Often, regardless of what they read, they do not consider themselves readers. They define themselves as not being good readers and, worse, as nonreaders—despite evidence to the contrary. Gina described herself in this way: "I'm very slow as a reader, even when I read by myself, inwardly. I would say I'm a nonreader." Ann pushed her on this point, asking, "You consider yourself a nonreader?" and Gina responded, "Nonreader. Yes. Even when I read the paper, which I hate reading because it gets me all dirty. I can read. I can read things if I like them." Here was an intelligent, accomplished woman, referring to herself as a nonreader even though she reluctantly admitted she could read things if she liked them.

4. Each reader has been and continues to be influenced by the instructional models they have experienced in school.

The readers we introduced earlier could often state rules that they had heard from instruction based on subskills and skills models of reading. As we begin working with any group of readers, we usually conduct the Reading Interview (Y. Goodman et al. 1987), which was developed to reveal how readers view the reading process. The Reading Interviews suggested that these readers held a subskills and skills model of reading: that reading must be taught in an explicit way, that reading is learned from parts to whole through a sequential hierarchy of skills, and that each skill must be attacked, reinforced, mastered, and tested before the next skill is presented.

When asked how they would help another student who was having difficulty, several of our seventh graders responded that they would help that student by using the same techniques and strategies that they had been taught. The following excerpt is both illustrative and typical.

Alan: If you knew someone was having trouble reading, how would you help that person?
Rudy: Probably pronounce it or something and sound it out.
Alan: What else?
Rudy: Have them turn the pages to see if they ran over it before—go back and see if they read it before, or saw the word.
Alan: What would a teacher do to help that person?
Rudy: Sound it out to them.
Alan: Would they do the same thing you would do? What else?
Rudy: Probably tell them the word.

The belief is that mastery of subskills precedes a focus on understanding the meaning of what is being read. From their point of view, readers need to know how to sound out and syllabicate in order to learn to read. They are concerned with learning how to attack words, memorizing from flash cards, and looking words up in the dictionary for pronunciation and meanings.

These readers believe in the skills model of reading often prevalent in special education and reading classes. They try to do all the things they believe they have been taught. Peter Board (1982), a researcher in miscue analysis who has studied such readers, believes that they have instruction-dependent personalities. They want to do what teachers tell them to do, and they can often describe their problems as they respond to their own miscues.

Tony, a second grader who speaks with the dialect of an African American child living in an urban inner city community, was reading the sentence *It's going to be at Mr. Vine's candy shop*. He read: *It's going to be* (slowly and haltingly), then regressed and read *It gonna be . . .* No! . . . *It's going to be . . . It going to be.* He repeated this segment of text a number of times, then looked up from his reading and said "I hate 'postrophe s's." Tony has heard his teacher remind him and the other students in his class that they have to carefully produce the final *s* and *d* sounds on words. He was trying hard to accommodate the rule but in so doing he lost the flow of the language and interrupted his focus on making meaning. In another story, when Tony came to *Mother smiled*, he paused for a few seconds, read *Mother* and then sounded out *smiled* without much success. He then looked up at the teacher, covered up *smil* and said, "If you take the *ed* off of this word will that let me know what it is?"

It is important to understand that these influences last far beyond the schooling years. At age 41, when Gina struggled with the word *treacherous*, she tried various beginnings, including *tr—, tre—*, and *trea—*, before she noticed the little word (*each*) within the big word (*treacherous*) and decided to pursue the oft-recommended word-attack strategy of "look for the little words in the big words." Of course, that strategy was no more successful for her than Tony's was for him.

5. Each reader has the potential for understanding the complexity of the reading process, the qualitative nature of making miscues, and the importance of reading for meaning.

Through RMA, all of the readers, regardless of the view of reading expressed initially, came to understand their power in constructing meaning when they read. As Gina shared with Ann during their final meeting, readers must begin to understand that they are in control of the reading process.

Ann: How have you changed as a reader?
Gina: I find that if I'm reading without understanding, I'll either change the article or go back and read, and say to myself, "Now try and understand it." Whereas, before I didn't used to.
Ann: What about the people you described as "clever" readers—do they make mistakes?
Gina: Yeah. I think they make mistakes in their ordinary, everyday reading. I think good readers always want to understand what they are reading. I think they understand what they are reading, but there might be one word that they have never heard of. Then they will try to learn that word. Some of them will put it into their vocabulary, others will say "OK, that's what it is."
Ann: If you're reading for pleasure, is it as important to fuss with words?
Gina: No, just go on to the next sex, or murder, or whatever. If you make too many mistakes where it is the wrong person, then it could confuse the plot. If you make too many mistakes, you may get the wrong person playing the wrong part. Which you have got to realize.
Ann: You realize that by doing what?
Gina: Going over it again . . . . By getting into the story, by what makes sense more than anything.

In the following transcript, Rolando, a seventh grader we introduced earlier, reveals a sophisticated understanding of the transactive nature of the reading process. He knows that all readers make miscues, and that each reader is potentially the best source of information about the reading strategies he or she uses.

Alan: Think of a hypothetical reader that's good. Do you think they ever come to something they don't know?
Rolando: Always, yeah . . . . Because I guess nobody has ever explored all the words. Maybe it's only someone that's very smart knows all the words, but still, if they're real smart, read all fast, they'll make a mistake—no doubt about it. Everybody has to probably make a mistake. Nobody's perfect.
Alan: If that person came to something they didn't know, what do you think they'd do?
Rolando: Again, I don't know. That matters who was reading. For me, I would just—the only thing I can answer is me, 'cause I know me. If you're going to answer that question you gotta ask every single person in the world about—if you want to find that. For me, I have to, you know, think about it, look it up or something, or just pass it and read another story. Or make a prediction!

Throughout this book, we document the ways in which readers come to these understandings. We also indicate that there are a variety of influences on a reader's coming to understand the complexity of the reading process.

6. Each reader has the ability to become a more proficient reader.

As readers change their views of the reading process, their reading strategies help them become more effective and efficient in the reading process. But if the readers do not continue to have opportunity to do a lot of reading or are in school or home settings where their reading miscues and strategies are not valued and understood, they can fall back into their earlier attitudes about reading and the reading process. At the end of her work with Ann, Marlene had come to understand this important point:

Marlene: Your way is different from a schoolteacher's. Their way is "Okay, read Chapter 1 and we'll talk about it tomorrow." But you only see me once a week. And I have a whole week to think about the story and the way it affected me when I was reading it, and the way I thought the author should have written it, or what I thought it should have sounded like.

Ann: How do you feel about your ability to continue to improve your reading?

Marlene: I can do it. It will take a lot of practice and reading a lot on my own.

We believe that revaluing holds more promise for these readers than does typical remediation. They need to define themselves as literate human beings, not as cheaters in the system. They need to become aware of their strengths as readers, rather than focusing on their weaknesses. They need to be made more consciously aware of a key aspect of reading: What you know is at least as important as what the author has to say. And these readers know a great deal. Unfortunately, they tend to discount, indeed distrust, their own knowledge and intuitions as they read. Equally detrimental, they denigrate the strategies they have that most resemble good readers' strategies, like skipping a word if you don't know it (or entire sections if they don't interest you) or neglecting to self-correct when meaning hasn't been disrupted. In short, they need to revalue the reading process itself, and they need to revalue themselves as readers. And, as teachers, we must remember that the object of reading instruction is not to eliminate miscues, but to help readers control the process—to help students become readers, not decoders or word attackers.

Another way of looking at this is that we want readers to discover the transactional sociopsycholinguistic model of the reading process (K. Goodman 1994). Kenneth Goodman has built his model of the reading process based on insights gained through using miscue analysis to examine readers. In so doing, he has said that "everything we know about reading we've learned from kids" (K. Goodman 1973, 3). But what can readers learn through engaging in a kind of miscue analysis? We believe they can discover a more holistic model of the reading process by listening to themselves read and learning to focus on meaning. In turn, they will become better readers. As readers define themselves as readers, they come to revalue themselves and the reading process. As teachers come to understand how students read, they also revalue the reading process and readers. In the next chapter, Ken provides us with a new term when considering the reader in trouble—we invite you to consider the concept of revaluing the reader rather than the concept of remediating the reader.

2

Principles of Revaluing

Kenneth S. Goodman

READERS LIKE CARLA, GINA, MARLENE, Rolando, and Kari help us understand that we must change our focus in dealing with those having trouble learning to read. Using a medical metaphor, we've treated those who do not respond well to reading instruction as sufferers from an illness. I'm not speaking only of those labeled *dyslexic,* a term I consider nonproductive. I'm also speaking about those labeled *remedial* in all its variations of degree. Both Gina and Marlene have been limited in their development as readers because they accepted and trusted the "diagnosis and remediation" metaphor; when the metaphor failed them, they assumed that they were the ones who had failed.

We've invented an endless variety of diagnostic tests to find out what's wrong with learners like Gina and Marlene. Consider the following incident, shared with me by Debra Goodman, about a second grader.

> Emily, a young second grader I knew, believed that she was a reader. A reading specialist discovered that she was reading holistically but had not yet discovered the alphabetic system of the English language. The teacher decided that Emily must face the fact that she was a nonreader. She arranged a meeting with the classroom teacher and the parent present.
>
> The so-called reading specialist wrote the sentence *I love Mommy* and helped Emily to read it. Then she wrote the sentence *I love dog Mommy* and asked Emily to read it. Emily read *I love Mommy.* "You see," the reading specialist announced triumphantly, "you don't know how to read!"
>
> This conference was very much like a group confrontation of an alcoholic or drug addict. Is Emily's belief that she can read a sickness? The implications are incredible. Maybe you don't really love your Mommy, after all. Maybe she shouldn't love you anymore because you can't read. The trauma that some kids go through in learning to read is almost criminal. I guess the theory is that you can't correct a problem unless you face it.

The insidious nature of labeling readers affects not just the young. As an adult, Gina believed that either dyslexia or learning disabilities had limited her ability to read, even though the condition had been undiagnosed when she was a child.

Gina: I don't think I had very good teachers, actually . . . . Don't forget, this was going back a long time when whatever I had, whether it was dyslexia or learning disabilities, they didn't really have.

Even at age 41, Gina held in her mind the image of herself as a child who was defective. Marlene was labeled as learning disabled in third grade, and she remained a special education student until high school graduation. Marlene also stated that she had dyslexia, and she felt victimized by an educational system that

---

Portions of this chapter appeared in Goodman, Kenneth S. "Revaluing Readers and Reading." *Topics in Learning and Learning Disabilities,* Volume 1, issue 4, 1982, pp 87–95.

did not recognize or properly treat her dyslexia. There was unmistakable bitterness in her voice as she shared her thoughts about her failure to learn to read well.

Marlene: Teachers were playing God, lawyer, doctor, everything, saying, "Oh, she's going to die when she's eighteen. You might as well take her out of school and put her in the state institution." I was healthy, it's just that they did not know what the word *dyslexia* was and they fought all the time with my mother when she said, "She has dyslexia. It is a reading problem."

What is startling about these disclosures is the power of labels like *dyslexic*, *learning disabled*, and *nonreader*, as though the labels themselves can explain why a student isn't reading as well as expected. Yet we know that few of the special tests that lend credibility to these labels are based on any solid understanding of what reading is and how it works. Test patterns found among readers with problems are assumed to be different from those in general populations who have not been studied with these tests, and causative patterns are assumed. When we do find the same patterns among more proficient readers, we assume that they too are disabled in some mysterious way that doesn't show—yet. The tests are designed to find things wrong with readers. And they do that well—so well that Carla at age 21 could tell us she read at the "fourth-grade level." She believed in the test results; she believed in the power of that information to define herself and to help us design instruction for her.

There's a much smaller variety of prescriptions available for dealing with syndromes the tests create. Everybody, regardless of diagnosis, gets basically the same prescription: "These readers need more structure," we are told. "Give them a strong dose of readiness followed by endless drills on phonics and word attack." The same patent medicines prescribed for the dyslexics are also hawked for the learning disabled, the mentally retarded, the bilingual, the myopic, the culturally diverse, and the plain vanilla remedial readers. After years of being on the receiving end of these "medicines," Carla, Gina, and Marlene could each recite the prescription. In early interviews with these women, we asked, "If you knew somebody who was having trouble reading, what would you do to help that person? What would you recommend?" Here are their answers.

Carla: Help them sound out words.

Gina: I would let them read, and I would point out things. You know, "What does that word say?" All the time. Like you do when you're teaching a child. Say the word over and over again; maybe get them to write it down. Maybe just sounding it out and saying it to you. I think that's all.

Marlene: Tell them to practice . . . . You sit down and read along with someone and if you get in trouble you have them say the word and keep going on. But if you keep missing that word, stop and spell the word, and say it, and go through that way.

Not surprisingly, these women would assist others in the ways they were assisted as children. Marlene's description of a practice session is probably similar to practice sessions she participated in herself. In her explanation of the practice routine, she assumes the role of the reader having difficulty, as well as the role of the helper (i.e., "you have them say the word . . . but if you keep missing that word . . .)." Even though these methods didn't help these women learn to read as well as they wanted, they persist in their trust of the skills-based instructional model—after all, the instruction hasn't failed, they have.

So enough already! Retrospective miscue analysis and the other strategies described in this book treat troubled readers as strong, healthy, and fully capable of learning how to read. If we can identify students with real, demonstrable physical problems, then we must provide medical or psychological help for dealing with those problems that can be cured or ameliorated and coping with those that cannot. But we cannot let ourselves as educators off the hook by blaming the readers for our lack of success in helping them to learn. The perspective we must adopt is one of building on strength. If we understand as educators some basic facts about how reading works and how it develops, we can build on strengths of all learners and support them as they grow into literacy.

We will use the term *readers in trouble* to refer to all those who are not doing as well as they think (or someone else thinks) they should do in the development of reading proficiency. The common denominator among such readers is that they have become their own worst enemies. They have acquired a view that the world is populated by two kinds of people: those who can read and those who cannot; those who can learn and those who cannot. They believe that, if they could just learn the phonics rules, just get enough word attacks, just master the skills, then they could do what good readers do easily and well. However, they believe they cannot because something is wrong with them; they just do not learn like "normal" people.

The key to helping readers in trouble is to help them revalue themselves as language users and learners and revalue the reading process as a transactive, constructive language process. They must set aside the pathological view of themselves, cast off the labels, and operate to construct meaning through written language using the strengths they have built and used in making sense of oral language or sign. To do that they need support and help.

Unfortunately, many educators have come to view reading as performance on tests, exercises, and workbooks. Teachers must put aside the instructional technology they have equated with reading and see reading instead as a process of making sense of written language. In reading there is a transaction between a reader and a written text. What the reader brings to the text—experience, attitudes, concepts, cognitive schemes—is as important as what the author brought to it in creating it. The reader's act is creative, too; meaning is created in response to the text.

We must understand that an authentic text is not just a string of equally important words to be perceived, recognized, or attacked in linear order. It is syntactically structured, semantically cohesive, and coherent. A printed text is an overall unity, a representation capable of varied interpretation and variable comprehension. Furthermore, texts exist in the context of culture, personal experience, and situation.

Reading is a process in which thought and language transact in a social context as the reader builds meaning. Readers are not the prisoners of their eyes. They have brains with which they seek sense as they read—they predict and infer where the meaning is going, what sentence patterns are coming, what words and phrases are expected, and what the text will look like. Making sense of print is the reader's goal as well as the framework in which perceptual, syntactic, and semantic information is processed. Readers are effective if they make sense of print.

Within the continuous preoccupation with meaning, the reader selects from the available cues only those that are most useful, predicts on the basis of knowledge of language and the world, monitors his or her own success, and corrects when necessary to make sense. The reader is always tentative but confident. He or she is self-monitoring to make sure predictions are confirmed, but he or she is willing to take the risks necessary to move to meaning. Risk-taking, self-monitoring, and self-confidence are the essence of a revaluing program.

READING: A UNITARY TRANSACTIONAL SOCIOPSYCHOLINGUISTIC PROCESS

HOW IS READING LEARNED?

Learning language is largely a matter of finding its underlying system, inferring its rules, and then being able to use them to express meaning and to understand it. Language is easiest to learn when it is whole, relevant, real, in context, and functional for the user. In this respect, written language is no different from oral language. One need not be unusually clever to learn to read and write any more than to learn oral language.

Only when learners are distracted from meaning by instruction or confronted by materials full of abstract nonsense is a disadvantage created. For those who may have mental or physical impairments, this disadvantage may be overwhelming. Learning letters is more difficult than learning words, which is more difficult than learning to remember or comprehend sentences. Understanding sets of unrelated sentences is more difficult than comprehending coherent stories or other meaningful texts.

Recent studies have demonstrated that children make a strong beginning as readers and writers as they encounter print in their environment and learn to understand its functions (Y. Goodman 1980). As they see print used, they come to know what it is for and what it means. The key to the learning is the universal search for order and comprehensibility that is characteristic of all humans. If teachers can grasp that, then they can understand the tremendous strength that all students bring to learning to read and write. That understanding can help teachers to revalue students not succeeding in school and to understand that their failure is the teachers' failure to help them use the strengths they have. All children seem to be remarkable language learners outside of school. If they appear less successful in school, it is because learning language has been made too hard for them in the quest to make it easier.

An Overemphasis on Skills

Skills have been the focus of the instructional programs troubled readers have repeatedly experienced. At the same time these students are trying to make sense of print they are also trying to read by the numbers: sounding out, attacking words, recognizing rules, using skills. Getting the words right becomes more important, for them, than making sense. Every unfamiliar word becomes a major obstacle to be identified before going on. The reader suffers from the "next-word syndrome"; each unconquered word is a symbol of defeat.

Readers in trouble are more likely to be the victims of too much skill use than not enough. They persevere on a single word, producing many nonword attempts before giving up. Many of them have had intensive instruction in phonics and word attack over and over as they moved through remediation programs. Although the effect of this training shows in their phonic near misses, their miscues are often interpreted by diagnosticians as proof that more phonics is needed.

Readers in trouble also tend to look to the teacher to tell them what to do next. The pattern is to wait a few seconds each time a problem word or phrase is encountered; then the teacher will supply the next word or an admonition to sound it out. The teacher may think he or she has helped by supplying the next word, but such repeated experiences only sustain the next-word syndrome and the basic feeling of defeat and inadequacy of the reader in trouble.

A Scenario for Failure

Readers in trouble in literate societies with schools universally available have experienced repeated cycles of failure. The natural history of each cycle is something like this: The students are not doing well in school. The less well they do, the more intensively the teacher applies the program. If students are not doing well on worksheets, flash cards, skill drills, and remedial exercises, then the teacher repeats the same ones or provides supplementary, similar ones. If the usual amount of time spent on such activities is not paying off, then more time is provided for them, either at the expense of other, more meaningful aspects of the reading period, such as free reading time, or of some other aspects of the curriculum, such as social studies, science, music, or art. If there are paraprofessionals available, then they are assigned to review and repeat with the readers in trouble what has not worked when the teacher did it. Recesses, lunch periods, after school time, even vacation periods are invaded in the name of helping readers in trouble to overcome their deficits.

Soon the classroom teacher gives up and the child is referred for remediation. Remediation usually begins with a heavy battery of tests that confirm that the reader is inadequately responding to skill instruction. The tests reveal patterns of weakness and deficiency. Remedial exercises are prescribed to eliminate the weaknesses. The exercises tend to be more abstract and fragmented versions of what did not work in the classroom (Taylor 1991).

Sometimes, at the beginning of remediation, there appears to be an upsurge of achievement and a flicker of hope and enthusiasm on the part of the learner. The student enjoys the special attention, particularly if the remedial teacher is warm and encouraging. Somewhat improved scores are achieved. As the remediation continues, however, the learner sinks once more into despair. The abstractness of the fragmented skill drills leads to frustration. What was fresh and new is recognized as the same dull, repetitive, and tedious exercises that have not worked before. Pep talks and admonishments to try harder build personal guilt. Furthermore, the teacher shows resentment at the ingratitude of the learner for all the personal care and attention.

Meanwhile, back in the class, the remedial student is missing important learning opportunities; the time spent on remediation is the time classmates are spending building concepts, reading, writing, doing. So the learner in trouble, in the name of building basic skill competence, is deprived of rich school experience. Ironically, the reader who rebels and acts out may be showing a healthier reaction than the one who withdraws or submits meekly to all this. At least such a rebel is showing a resistance to accepting full responsibility for failure.

The answer to this dismal scenario is revaluing. The students must be helped to revalue themselves as learners. They must revalue the process of reading as the construction of meaning in response to print. They must come to appreciate their own strengths, to recognize the productive strategies they already can use, and to build positively on those. They must come to put in perspective their transactions with authors through texts. Then they can put proper value on themselves and understand that no one can easily read and comprehend everything and that what one knows before reading constrains what one can know after reading. They need to know that some texts are difficult to read because they are poorly written, and others are difficult because they contain new, complex ideas. They need to know that, while everybody can find interesting, entertaining, or useful things in print, not everybody has to like everything they read. Finally, they need to realize that the easiest things for them to read are going to be the very ones that they have the most interest in and the most background for and from which they get the most pleasure.

The Need for Revaluing

Revaluing is not going to happen simply, easily, or quickly. It requires great patience and gentle support from teachers to help students in a long, slow rebuilding of the sense of self and sense of reading. Essentially, a revaluing program involves getting readers to read real, meaningful texts, to strengthen and gain new appreciation of the productive strategies that lead to comprehension, and to drop

THE ENVIRONMENT FOR REVALUING

the nonproductive strategies. Teachers can turn the conflict that readers in trouble experience every time they attempt to read into a positive force to achieve the revalued reading. Piaget (1971) talks about disequilibrium, a point in learning when the learner has unresolved conflicts and has not yet accommodated. Readers in trouble have been in this unbalanced state for so long that it has become reading for them.

From Skills to Meaning

However, the very conditions of their discomfort contain the seeds of productive resolution: Here is a written text created by an author to represent a message coherently. Here is a reader trying to make sense of the text no matter what else he or she is doing. Patiently, in the context of supporting the reader's search for meaning, the teacher helps the reader to shift away from word identification, from sounding out, from teacher dependence. Patiently, the teacher helps the troubled reader to trust his or her own linguistic judgment, to have faith in the predictions and inferences that are coming to mind, to take risks, to self-monitor by constantly applying the key test: Does that make sense? Gradually the reader finds that the text is making sense. An accommodation takes shape in which graphophonic, syntactic, and semantic cues are used selectively to the extent that they are useful. Any exaggerated value attached to any one cue, cue system, or strategy gives way to putting each in its proper perspective.

The Teacher as Catalyst

The teacher, carefully monitoring this conflict between productive and non-productive strategies, between getting the next word and making sense, can be a catalyst. The teacher tips the balance by supporting the troubled readers' intuitions, by appreciating when something has worked, or by asking a timely question at a point where the reader falters: What's happening in the story? What do you already know about____? Did that make sense? Why not?

The teacher starts by learning about the learner. That does not mean diagnostic tests. It means asking learners what they read. It means inviting them to read a variety of things that vary in content, function, and complexity. It may mean, if the student has made some kind of start at becoming successful as a reader, using some variation of miscue analysis (Y. Goodman et al. 1987). The teacher moves slowly and supportively to overcome the fear and despair. Often, as students relax, they reveal themselves to be much more capable than either they or the teacher had supposed.

One problem that may be faced at the beginning of a revaluing program is that the learners have so strongly internalized an expectation of how reading will be taught that they reject anything else. The reader must come to trust the teacher and learn new ways of evaluating his or her own progress. The teacher must let the learner see how progress comes through a focus on trying to make sense of meaningful texts. This focus, of course, is at the center of revaluing.

Building Self-Confidence

In starting to work with any reader in trouble, the teacher must take care not to assume that the reader is devoid of reading ability. Group or individual test scores are untrustworthy, since all they may reveal is the students' great fear of failure and the ease with which they become discouraged and give up. It is only after the reader has relaxed and begun to participate fully that any trustworthy insights may be drawn. At the beginning the instructional situation must be made completely nonthreatening. For some readers who are in serious trouble, it will be sufficient, as a beginning, to encourage them to follow as the teacher or aide reads.

As the reader gains confidence and begins to reveal interests, focus may shift to a variety of kinds of reading: signs, catalogs, manuals, menus, TV guides, and the like. The teacher will seek evidence of a particular reader's interest and supply materials, either narrative or expository, that will be highly motivating—materials that are interesting and will help build self-confidence.

To be successful in helping troubled readers, teachers must take their lead from the students. The teacher monitors the learner, letting the learner set the pace and direction, but offering the right help at the right time. This process is not unlike what parents do intuitively as they support the oral language development of preschool children.

Difficult Textbooks

Coping with school textbooks, especially in upper elementary and secondary grades, is a problem that most troubled readers face even as they are improving in their ability and self-confidence. In fact, it is often discouraging for students to realize that, although they know they are reading much better, they still cannot handle grade level textbooks. In dealing with this problem, as in all aspects of working with troubled readers, it is necessary for the teacher to be absolutely honest with the students. However, the students need to understand that it is not simply because they are ineffective readers that this problem occurs. Textbooks are difficult to read for many reasons.

1.   The textbooks may be poorly written. Too many subject matter textbooks are still written by authorities who do not write clearly and concisely with the nature of the intended readers in mind. Often vocabulary is used that is unnecessarily technical and obscure or not properly developed, illustrated, and defined.

2.   The textbooks may present too much information too superficially and too rapidly. This is, of course, a problem that will vary with the background and interest of the learner and the skill of the teacher in providing experiences to help students read and understand the book. The problem may not be a general weakness in reading but rather too little background for the concepts presented.

Helping students realize that it is not always their fault as readers that they have trouble learning from textbooks is itself an important part of revaluing. Readers in trouble often think that good readers understand everything they read the first time they read it. Even when readers in trouble have reasonably good comprehension, they think they failed because they cannot remember every little detail.

Strategies

Readers in trouble also need other kinds of coping strategies: 1) knowing how to read for the gist of a text rather than every detail and knowing how to skim and survey materials to decide whether they are worth pursuing; 2) knowing how to reread to focus on what is important in difficult materials; 3) knowing how to frame questions to ask the teacher when they do not understand; 4) knowing how to find information in simpler, easier-to-read reference books; and 5) knowing how to get information from sources other than books.

Part of the solution for dealing with difficult school textbooks lies with teachers understanding why students have difficulty with them. Misuse of textbooks by teachers (expecting students to learn from them without the teacher's help) causes as much difficulty for readers as the ineffective use of reading strategies.

Writing

Teachers of readers in trouble often find that, as their students improve in reading, they become enthusiastic writers. Troubled readers are seldom expected to write much, so they usually have had little experience in writing. Their first efforts will look like those of other inexperienced writers, full of invented spelling and unconventional punctuation. Encouraging students to keep journals will create a nonpressured opportunity to write without worrying about accuracy. Students can then move on to a variety of other forms of expository and creative writing. The key to writing development for troubled readers is to emphasize function by focusing on the most useful and meaningful forms of writing.

THE CHALLENGE FOR EDUCATORS

It will not be enough merely to turn troubled readers into reluctant readers. Schools have already produced too many people who can read but do not choose to do so. Reading for troubled readers has been difficult, tedious, and nonproductive, and its development has been associated with much embarrassment and pain. Teachers must patiently help such students to find reading materials that give them personal satisfaction and pleasure. They must help them realize that reading is something they can do when traveling, when waiting, when there is some time available for a quiet, personal activity, or when there is nothing interesting on television or nobody to talk to. Students must reach the point where they choose to read when there is nobody to make them do it before educators can really claim success.

Teachers can make the difference in whether readers in trouble find their way out or not. However, to be successful they will need the help of parents, colleagues less directly concerned with literacy, and the students themselves. All must come to revalue the readers and the reading process.

3

Understanding the Reading Process

Ann M. Marek
Yetta M. Goodman

DURING THE 1960s, KENNETH GOODMAN pioneered a research tool known as miscue analysis to investigate the reading process. Miscue analysis provided a scheme for analyzing oral reading behavior as a "window" on the reading process (K. Goodman 1973). He deliberately chose to use the term *miscue* to avoid the negative connotations of terms like *error* or *mistake* and to emphasize his belief that all reading is cued by language and personal experience and is not simply random, uncontrolled behavior (Y. Goodman et al. 1987). In its most exhaustive form, miscue analysis is conducted using the Goodman Taxonomy of Reading Miscues, a procedure that considers eighteen questions in analyzing the complex relationships between expected responses to the text and observed responses. Miscues are defined as those instances when the reader makes an observed response that differs from what is expected. In miscue analysis *expected responses* are not simply defined as "the printed text"; rather, expected responses are what the analyst expects a reader to read, based upon the analyst's own linguistic perspective. The taxonomy includes questions such as the following that provoke analysis of the relationship between the linguistic qualities of each miscue and the strategies readers use.

- Do miscues result in sentences that are semantically and syntactically acceptable? That is, do the miscues result in sentences that make sense and sound like language?
- Do miscues cause grammatical transformations?
- To what degree do miscues retain the grammatical function of the text items?
- To what degree do miscues retain a semantic relationship to the text items?
- To what degree do miscues retain graphic and phonological similarity to text items?
- In what ways do readers use strategies such as self-correcting and predicting?

Ken continues to test and adapt his theory and model of the reading process, adjusting the taxonomy to take new findings into account (K. Goodman 1984, 1994). The Goodman Taxonomy, with its complex system of questions, reflects current knowledge and theory in linguistics, psycholinguistics, and sociolinguistics. A current version of the taxonomy is included in the *Reading Miscue Inventory* (Y. Goodman et al. 1987).

A less rigorous method for analyzing miscues, the Reading Miscue Inventory (RMI), has been formulated by Yetta Goodman and Carolyn Burke (1972a) and revised by Yetta, Carolyn, and Dorothy Watson (1987). The original RMI version published in 1972 was an attempt to bring the power of miscue analysis to teachers working with students in classrooms or other instructional settings. It was developed with the help of teachers, special educators, and reading specialists, and collaborations with these educators over the years have led to the publication of four new forms of miscue analysis included in the 1987 version of the RMI. Procedure I, the RMI version closest to the original version, was used in much of the research reported in this volume and includes six questions derived from the taxonomy. These questions will be discussed later in this chapter. The three new alternative forms of miscue analysis represent attempts to make miscue analysis simpler and less time consuming. Although each of these versions is somewhat simpler than the original RMI, they can be used as a short cut only by teachers and researchers who have an understanding of the major concepts of miscue analysis. Research has demonstrated that the use of simplified versions of miscue analysis without a corresponding understanding about the reading process will not help teachers understand reading or evaluate their readers (Long 1984). Learning to use miscue analysis in its original form will provide teachers/researchers with insights into language, language learning, and reading. Once they have gained this knowledge, teachers/researchers can then select from among the versions of RMI the procedure most useful to them at a given moment. Since retrospective miscue analysis engages readers in analyzing their own miscues, it also requires that the facilitator (whether it is a teacher/researcher or another student) understand the ways in which readers transact with written texts.

Since its inception, miscue analysis has influenced literally thousands of teachers/researchers as they observe readers' transactions with print. Hundreds of formal miscue analysis studies have been conducted over the past 30 years. Ken and other researchers (see *Annotated Chronological Miscue Analysis Bibliography*, Brown et al. 1994) have studied readers across many dimensions of diversity, including:

- age (from preschool through the elderly)
- linguistic diversity, including speakers of various dialects of English (Downeast Maine, Hawaiian Pidgin, rural and urban English of African Americans), and speakers of languages other than English (Spanish, Chinese, Japanese, American Sign Language, Yiddish, and Hebrew, to name just a few)
- ability level (from the least proficient through the most proficient readers, as rated by their teachers, standardized reading achievement tests, and other measures)
- curriculum orientation (students in classrooms whose orientation toward reading instruction is phonics based, skills based, whole language, literature studies, bilingual/biliterate, or combinations of these)

The research has informed us about the complex relationships among reader, text, and writer and has led to the development of the Goodman model of the reading process (K. Goodman 1984, 1994). This model represents reading as a process of constructing meaning from text. According to Ken, "readers utilize three information systems in constructing their texts and comprehending. Learning to read is at least partly gaining control over these systems and their interactions in the context of literacy events" (1984, 102). The three information systems referred to include the graphophonic system of relationships between orthography and phonology, the syntactic system of grammatical structures in text, and the semantic system—the "whole system by which language may represent highly complex social and personal meaning" (K. Goodman 1994, 1121).

Using these sources of information, readers must apply several cognitive strategies to construct meaning. These strategies are described as:

1. Initiation or task recognition—the overt decision to initiate reading, sometimes inspired by the recognition that something in the visual environment is readable.

2. Sampling and selection—the efficient selection of information to process during reading, based upon "everything the reader knows relevant to language, to reading, and to the particular task" (K. Goodman 1984, 104).
3. Inference—the strategy of using what is known to guess the unknown.
4. Prediction—the ability to anticipate what language may be coming.
5. Confirming and disconfirming—the self-monitoring strategy used to decide whether predictions and inferences have been validated.
6. Correction—the ability to reconstruct text when predictions and inferences have been disconfirmed.
7. Termination—the deliberate decision to discontinue reading.

Ken has described the transaction between the information cueing systems and the strategies used by readers:

> Readers develop sampling strategies to pick only the most useful and necessary graphic cues. They develop prediction strategies to get to the underlying grammatical structure and to anticipate what they are likely to find in the print. They develop confirmation strategies to check on the validity of their predictions. And they have correction strategies to use when their predictions do not work out and they need to reprocess the graphic, syntactic, and semantic cues to get to the meaning. (1984, 9)

And central to his theory is the notion of efficiency in reading.

> Readers use the least amount of available text information necessary in relation to the reader's existing linguistic and conceptual schemata to get to meaning. (1994, 1114)

Whereas the Goodman model recognizes and values efficiency in reading, traditional remedial instruction often emphasizes a need for readers to look more carefully at the letters in words and to read more slowly, more cautiously.

This model of the reading process is particularly compelling because it has been derived from three decades of empirical research using miscue analysis. The insights provided through research using miscue analysis include the following:

1. The purpose of reading is constructing meaning.
2. In the process of constructing meaning, all readers make miscues.
3. There is only one reading process in which three types of information (graphophonic, syntactic, and semantic) are dealt with in an integrated way.
4. This integration is achieved through the processes of sampling, inferring, predicting, confirming, and self-correcting.
5. Highly proficient, average, and non-proficient readers all use the same processes. The differences in their success at constructing meaning from print are a consequence of how they control these processes, not in the processes they use.
6. The major differences between proficient and non-proficient readers are a function of how well they control the semantic and to a lesser extent the syntactic information. There are few differences in the degrees of control that children at different levels of reading proficiency display over the graphophonic information.

Miscue analysis has taught us a great deal more than this, but these findings are particularly important in dealing with readers who need to revalue reading and revalue their own abilities as readers. Too often, readers in trouble believe that they are fundamentally different from those they describe as good readers. Yet miscue analysis reveals that readers at all proficiency levels are more similar than different. There is a single reading process, and the differences among readers are related to how well readers control that process in any given text, at any given time. And readers in trouble can benefit from knowing what the experts know about reading: that all readers make miscues, that miscues vary in the extent to which they disrupt meaning construction, and that a focus on constructing meaning will produce the highest quality miscues.

But how do miscues provide these insights? What questions are asked about miscues? How do the answers help us understand the reading process? In the next section, we describe miscue analysis procedures and share examples of miscues made by Carla when reading "Anita's Gift" (Morgan 1955) to illustrate the power of the analysis. It is not our intention to explain miscue analysis thoroughly enough that a reader new to this process would be able to conduct an analysis. For indepth information regarding miscue analysis procedures, consult *Reading Miscue Inventory: Alternative Procedures* (Y. Goodman et al. 1987). But since familiarity with miscue analysis is necessary for understanding retrospective miscue analysis, we provide the following introduction.

RMI—PROCEDURE I

Each version of miscue analysis involves the collection and examination of a complete oral reading experience followed by a retelling. Though the same reading process is at work when observed responses match expected responses, it is only when observed responses deviate from expected responses that we can see the reading process at work. Miscues are simply defined as observed responses which differ from what the person listening to the reading expects to hear—acknowledging that what someone expects to hear is influenced by that person's own linguistic background and expectations about text. Dialect variability provides many examples of when a person listening to a reader has certain expectations about what the reader will read in response to the text. Consider the pronunciation of the word *can*. English speakers from around the world may pronounce the word variously to rhyme with *kin*, *ken*, or *kan*, depending upon dialect conventions and, to some extent, depending upon the sentence in which the word is used. What may sound like a miscue to one analyst may fit the expectation of another analyst and not be marked as a miscue. Miscue analysts endeavor to be conscious of the ways in which their own linguistic background affects the set of expectations they bring to analyzing a reader's observed responses.

> It is important to keep in mind that teacher/researchers who are involved in analyzing or evaluating miscues bring their own language, concepts, and knowledge about language and cognition to the interpretation of miscue analysis and that this interpretation influences the analysis and evaluation of miscues. What is in the text is always an interpretation based on expectations by the reader, anyone listening to the reader, or anyone evaluating or examining reading. For this reason, it is best to avoid the common-sense notion that what the reader was supposed to have read was printed in the text. (Y. Goodman et al. 1987, 60)

Selecting Materials

Usually, the material selected for miscue analysis is unfamiliar to the reader, but it should be potentially understandable—that is, the content should relate to the reader's experiences and it should be written in language that is accessible to the reader. The text should also be difficult enough to challenge the reader, but not so difficult that the reader is unable to read the material independently. Generally, a minimum of 25 miscues must be generated in order to obtain a picture of the reader's strategies.

An entire cohesive printed text (story, article, chapter, and so on) that is interesting and well written is selected. The length of the text may vary considerably, depending upon the age and proficiency of the reader, but if possible, passages should be at least 500 words long. Of course, passages for very young readers might be much shorter, but it is important with readers of all ages not to underestimate their ability to read a substantial amount of text. A significant study by Menosky (1971) revealed that the quality of miscues changes after the first 200 words in a text. As readers become familiar with the content and the writing style, their predictions are more effective, they self-correct more miscues that do not make sense, and they make fewer corrections on miscues that retain syntactic and semantic acceptability. In short, they produce more high-quality miscues. Therefore, it is critical that texts be of sufficient length to allow readers to become immersed in the piece and to demonstrate their most effective and efficient strategies.

Key pt

Conducting the Reading Miscue Inventory (RMI) Session

In preparation for the RMI session, the teacher/researcher prepares a typescript of the text to mark during the reading. The typescript is a triple-spaced, typewritten version of the original source that maintains the same line endings and page endings as the original material. The setting should be as free from distractions as possible, and a high-quality tape recorder must be used to record the reading. Since the bulk of the analysis will be done after the RMI session, it is imperative that the tape recording be clear.

The reader is then asked to read the entire selection from original source material if possible, without any assistance from the teacher/researcher, and provide a retelling (or other presentation) of the text at the conclusion of the session. The teacher/researcher may wish to have an outline of the text, including major characters, events, and themes, for reference during the retelling. To score the retelling, teachers/researchers may assign 100 points across such categories as characters, events, and themes, and then evaluate the retelling against the 100-point scale. Such an analysis produces a retelling score, which reflects in part what it is a reader has come to understand. Other teachers/researchers may wish to utilize a holistic scoring scale (Irwin & Mitchell 1983), where retellings are rated on an even-numbered (1–4) or an odd-numbered scale (1–5). Holistic ratings may be based upon the teacher/researcher's familiarity with other readers' retellings of a particular text, or with the same student's retelling of other texts.

While the student reads, the teacher/researcher marks every miscue she hears directly on the typescript. The following marking system is used:

1. text item substitution

    There
    Where is Sven?

2. complex substitutions

    anything
    . . . nothing has any weight in space.

3.   substitutions often called reversals

Was/something\wrong with Papa?

4.   substitutions involving bound morphemes

ing
. . . and keep house

5.   omissions

He worked (at home) every afternoon.

6.   insertions

off
When the chair rocked the boy fell.

7.   repetitions (a rereading without correction)

Ⓡ
She pulled him up . . .

8.   correction

Ⓒ *Talking*
Taking Anita by the hand . . .

9.   nonword substitutions

$gorun
. . . between the roof and the ground . . .

All miscues are marked on the typescript, although only a subset are actually coded for miscue analysis. For example, pauses and misarticulations are marked, but are not coded in miscue analysis. In Procedure I of the RMI, miscues which are coded include: substitutions (including reversals and bound morphemes), omissions (including uncorrected partials), insertions, and intonation shifts that cause changes to the syntax or meaning of the text (Y. Goodman et al. 1987, 76). Each of these miscues is coded even if eventually corrected (the analysis will take into consideration whether the miscue was corrected). The first complete observed response is the response that is selected for coding.

Each miscue selected for coding is transferred to a coding sheet. The coding sheet contains columns that refer to the questions asked about each miscue (see below).

Coding the Miscues

MISCUE ANALYSIS PROCEDURE I CODING FORM   © 1987 Richard C. Owen Publishers, Inc.

		1	2	3	4	See 2, 3, 4			See 1, 2, 4				5			6		
READER CARLA DATE 10-15-83		SYNTACTIC ACCEPTABILITY	SEMANTIC ACCEPTABILITY	MEANING CHANGE	CORRECTION	MEANING CONSTRUCTION			GRAMMATICAL RELATIONSHIPS				GRAPHIC SIMILARITY			SOUND SIMILARITY		
TEACHER AGE/GRADE SCHOOL						No Loss	Partial Loss	Loss	Strength	Partial Strength	Overcorrection	Weakness						
SELECTION Anita's gift																		
LINE No./MISCUE No. READER	TEXT												H	S	N	H	S	N
see	seem																	
a. TOTAL MISCUES ___ b. TOTAL WORDS ___ a ÷ b × 100 = MPHW ___		COLUMN TOTAL																
		PATTERN TOTAL																
		PERCENTAGE																

(Goodman, Watson, Burke)

In Procedure I, six questions are asked about each miscue. A miscue produced by Carla while reading *Anita's Gift* is provided as an example:

The little family was very quiet at

ⓒ   see

breakfast and did not seem to be hungry.

An unsophisticated analysis of this miscue might sound something like this:

Seem and *see* are graphically very similar, and the reader who made this miscue was simply not looking closely enough at the visual display. When the reader noticed the *m* after having said *see*, she corrected her error. Reading instruction focusing on paying more attention to the print would remediate this kind of mistake.

But miscue analysis will lead to a more complex explanation for the miscue and a very different recommendation for reading instruction.

Procedure I Questions

Let us consider the Procedure I RMI questions and how they would be answered for this miscue.

Question 1. Does the miscue occur in a structure that is syntactically acceptable in the reader's dialect?

The first complete production of the miscue is selected for coding, so this miscue would be coded as a substitution of *see* for *seem* and would be read for analysis as *The little family was very quiet at breakfast and did not see to be hungry.* To judge syntactic acceptability, the analyst asks whether the miscue fits within the syntax of the sentence and within the entire story. Frequently, when a word that serves one grammatical function is substituted by a word that serves another grammatical function, syntactic acceptability is disrupted. If the miscue is found to be syntactically unacceptable within the sentence, the sentence is then read to determine whether the miscue has partial acceptability—that is, whether it is syntactically compatible with the portion of the sentence leading up to it or whether it is compatible with the portion of the sentence following it. Allowing for "partial" acceptability reveals a great deal about the reader's use of prediction and self-correction strategies. In this example, the miscue is partially acceptable and is coded as P. It is syntactically acceptable with the portion of the sentence leading up to the miscue: *The little family was very quiet at breakfast and did not see . . .* But the verb form of *see* is incompatible with the *to be* which follows.

In this instance, *seem* is a copulative verb that asserts that something is or appears to be. Copulative verbs act as connecting links between the subject and either a predicate noun (which renames the subject) or a predicate adjective (which describes the subject). Here, the subject *family* is linked by the verb *seem* to the predicate adjective *hungry*.

The verb *see*, however, is not a copulative and it is incompatible with the predicate adjective that follows it in the sentence. In its transitive form, *see* most commonly is complemented by a direct object. The easiest way to identify a direct object is to say the subject and verb and then ask the question "What?" The little family did not see what? If this was the prediction Carla was building (that the word would be *see* and that it would be followed by a direct object), it is easy to see why the *to be* copulative and predicate adjective *hungry* caused her to disconfirm her earlier prediction and to self-correct.

Could Carla explain her behavior in these linguistic terms? Of course not. But the knowledge she has about English grammar as a speaker of the language, combined with her drive to make sense of text, leads her to reprocess the text and self-correct.

For Question 1, the choices for miscue coding are:

Y—The miscue occurs in a structure that is completely syntactically acceptable within the sentence and within the text.

P—The miscue occurs in a structure that is either syntactically acceptable with the first part of the sentence or is syntactically acceptable with the last part of the sentence. Or the miscue is syntactically acceptable within the sentence, but not within the complete text.

N—The miscue occurs in a sentence that is not syntactically acceptable.

The miscue *see* substituted for *seem* is coded as P, since it occurs in a structure that is syntactically acceptable with the first part of the sentence; the coding is reflected on the sheet as follows:

MISCUE ANALYSIS PROCEDURE I   CODING FORM   © 1987 Richard C. Owen Publishers, Inc.

READER CARLA DATE 10-15-83	SYNTACTIC ACCEPTABILITY (1)	SEMANTIC ACCEPTABILITY (2)	MEANING CHANGE (3)	CORRECTION (4)	MEANING CONSTRUCTION (See 2,3,4)			GRAMMATICAL RELATIONSHIPS (See 1,2,4)				GRAPHIC SIMILARITY (5)			SOUND SIMILARITY (6)		
TEACHER AGE/GRADE SCHOOL					No Loss	Partial Loss	Loss	Strength	Partial Strength	Overcorrection	Weakness	H	S	N	H	S	N
SELECTION Anita's gift																	
LINE No./MISCUE No. READER TEXT																	
see seem	P																

Question 2. Does the miscue occur in a structure that is semantically acceptable within the reader's dialect?

In a way, words in English have no meaning outside the syntactic context in which they are used. In Ken Goodman's words, "A text cannot be comprehensible to a reader without being grammatical to that reader" (1994, 1119). For example, we could ask someone what *can* means, and that person would have to ask, "How is it used?" It has a different meaning in each of the following sentences:

- I can take out the trash.
- I took out the trash can.
- Can the guy who took out the trash.

Because semantic acceptability depends on syntactic acceptability, miscue researchers have determined that semantic acceptability cannot be coded "higher" than syntactic acceptability. Therefore, if syntactic acceptability is coded as Y, semantic acceptability may be either Y, P, or N. But if syntactic acceptability is coded as P, semantic acceptability may only be P or N. And if syntactic acceptability is N, semantic acceptability must also be N.

In the miscue above, the verb form substitution of *see* for *seem* is acceptable only with the portion of the sentence leading up to and including the miscue, so we coded the miscue P for syntactic acceptability. Semantic acceptability, therefore, will be either P or N. In this instance, one can imagine a semantically acceptable structure that could have begun *The little family was very quiet at breakfast and did not see . . .* For example, the sentence could have been:

- The little family was very quiet at breakfast and did not see the man approach the front door.

or

- The little family was very quiet at breakfast and did not see a solution for their problems.

The choices for coding Question 2 are:

Y—The miscue occurs in a structure that is completely semantically acceptable within the sentence and within the text.

P—The miscue occurs in a structure that is either semantically acceptable with the first part of the sentence or is semantically acceptable with the last part of the sentence. Or the miscue is semantically acceptable within the sentence, but not within the complete text.

N—The miscue occurs in a sentence that is not semantically acceptable.

The miscue is therefore coded as P, since it occurs in a structure that is semantically acceptable with the first part of the sentence.

The coding sheet now reflects analysis of the first two questions:

MISCUE ANALYSIS PROCEDURE I CODING FORM   © 1987 Richard C. Owen Publishers, Inc.

		1	2	3	4	See 2, 3, 4			See 1, 2, 4				5			6		
READER CARLA DATE 10-15-83		SYNTACTIC ACCEPTABILITY	SEMANTIC ACCEPTABILITY	MEANING CHANGE	CORRECTION	MEANING CONSTRUCTION			GRAMMATICAL RELATIONSHIPS				GRAPHIC SIMILARITY			SOUND SIMILARITY		
TEACHER AGE/GRADE SCHOOL																		
SELECTION Anita's gift																		
LINE No./MISCUE No.						No Loss	Partial Loss	Loss	Strength	Partial Strength	Overcorrection	Weakness						
READER	TEXT												H	S	N	H	S	N
See	seem	P	P															

Question 3. Does the miscue result in a change of meaning? This question is asked only if the miscue has been coded completely syntactically and semantically acceptable. Over the years, teachers/researchers using miscue analysis have determined that the extent of meaning change is a legitimate question only when the reader has produced acceptable structures. Most miscue analysts agree that evaluating meaning change in the absence of a coherent structure is a difficult if not invalid judgment. The purpose of the question is to evaluate the extent to which an acceptable structure changes ideas, incidents, characters, facts, concepts, and so on, within the text. Of course, because reading is an active construction of meaning, the analyst has constructed her own meaning and is judging the reader's construction against her own. As a result, judgments of meaning change are the most likely to vary among analysts, and they can have spirited disputes about the extent of meaning change. But this difficulty does not compel us to eliminate the question—after all, the very difficulty involved in reaching consensus among analysts helps them appreciate the personal construction of meaning within the context of a more general, social construction of meaning.

However, since Carla's miscue was judged partially acceptable both syntactically and semantically, the question regarding change of meaning is not coded.

But consider the following miscue:

"There's nothing we can do now, Anita. It's

too late. The store's closed. Nothing to do

but go home and go to bed. I have money to pay

for the flowers and—well, if he's a kind man,

will
it may be all right."

In this instance, Carla has substituted *will* for *may*. The substitution fits both within the sentence and within the story and is fully acceptable syntactically and semantically. Since it would be coded Y for syntactic acceptability and Y for semantic acceptability, we would consider the question of meaning change. The coding choices for Question 3 are:

Y—There is inconsistency, loss, or change of meaning of a *major* idea, incident, character, fact, sequence, or concept.
P—There is inconsistency, loss, or meaning change of a *minor* idea, incident, character, fact, sequence, or concept.
N—Within the context of the entire passage, no change in meaning is involved.

The analyst must ask, "How significant is the shift in meaning represented by the miscue?" In the story, the character who is speaking, Pablo, is attempting to reassure his little sister, Anita, that they can make amends to a flower shop owner from whom Anita inadvertently stole flowers. Central to the plot of the story is the family's fear of retribution for Anita's theft and their relief when the shop owner understands her mistake—after all, she thought flowers in New York were free just like they are in Puerto Rico. In the text, Pablo says *if he's a kind man, it may be all right*. Pablo reveals his uncertainty that even a kind man will forgive Anita for stealing flowers, however innocent her act.

But if, as in the miscue, Pablo says *it will be all right*, then the character is presented as rather confident of a successful resolution. In some sense, a display of confidence might lessen the tension the author is attempting to establish as the family awaits morning and their opportunity to resolve the conflict. The author, however, builds tension in other ways in the next paragraphs. He describes the restless night Pablo spent and his wish to be running the other way as he and Anita approach the flower shop the next morning. Since uncertainty about the outcome is established through subsequent passages, it is doubtful that this miscue would result in a significant shift in meaning, though clearly some change has been made. Code the miscue P for meaning change, as follows:

MISCUE ANALYSIS PROCEDURE I   CODING FORM   © 1987 Richard C. Owen Publishers, Inc.

						1	2	3	4	See 2, 3, 4			See 1, 2, 4				5			6		
READER	CARLA			DATE 10-15-83		SYNTACTIC ACCEPTABILITY	SEMANTIC ACCEPTABILITY	MEANING CHANGE	CORRECTION	MEANING CONSTRUCTION			GRAMMATICAL RELATIONSHIPS				GRAPHIC SIMILARITY			SOUND SIMILARITY		
TEACHER		AGE/ GRADE		SCHOOL																		
SELECTION	*Anita's gift*									No Loss	Partial Loss	Loss	Strength	Partial Strength	Overcorrection	Weakness						
LINE No./MISCUE No.		READER		TEXT													H	S	N	H	S	N
		See.		*Seem*		ρ	P	--														
		will		*may*		Y	Y	P														

Returning to our original example, it should be clear at this point that the *see* for *seem* substitution is not simply carelessness—rather, it demonstrates the success with which Carla is able to predict semantic and syntactic structures. But what happens when her good predictions aren't confirmed? Consider the next RMI questions.

Question 4. Is the miscue corrected?   To establish whether or not the reader attempts to correct the miscue, the analyst determines the following:

Y—The miscue is corrected.

P—There is either an unsuccessful attempt to correct, or the expected response is read and then abandoned.

N—There is no attempt to correct.

In Carla's miscue, after saying *see* for *seem* she regresses to the point between *and* and *did*, repeats the sentence portion, self-corrects the miscue, and continues to the end of the sentence. In this case, she makes a complete correction of the miscue, so this question is coded with Y. Occasionally, readers will make an unsuccessful attempt to correct a miscue, or they will read the expected response and then abandon it. In either of these instances, the miscue is coded P for partial correction. If no attempt is made to correct the miscue, it is coded with an N.

Of course, we now understand that Carla was not simply substituting one word (*see*) for another (*seem*) based on their graphic similarity, although she may have used some of the graphic cues from *seem* to support her prediction. And it is not likely that she simply looked closer at the word, noticed the *m*, and restated the word. Rather, she had successfully predicted a sentence ending which could have been written by the author. However, because the words *to be* signal that her prediction is not working out, she regresses to a point where meaning can be reprocessed and self-corrects this miscue. Just because we don't hear Carla say the words *to be hungry* does not mean she hasn't processed them. She has made a prediction (*The little family was very quiet at breakfast and did not see . . .*), disconfirmed that prediction (*did not see . . . to be hungry???*), and corrected by reconstructing the text when her predictions and inferences were disconfirmed. Question 4 is reflected on the coding sheet as follows:

MISCUE ANALYSIS PROCEDURE I   CODING FORM   © 1987 Richard C. Owen Publishers, Inc.

READER CARLA DATE 10-15-83			1 SYNTACTIC ACCEPTABILITY	2 SEMANTIC ACCEPTABILITY	3 MEANING CHANGE	4 CORRECTION	See 2, 3, 4 — MEANING CONSTRUCTION			See 1, 2, 4 — GRAMMATICAL RELATIONSHIPS				5 GRAPHIC SIMILARITY			6 SOUND SIMILARITY		
TEACHER AGE/GRADE SCHOOL							No Loss	Partial Loss	Loss	Strength	Partial Strength	Overcorrection	Weakness	H	S	N	H	S	N
SELECTION Anita's gift																			
LINE No./MISCUE No.	READER	TEXT																	
	See	seem	P	P	--	Y													

Question 5. How much do the two words look alike?

To answer this question, the analyst divides the text item and the miscue into three parts:

H—A high degree of graphic similarity exists between the miscue and the text.

S— Some degree of graphic similarity exists between the miscue and the text.

N—No degree of graphic similarity exists betweeen the miscue and the text.

A high (H) degree of similarity exists if two parts of the text look like two parts of the miscue and appear in the same location (beginning, middle, or end); some (S) similarity exists if one part of the text looks like one part of the miscue or if there is the same general configuration and a letter in common; no (N) similarity exists if there are no letters in common.

Carla's substitution of *see* for *seem* is highly similar, with three of the four letters the same, and is coded H on the coding sheet:

MISCUE ANALYSIS PROCEDURE I   CODING FORM   © 1987 Richard C. Owen Publishers, Inc.

READER: CARLA DATE 10-15-83			1 SYNTACTIC ACCEPTABILITY	2 SEMANTIC ACCEPTABILITY	3 MEANING CHANGE	4 CORRECTION	See 2, 3, 4 — MEANING CONSTRUCTION			See 1, 2, 4 — GRAMMATICAL RELATIONSHIPS				5 GRAPHIC SIMILARITY			6 SOUND SIMILARITY		
TEACHER AGE/GRADE SCHOOL							No Loss	Partial Loss	Loss	Strength	Partial Strength	Overcorrection	Weakness	H	S	N	H	S	N
SELECTION: Anita's gift																			
LINE No./MISCUE No. READER		TEXT																	
	see	seem	P	P	—	4								✓					

Question 6. How much do the two words sound alike? Sound similarity is portioned and coded just like graphic similarity. The analyst must keep the reader's dialect in mind when coding sound similarity and not judge the reader against the analyst's dialect preferences. Coding choices are as follows:

H—A high degree of sound similarity exists between the miscue and the text.
S— Some degree of sound similarity exists between the miscue and the text.
N—No degree of sound similarity exists between the miscue and the text.

Carla's substitution sounds highly similar to the expected response and is coded H on the coding sheet.

MISCUE ANALYSIS PROCEDURE I   CODING FORM   © 1987 Richard C. Owen Publishers, Inc.

READER: CARLA DATE 10-15-83			1 SYNTACTIC ACCEPTABILITY	2 SEMANTIC ACCEPTABILITY	3 MEANING CHANGE	4 CORRECTION	See 2, 3, 4 — MEANING CONSTRUCTION			See 1, 2, 4 — GRAMMATICAL RELATIONSHIPS				5 GRAPHIC SIMILARITY			6 SOUND SIMILARITY		
TEACHER AGE/GRADE SCHOOL							No Loss	Partial Loss	Loss	Strength	Partial Strength	Overcorrection	Weakness	H	S	N	H	S	N
SELECTION: Anita's gift																			
LINE No./MISCUE No. READER		TEXT																	
	see	seem	P	P	—	4								✓			✓		

Patterns

After the six questions are considered for each miscue, the patterns of relationships among the questions are analyzed to indicate the reader's degree of proficiency in using reading strategies. Two sets of patterns are examined.

Patterns for Constructing Meaning These patterns reflect the reader's attempts to make sense of the text in relationship to the expected meaning. Again, the "expected" meaning is whatever the analyst believes the author intended, and analysts need to be sensitive to this fact. The answers to Questions 2, 3, and 4 form the basis for the patterns. The patterns fall into several categories that indicate the influence of the miscues on the construction of meaning:

NO LOSS—These patterns include miscues that are semantically acceptable with no meaning change or, if not acceptable, are corrected.
PARTIAL LOSS—These patterns usually include those miscues that are semanti-

cally acceptable but cause some meaning change or are only partially semantically acceptable. These miscues are not successfully corrected.

LOSS—These patterns are largely those that are semantically unacceptable and not successfully corrected.

Patterns for Grammatical Relationships   These patterns reflect the reader's ability to focus on syntax and semantics and to make corrections when necessary. The answers to Questions 1, 2, and 4 are used to establish one of the following patterns:

STRENGTH OF GRAMMATICAL RELATIONSHIPS—Strength is indicated when miscues are syntactically and semantically acceptable or, if not, are corrected.

PARTIAL STRENGTH—Partial strength is indicated when miscues are acceptable syntactically but not fully semantically acceptable and not corrected.

OVERCORRECTION—Overcorrection is indicated when miscues are fully acceptable syntactically and semantically, yet the reader self-corrects.

WEAKNESS—Weakness is indicated when miscues are not fully acceptable syntactically or semantically and are not successfully corrected.

In *Reading Miscue Inventory: Alternative Procedures*, instructions are provided about how to calculate percentages among the various patterns to build a profile of the reader's strengths. These statistics are useful for some purposes. The profile, along with the retelling information, reveals the qualitative nature of the miscues, provides a comprehensive picture of the reader's ability to transact with that particular text, and gives teachers/researchers a great deal of insight into the reading process at work. It can also document a reader's development over time and across genre types. Carla's patterns are shown on the coding sheet.

MISCUE ANALYSIS PROCEDURE I   CODING FORM   © 1987 Richard C. Owen Publishers, Inc.

READER CARLA DATE 10-15-83	1 SYNTACTIC ACCEPTABILITY	2 SEMANTIC ACCEPTABILITY	3 MEANING CHANGE	4 CORRECTION	See 2, 3, 4 MEANING CONSTRUCTION			See 1, 2, 4 GRAMMATICAL RELATIONSHIPS				5 GRAPHIC SIMILARITY			6 SOUND SIMILARITY		
TEACHER AGE/GRADE SCHOOL SELECTION Anita's gift LINE No./MISCUE No. READER TEXT					No Loss	Partial Loss	Loss	Strength	Partial Strength	Overcorrection	Weakness	H	S	N	H	S	N
see seem	P	P	–	4	✓			✓				✓			✓		

RMI—PROCEDURE III

Teachers/researchers familiar with Procedure I of the Reading Miscue Inventory have over the years invented streamlined versions of the RMI to suit their purposes and to minimize the time involved in coding the miscue data. The 1987 revision of the original RMI (Y. Goodman et al.) includes three versions of the RMI in addition to Procedure I. Because several of the case studies presented in this book (see Chapters 7 through 10) utilize Procedure III of the RMI, a summary of that procedure follows.

Procedure III provides insights into the strengths and weaknesses of readers, but because the unit of analysis is the sentence as the reader finally produced it, it provides less detail than Procedure I about a reader's strategy use. The process for tape-recording the reading and the retelling is the same as in Procedure I; however, in Procedure III, the typescript itself is used both for marking miscues and coding of each sentence both in the right-hand margin (see below). The teacher/researcher reads each sentence as the reader left it and codes the sentence by asking the following questions:

Question 1: Syntactic Acceptability. Is the sentence syntactically acceptable in the reader's dialect and within the context of the entire selection? The possible codings are Y (the sentence as finally produced by the reader is syntactically acceptable) or N (the sentence is not syntactically acceptable).

Question 2: Semantic Acceptability. Is the sentence semantically acceptable in the reader's dialect and within the context of the entire selection? (Question 2 cannot be coded Y if Question 1 has been coded N.) The possible codings are Y (the sentence as finally produced by the reader is semantically acceptable) or N (the sentence is not semantically acceptable).

Question 3: Meaning Change. Does the sentence, as finally produced by the reader, change the meaning of the selection? (Question 3 is coded only if Questions 1 and 2 are coded Y.) The coding choices are N (there is no change in meaning), P (there is a minor change of meaning), or Y (there is a major change of meaning).

Question 4: Graphic Similarity. How much does the miscue look like the text item? Substitution miscues are coded as H (high degree of graphic similarity), S (some degree of graphic similarity), or N (no graphic similarity between the miscue and the text). The codings (H, S, or N) are placed in a circle directly above the word-level substitutions on the typescript.

Following is an example from the RMI of how this marking and coding would appear for two sentences on the typescript:

Once upon a time there was a woodman

who thought that no one worked as hard as

he did. One evening when he came home   1. YN —

from work, he said to his wife, "What do you

do all day while I am away cutting wood?"   2. YYN

The summary of statistics for Procedure III can be placed at the bottom of the typescript, and it would include:

Syn. Accept.	#Y__	Y__%	#N__	N__%			# Sentences Coded __
Sem. Accept.	#Y__	Y__%	#N__	N__%			# Sentences Coded __
Meaning Change	#Y__	Y__%	#P__	P__%	#N__	N__%	# Sentences Coded __
Graphic Sim.	#H__	H__%	#S__	S__%	#N__	N__%	# Miscues Coded __

To compute syntactic acceptability, count the number of sentences coded Y and enter this number in the appropriate column; do the same for the number of sentences coded N. Then add these two subtotals and enter in the right-hand column. Then divide the subtotals of N and Y by the total number of coded sentences to calculate percentages; enter these in appropriate columns. Semantic acceptability, meaning change, and graphic similarity are calculated in the same way. Teachers/researchers may wish to calculate the total number of miscues per hundred words, through dividing the number of individual miscues by the total number of words in the text. The retelling may be evaluated as described in Procedure I.

Miscue Analysis Insights into Carla's Ability

We now appreciate Carla as a sophisticated language user, able to predict the author's linguistic structures based on her own knowledge about language and the way it is represented in texts. She is able to sample the print, focus on meaning, and reprocess text when the structures she is producing don't make sense and don't sound like language. Her retelling score was 90, reflecting her ability to integrate and comprehend what she was reading.

However, an analysis of each of her miscues present a profile of a reader who is not using these effective strategies all of the time. Consider the following statistics, based on an analysis using Procedure III of the RMI:

1. Carla made 167 miscues in 1,394 words—12 miscues per 100 words.
2. She made 162 substitutions:

   67 percent of the substitutions had high graphic similarity
   32 percent had some graphic similarity
   1 percent had no graphic similarity
3. Some of the substitutions were nonwords, noted with a $, like the following examples:

                          $drust
   And so he burst into the apartment that night

   without the least idea of what he would find

   within those four walls of home.

                    • • •

                                        $siction
   They stopped while Pablo looked the situation

   over.

4. Other substitutions were semantically unacceptable and not corrected:

                                    trees
   This brought a fresh flood of tears from Anita.

                    • • •

We give them away just as little sister here

brought
thought people in New York do.

5.   A few of the substitutions were high-quality substitutions that retained syntactic and semantic acceptability:

shiver
He felt a shudder run through Anita and put

his arm protectingly across her shoulders to

keep her warm.

•   •   •

But for now, if Anita will come sometimes on

Saturday nights at six, I will give her a few

blooms
blossoms to take to her mamita, flowers that

will not keep in the shop over Sunday.

•   •   •

quietly
But Grandmother answered quickly, "Not because

he is from one place or another, daughter, is

anyone kind, but because kindness is in his

heart toward all people."

What strikes us about Carla's profile is the extent to which she is relying on graphophonic cues when reading. A total of 99 percent of her substitution miscues had at least some similarity to the text items, and 67 percent of the miscues were highly similar to the text. The examples of nonword substitutions, as well as uncorrected and unacceptable substitutions, show how very much Carla is struggling to produce words that look like the text. Even her high-quality substitutions show considerable attention to graphophonic cues. We conclude from this analysis that the *last* thing Carla needs is to pay more attention to the letters in words. It appears as though her preoccupation with letters and words is sometimes taking her attention away from making sense. For example, each of the nonword substitutions was not corrected. Yet we know from several other miscues that Carla is able to self-correct when she is focusing on constructing meaning. The instructional implications we draw from her miscue analysis include the following:

1. Carla needs to read whole, authentic texts so that she can focus on making sense of real texts.
2. Carla needs to recognize that many of her miscues reveal her strengths as a reader: her ability to make good predictions and to reprocess text when those predictions are disconfirmed. Those strengths should form the basis for any instruction.
3. Carla needs to trust that texts will make sense and that she should not tolerate nonsense. Often readers in trouble spend so much time working with fragmented language that they forget that reading is supposed to make sense.
4. Carla needs to understand the power of one consistent strategy: Make it make sense to you and settle for nothing less.

Furthermore, everything we learned through miscue analysis can be accessible to Carla as well. We are remiss when we fail to share with readers what we know about language, about reading, and about learning. Finding ways to share our understanding can be difficult; obviously, a lecture on sociolinguistic or psycholinguistic theory will be useless. But a technique like retrospective miscue analysis, where readers ask themselves a series of questions about their miscues in the presence of a facilitator who understands the complexity of the reading process, can significantly demystify the process and restore readers' confidence in their abilities as language users. The procedure is described fully in Chapter 4.

4

Retrospective Miscue Analysis

Yetta M. Goodman
Ann M. Marek

MISCUE ANALYSIS HAS BECOME A powerful heuristic tool for teachers and researchers as they build understandings about the reading process. As Kenneth Goodman predicted years ago (1973), miscue analysis has become a window on the reading process, providing knowledge to build and expand on a transactional sociopsycho-linguistic model of reading (K. Goodman 1984, 1994). Miscue analysis provides a base upon which teachers/researchers construct theories about how reading works, discover how students read, and explore readers' knowledge about language. Such knowledge helps teachers support students in the development of effective and efficient reading strategies.

Miscue analysis can also be used by students to gain insights into themselves as readers. In this chapter, we discuss ways to involve readers, especially those who have had difficulty learning to read in school settings, in using miscue analysis to help them revalue their abilities as readers and at the same time come to new understandings about language use and the reading process. We also suggest ways for teachers/researchers to learn more about the reading process by eavesdropping on readers who are examining their own reading. Since this revaluing procedure involves readers listening to, thinking about, and talking about the miscues they made during a previous oral reading, it is called *retrospective* miscue analysis (RMA). Retrospective miscue analysis was initially developed by a Canadian secondary school reading specialist, Chris Worsnop, in the 1970s (see Chapter 12). The use of RMA has expanded over the past twenty years, and in this chapter we describe a variety of purposes and methods for engaging students in retrospective miscue analysis.

When talking about the various uses of RMA, it is helpful to acknowledge that the participants in RMA wear different hats or have different roles to play at differ-ent times depending upon their purposes for conducting the RMA sessions. When classroom teachers such as Debra Goodman, Don Howard, and others organize the use of RMA in classroom settings for instructional purposes, they take a teacher stance. In such instances the focus is on how to maximize the positive effects of RMA on students' learning.

As more teachers have developed strong research interests and more full-time researchers have become aware of the importance of instruction taking place in authentic settings, the teacher and researcher roles are not easily separable. Sarah Costello has assumed a research stance, as shown by her work with Bernice (see Chapter 10), and Ann Marek researched RMA to help Marlene and Gina revalue themselves as readers (Chapters 5 and 6). Because of these overlapping roles, we use the term *teacher/researcher*. In a sense, each person needs to be clear about the primary purpose of their work with RMA. We will note where teachers/researchers have different questions and issues to consider, but we use the conjoined noun (teacher/researcher) to represent the blurring of the roles of inquirers interested in RMA. At all times, the stance the teacher/researcher takes in using RMA will be influenced by the questions and purposes that are most significant, and those decisions will in turn influence the organization of the RMA procedures.

Retrospective miscue analysis is a dynamic tool, and we anticipate that teachers/researchers will adapt the procedures described in this book. One basic requirement, however, in using and adapting RMA is that teachers/researchers understand the theoretical issues underlying miscue analysis (K. Goodman 1994) and are knowledgeable about conducting miscue analysis (see Chapter 3 and Y. Goodman et al. 1987). This knowledge is critical in responding appropriately to readers as they analyze their own miscues. Teachers/researchers draw upon their theoretical understandings of the reading process to help readers revalue themselves as readers.

THE PURPOSES OF RETROSPECTIVE MISCUE ANALYSIS

Retrospective miscue analysis allows readers to become overtly and consciously aware of their own use of reading strategies and to value their knowledge of the linguistic systems they control as they transact with written texts. It provides readers with an opportunity to know themselves as readers, to observe and evaluate their transactions with texts, to talk about their views with others, and to revalue their strengths as learners and language users (K. Goodman 1986; Y. Goodman & Marek 1989) (see Chapter 2).

Retrospective miscue analysis, as an instructional tool, helps readers build insights into themselves as readers and into the reading process in general. In instructional settings, it provides opportunities for students to self-evaluate and for teachers to evaluate information that may be used to plan instructional aspects of a reading program.

The role of the teacher in RMA discussions requires sensitivity toward the readers and an understanding of the reading process in order to conduct RMA discussions. Teachers are learners during these discussions, discovering more about themselves as teachers and honing their observational abilities as they learn to listen and observe carefully and thoughtfully. They become sensitive to the importance of critical moment teaching, and they know when a reader needs to be supported, when a good question can be raised, when an alternate strategy could be suggested, or when some phenomenon should be ignored and left for another session. Teachers relinquish control over the reader during RMA sessions and help readers assume responsibility for their own decisions concerning which strategies are most helpful at any particular point in time during the reading. Through gentle but provocative questioning, the teacher focuses the reader on self evaluation in such a way as to create conflict within the reader that pushes the reader to reconsider the strategies that interfere with his or her construction of meaning.

RMA is also a research tool that reveals information about the ways in which readers respond to their own miscues as they read and the ways in which a conscious awareness of the role of miscues influences reading development. Researchers can examine how text differences such as formats, genres, language structures, and content affect readers' miscues. They can also examine the language, questioning techniques, and instructional strategies used by teachers and students to understand how language and instruction influence the views and responses of the students.

RMA GENERAL PROCEDURES

General procedures for conducting retrospective miscue analysis sessions are presented below with suggestions for adaptations for instructional and research purposes. The general procedures include descriptions of:

- Initial Session with Reader
- Preparation for the RMA Session
- Conducting the RMA Session
- Follow-Up of the RMA Session

A detailed outline for the Retrospective Miscue Analysis Session is included at the end of the chapter.

Initial Session with the Reader

As with all interactions with students, the initial encounter during the first session with the reader establishes a warm and positive relationship. We strongly believe that readers need to understand the purpose of the instructional program or research project and know what is involved in terms of their time and responsibility. The reader should agree to participate willingly. The teacher/researcher then interacts with the reader to discover what the reader believes about himself or herself as a reader, the lengths and types of literacy events the reader engages in, and the occupational and avocational interests of the reader. In general, the teacher/researcher sets a tone that helps the reader feel comfortable.

Conducting the *Reading Interview* (Y. Goodman et al. 1987) (Appendix A) provides useful information about students' literacy histories, the influences of reading instruction, and their perceptions about themselves as readers (and writers) and about the reading process. A range of reading material is often available at the initial reading session to discover what kinds of reading materials the reader is interested in and to involve the student in the selection of the reading material.

The initial session usually includes the tape recording of an oral reading of a whole story or article, followed by a retelling using the steps of miscue analysis as presented in the *Reading Miscue Inventory* (RMI) (Y. Goodman et al. 1987). For younger readers or if the initial session has taken longer than anticipated, a second session may be set up to collect the RMI. The reader is given a selection to read which is considered within the language and conceptual knowledge of the reader, but which is unfamiliar and somewhat challenging. The selection of the material is made based upon the teacher/researcher's knowledge about the interests and abilities of the readers (see Chapter 3, this volume). Ranges of reading genre and presentational formats may be used throughout the RMA sessions to gain information about the readers' responses to different texts.

The reader reads the text without any aid from the teacher/researcher. The teacher/researcher marks the miscues on a typescript that is a replica of the actual reading material. Following the oral reading, the reader provides a retelling, which is usually oral, although for specific purposes other kinds of presentations, such as written retellings, webs, drawing, or sketches, are used. After the unaided retelling, the teacher/researcher extends the retelling by asking the reader open-ended questions. (For a more detailed discussion of retellings, see the *Reading Miscue Inventory*; Y. Goodman et al. 1987.) The reading and retelling are tape-recorded.

As students become familiar with the procedures, it is possible to organize the sessions so that two students working together conduct the RMI session.

For Research Purposes   The selection of materials, the types of readers, and the retelling/presentation formats are all adaptable depending upon the researcher's questions. Thorough records are kept documenting dates and contextual setting. The data are organized so that they can be retrieved for in-depth analysis and comparison over time. The important issue is that the rationale for the questions and any adaptation to the procedures are grounded in miscue analysis theory.

Preparation for the RMA Session

The teacher/researcher listens again to the tape recorded RMI reading and retelling episode, checks the miscue markings on the typescript of the story, and either makes a transcript of the retelling or notes aspects of the retelling that shed light on the miscues and the reader's comprehension that will be helpful in planning the RMA session. The miscues are coded using one of the miscue analysis procedures (Y. Goodman et al. 1987) to establish a profile of the reader's use of strategies and language cueing systems. It is important to be well acquainted with all aspects of the reader's RMI. The teacher/researcher then makes a plan regarding the direction that the RMA session will take and arranges a time for the RMA session with the reader. For example, in some cases students are in control of the miscue selection process and involved in listening for the miscues and deciding which miscues will be examined, while for other purposes the readers will only hear the miscues that the teacher/researcher preselects.

Teachers may wish to focus a reader's attention on particular kinds of miscues (i.e., omissions that result in semantically and syntactically acceptable sentences), thus establishing a theme for the kinds of miscues that will be discussed. In this way, the RMA session becomes similar to a strategy lesson session (Y. Goodman et al. 1996). (See "Miscue Selection" below for further discussion.) At other times, the teacher/researcher may observe and participate without taking control of the session while a pair or small group of students work together to decide which miscues they want to discuss. The students then stop the tape recording where they wish and participate in a discussion concerning the quality of miscues and the role of miscues in the reading process.

Deciding when to schedule the first and subsequent RMA sessions will depend upon various factors, including the time and availability of the teacher/researcher and the readers. Schedules for younger children may include shorter and more frequent sessions than those for older readers. Younger children should probably not participate in an RMA session on the same day that the RMI takes place or there should be a substantial break between the RMI and RMA sessions.

For Research Purposes   It might be helpful to examine the ways length of time between the RMI and the RMA sessions or between the RMA sessions affect readers' responses. An important question to explore would be to compare the differences and similarities between those sessions in which readers select their own miscues and those in which the teacher/researcher preselect miscues for discussion.

Preselection of RMA Session Miscues   When the teacher/researcher chooses to preselect miscues for analysis during the RMA session, we recommend that five to ten miscues be selected for discussion with the reader. In selecting the miscues, the teacher/researcher must take into consideration the characteristics of the reader. For example, if the reader has low self-confidence, the teacher/researcher should select high-quality miscues that are fully acceptable semantically and syntactically and left uncorrected or miscues that are unacceptable and are self-corrected. Other suggestions for preselecting miscues are presented in the chart below.

Reader Characteristics	Suggested Miscue Selection
Reads slowly, hesitantly; makes miscues that have high graphophonic similarity to the text but may disrupt meaning	Select miscues that are acceptable and have little or no graphophonic similarity
	Select insertion and omission miscues that are acceptable
Seldom attempts self-correction	Select miscues that demonstrate effective prediction, disconfirmation, and self-correction strategies; contrast with miscues where self-correction is not attempted

Produces nonword substitutions for words in the reader's oral vocabulary	Select miscues where persistence resulted in semantically and syntactically acceptable miscues; contrast with nonword substitutions
Consistently corrects miscues that are syntactically and semantically acceptable (overcorrection)	Select fully acceptable miscues where correction is unnecessary
Satisfied with focus on surface features of the text rather than focus on making sense	Contrast miscues that do/don't make sense
	Select miscues that highlight manipulation of syntax in insertions and omissions
Is not consistently reading efficiently	Select miscues that highlight efficient strategies
Is unaware of the strength shown in making higher quality miscues in the middles and ends of texts	Select miscues that highlight the increasing quality of miscues as the text progresses

We believe that with students who lack confidence, the teacher/researcher should initially preselect miscues and select high-quality miscues that focus readers' attention on their strengths. These are miscues most often missed by readers and teachers alike. Eventually, the selection of miscues may shift from the teacher/ researcher to the reader, and this process is described below. When RMA is organized for students to work in pairs or small groups, readers will probably be in control of selecting their own miscues at an earlier point in the process.

Teachers will build knowledge about the kinds of miscues to preselect for different readers as they gain experience in conducting RMA sessions. Examination of the transcripts of the sessions helps teachers evaluate their own procedures, their questioning techniques, and the miscue selection process. As teachers help the reader focus on high-quality strategies, in comparison to less effective and efficient ones, they often create a useful disequilibrium that the reader has to accommodate. As readers become more consciously aware of the reading process and of the strategies that help them focus on constructing meaning, they lessen their reliance on strategies (like looking more carefully at the letters in a word and spending an inordinate amount of time attacking it) that are in fact interfering with proficient reading.

For Research Purposes   It would be helpful to study the differences between readers' responses to preselected or self-selected miscues. Or researchers might examine how teachers decide which miscues to preselect and what effect their selection has upon the reader's development of more efficient and effective strategies.

Conducting the RMA Session

Two tape recorders are arranged. The original reading material is on hand, as are two copies (or more depending on the number of participants) of the type-script of the reading material. One typescript of the text is unmarked—the other is marked with the reader's miscues (if miscues are preselected). In some instances, the readers may become involved in marking their own miscues on the typescript, whether the miscues have been preselected for analysis or whether the readers are selecting the miscues during the RMA session itself. These readers usually have become familiar with the most common miscue markings (that is, markings for omissions, insertions, substitutions, repetitions, and corrections), and they mark miscues in ways that are quite similar to standard miscue analysis protocol. One tape recorder is used to replay the original reading session in order to listen to and discuss particular selected miscues. The other tape recorder is left on to preserve the discussions during the RMA session.

It is important to have all the materials available from the beginning, including pencils and paper for note taking. Tables and chairs should be arranged so that participants are seated comfortably throughout the session. If possible, a quiet and separate room for the session will aid in obtaining a good tape recording. Physical arrangements and other procedures will need to be adapted depending on whether the RMA occurs in a one-on-one setting, in pairs, in small groups, or as a total class experience.

It is important to be honest with the students regarding the purpose of the procedure, how long the session will last, how many sessions there will be, and what the student can expect during the session. Readers are most comfortable in research and instructional settings when they know what is expected of them, what their role is in the process, and how and when sessions will occur. Therefore, a printed guide including an overview of and general procedures for the sessions, a timetable for each session and the total number of sessions, and a list of the RMI questions should be presented to each participant. These guides should also be available for interested parents and teachers.

For Research Purposes   As researchers interact with readers, procedures change. Careful documentation of such changes may help to establish new or expanded directions and formats for RMA sessions.

RMA Participants and Interactions during the RMA Session   The tape recorder that will be left on continuously is turned on. The participants in the RMA session, usually one or more readers and a teacher/researcher, turn on the tape recording of the reader and listen to the original reading, following a typescript of the original text. When miscues have been preselected by the teacher/researcher, the typescript will show marked miscues. When students are listening to the tape recording and selecting their own miscues, they may be invited to mark their own miscues.

The power of students working together cannot be underestimated. A small group of students can work together with the teacher in the beginning so that the teacher can demonstrate the possible direction an RMA session might take. Sarah Costello (1992; see Chapter 14) and Chris Worsnop (1980; see Chapter 12) describe different groupings within the RMA setting. Eventually, the students themselves may conduct the RMA sessions without a teacher present. Conferences should be held regularly with the students to monitor what they are gaining from the experience. Logs may also be kept by the participants. Teachers should also sit in on RMA sessions periodically to see that the experience is a dynamic one and not becoming a boring routine. Some teachers may hold an RMA session with a whole class on occasion. It would be necessary to gain a student's permission to be used as an example in such a setting.

For Research Purposes   The role of collaborative learning during RMA sessions can become a focus. It would be helpful to know whether the ways in which different readers are involved in selecting miscues and the order in which they are included in the discussion and in answering the RMA questions influence aspects of RMA. When more than one student is involved in RMA, it would be interesting to know whether RMA results would be affected if the students who are listening to the reading have read the material previously. Depending upon the research questions, these variations may be held constant from one session to another, or may be changed depending on reader differences such as age or proficiency.

Miscues Selected by Readers   If the teacher/researcher has not preselected miscues, the reader is told to stop the tape recorder whenever something unexpected in the reading is heard. The teacher should decide whether the reader will be in total control of stopping the tape recorder when a miscue is heard or whether the teacher will stop the recorder if the reader does not stop it at a particular miscue. Students do not have the same notion about miscues as teachers/researchers do. Different readers attend to miscues in different ways. Students' attitudes about themselves as readers may be involved in making such decisions.

For Research Purposes   Allowing readers to be in control of selecting miscues by stopping the tape recorder whenever a miscue is heard may give researchers an opportunity to explore the different kinds of miscues selected by different kinds of readers. The responses readers make during RMA sessions provide an abundance of metalinguistic and metacognitive statements. The analysis of such statements will add a good deal to our understanding of the ways in which different readers can consciously respond to the reading process.

Discussion and Response to Miscues   Each time the tape recorder is turned off to discuss a miscue, the reader is encouraged to explore with the teacher/researcher what occurred and why. Certain questions based upon the ones used in RMI coding procedures are then asked of the reader about each selected miscue. This process of identifying and discussing miscues continues throughout the RMA session.

Following are suggested questions that may be used to guide the discussion about each miscue. Not all of them will necessarily be used during each session—some may prove to be more useful than others. Each question is designed to help the reader focus on their use of reading strategies and language cueing systems:

1. Does the miscue make sense?
2. Does the miscue sound like language?
3. a. Was the miscue corrected?
    b. Should it have been?

If the answer to Questions 1 and 3a was "No," then ask:

4. Does the miscue look like what was on the page?
5. Does the miscue sound like what was on the page?

For all miscues, ask:

6. Why do you think you made this miscue?
7. Did that miscue affect your understanding of the text?

Each question is usually expanded into a discussion by asking "Why do you think so?" or "How do you know?"

It may be necessary to have the reader reread a few paragraphs prior to the miscue portion of the text. If students do not understand the questions, teachers/researchers need to rephrase or modify the questions as necessary. It is important, of course, that the theory which informs these procedures and questions be kept intact as adaptations are made. Questions are asked to help students focus on the reading process. Often, if the answer to the question "Does this make sense?" is "Yes," the discussion revolves around the positive nature of high-quality miscues, and subsequent questions are not asked. The question that focuses on sound and graphic similarity is used to demonstrate occasions when students may over-rely on graphophonic information (e.g., "No, it doesn't make sense or sound like language, but it looks and sounds a lot like the text."). Some students need to be helped to realize that an over-reliance on graphophonic information rather than on meaning is not a very productive strategy. This is especially true for students who repeatedly have been exposed to skills-based instruction.

Teachers/researchers will want to experiment with the kinds of questions to use with their students. Depending on the age of the students and the intensity of the sessions, questions may vary. If students are encouraged to question each other in collaborative sessions, a list of possible questions may be printed to facilitate the sessions.

After the RMA session, the reader reads and retells another selection for RMI purposes, which the teacher/researcher analyzes using RMI procedures. The selection is used during the next RMA session. If the RMA session has lasted too long or the reader is a young child, another session may need to be scheduled to collect the RMI.

For Research Purposes   There are many aspects of the discussion and responses which invite analysis. The researcher may want to explore only certain segments of the RMA session, or focus on one student or the teacher in depth. Decisions about whether questions will vary or remain standard from one setting to another, as well as the roles of the Reading Interview and the retelling or other presentational forms during the questioning and discussions are all possible aspects to be explored.

Follow-up on the RMA Session

For some purposes, the teacher/researcher may transcribe all or portions of the recording of the RMA session, and plans are made for further sessions. The planning of each RMA follow-up session needs to take into consideration the insights the reader has expressed during the previous RMA session, the miscues the reader has made in the latest RMI, and the goals for the instructional program. In subsequent sessions, students can be encouraged to bring their own reading material to the RMA session unless the teacher prefers to use a core of reading materials to have typescripts for miscue markings available in advance. Photocopies of the page from the reading material can be used for a typescript when the reader has selected his or her own material and there is no time to produce a typical typescript.

For Research Purposes   Follow-up activities will depend upon whether the RMA is a one-time experience for the readers or whether there are to be subsequent RMA sessions. Some research questions may be answered in only one RMA session—others may require a series of sessions.

FURTHER CONSIDERATIONS

Teachers/researchers who have used miscue analysis, especially for readers in trouble, are very aware of the negative attitudes that readers often have about themselves as readers. It is not uncommon to hear such readers declare that they are poor readers because they omit words, make mistakes, don't remember everything they read, don't know every word, don't look up new words in the dictionary, read too fast, read too slow, substitute words, or rearrange sentences as they read. It becomes obvious that, if the readers could become consciously aware that such behaviors are expected in reading and that *all* readers use these strategies as they read, then the readers might revalue themselves as readers and the process of reading as well. Using RMA for instructional purposes is designed to do just that.

Sometimes the teacher may be using RMA for evaluating student growth or for investigating the developmental nature of reading. In such cases, the teacher may have purposes for the RMA sessions that are similar to the researcher's purposes. As the teacher and the students become more familiar with RMA, their own purposes may change over time, and this will affect the way the RMA procedures are used. The age of the student will also affect some aspects of RMA. Even working with adults, when Ann found some questions were more easily understood than others and some procedures more threatening than others, she made adaptations accordingly. As students and teachers become more sophisticated with the use of RMA, new questions or procedures may be generated to highlight their growing understanding about the reading process.

OUTLINE: RETROSPECTIVE MISCUE ANALYSIS SESSION

I. **Initial Session with Reader**
    Arrangements and Materials: Tape recorder, background information sheet, paper for taking notes, reading and interest interviews, text for reading, and a typescript for marking miscues
    Procedures:
    1. Establish rapport
    2. Collect background information
    3. Conduct Reading Interview (Appendix A)
    4. Tape-record reading and retelling (may be conducted at a separate, subsequent session)

II. **Prepare for RMA Session**
    Arrangements and Materials: Tape recorder, tape of previous reading, typescript of text, RMI coding forms, RMA session organizer
    Procedures:
    1. Check and mark typescript from previous reading
    2. Code miscues
    3. Preselect miscues for RMA session
    4. Find and mark numbers on tape recorder for session organizer
    5. Prepare RMA session organizer (Appendix B)

III. **Conduct RMA Session**
    Arrangements and Materials: Two tape recorders, tape of previous reading, marked and unmarked typescripts of previous reading, two blank tapes, new reading material and typescripts
    Procedures:
    1. Tape-record RMA session
    2. Use RMA session organizer to locate and identify preselected miscues
    3. Mark the miscue with student on blank typescript
    4. Discuss miscues using RMA questions as guides
    5. (Optional) Tape-record new reading and retelling for a subsequent RMA session (may be conducted at a separate, subsequent session)

IV. **Analyze RMA Session**
    Materials: Tape recorder, tape of RMA session, RMA response forms
    Procedures:
    1. Listen to RMA session tape recording and take notes on the RMA response form (Appendix C)
    2. Transcribe significant portions of tape recordings
    3. Begin preparation for next RMA session

Part II

RESEARCH IN REVALUING

RESEARCH IN RETROSPECTIVE MISCUE ANALYSIS has focused on helping individual readers understand the reading process and examine their beliefs about themselves as readers. Miscue analysis provides a careful analysis of changes over time in their reading as they transact with written texts. Miscue analysis research, therefore, lends itself to be presented in case study formats. We have purposely chosen to include a broad range of case studies because we hope that, by presenting different readers in this way, we establish significant retrospective miscue analysis concepts.

Although we believe that the underlying reading process is the same (see Chapter 3), all readers provide unique profiles based on their history as readers, their history of reading instruction, and their definition of themselves as readers. Teachers and specialists who work with readers appreciate the unique reading responses, proficiencies, and belief systems that they face with every student with whom they work. We include in this part of the book readers of varying ages from middle school through adults, readers of varying experiential and language backgrounds, and readers who vary in reading proficiency.

These case studies provide examples of retrospective miscue analysis as an instructional strategy to support readers' development. Examples and discussions of readers' miscues presented through the voices of teachers/researchers tell powerful stories of the revaluing process and of the influence of retrospective miscue analysis not only on the reader but also on the teachers/researchers. Ann Marek did the foundational research design for the RMA studies, and her work is presented first in this section. Next, we describe the National Council of Teachers of English research and the case studies that emerged from that work. Each author uses the same procedures and analyses but answers his or her own research questions. Finally, we share David Weatherill's description of his work with Lucas, one of the earliest reported RMA studies.

Ann shares the design of the case study research she conducted with two adult readers and shows how retrospective miscue analysis helped one of them, Gina, discover the reading process and to revalue her abilities as a reader.

CHAPTER 5: AN ACCOMPLISHED PROFESSIONAL: A READER IN TROUBLE

In another case study, Ann shows Marlene, another adult reader, engaging in retrospective miscue analysis sessions in a dramatic reshaping of her orientation toward reading and herself as a reader.

CHAPTER 6: SURVIVING READING INSTRUCTION

The research discussed here by Yetta Goodman and Alan Flurkey shows how retrospective miscue analysis is used to explore the reading process with seventh graders who use this knowledge to revalue themselves as readers. They explore important issues concerning the role of readers' metalinguistic awareness and challenge the concept of good and poor readers.

CHAPTER 7: RETROSPECTIVE MISCUE ANALYSIS IN MIDDLE SCHOOL

CHAPTER 8: REVALUING AND REVELATIONS

Alan Flurkey describes in detail his work with Rolando, a seventh grader who participated in the study described in Chapter 7. Rolando, labeled a poor reader, shows how much knowledge readers have about the reading process and suggests that perceptions about students need to be carefully considered.

CHAPTER 9: STRATEGIES AND METAPHORS

Joel Brown presents a case study of Kari, another student included in our study of seventh-grade readers. Kari reveals her personal responses to the reading process and also shows her insights into her early experiences as a remedial reader in school.

CHAPTER 10: BUILDING CONFIDENCE IN A PROFICIENT READER

Bernice, a proficient reader in the seventh-grade study, is profiled in this chapter by Sarah Costello. This case study shows how a good reader's nonproductive views of reading impact the way she defines herself as a reader.

CHAPTER 11: REVEALING STRATEGIES FOR A GOOD READER

David Weatherill shares his work with eleven-year-old Lucas and describes the insights teachers may gain when they use retrospective miscue analysis to evaluate students who are capable readers. He also makes suggestions for instruction for readers like Lucas.

5

An Accomplished Professional: A Reader in Trouble

Ann M. Marek

ADULT READERS WHO SEEK SUPPORT from remedial reading centers often possess misconceptions about the nature of the reading process and their accomplishments relative to that process. As Yetta and I have discussed, extensive research has documented that, for proficient and non-proficient readers alike, reading involves constructing meaning from print and in the process making miscues (K. Goodman and Y. Goodman 1977). Just as the number and quality of miscues varies, so also does the degree of comprehension. Thus, in actuality, even for good readers, reading is not a perfect rendering of text that results in a complete, unabridged recollection of what has been read. Through using retrospective miscue analysis (RMA) as an instructional strategy with adult readers, I hoped they would see that many of the strategies they employ are effective, while others disrupt meaning and are ineffective. I thought that if they began to see error as a qualitative rather than quantitative issue, their awareness of the reading process and of their own strengths and weaknesses might bring about a positive change in the reading strategies they employ. Most important, I wanted them to dismantle the notion that good reading is represented by error-free reproductions of text.

In the case studies I describe in this chapter and in Chapter 6, I demonstrate how retrospective miscue analysis can be used to develop this awareness in order to help adult readers improve their reading strategies and revalue themselves as readers. But first I want to share the specific RMA procedures I used to conduct the research. Yetta and I believe that RMA procedures should be adapted as necessary to suit a given teacher/researcher's purposes. Since my work was foundational in exploring the effectiveness of the strategy, I chose to preselect the miscues the readers would analyze, and I followed a consistent format in conducting the sessions. I used the same procedure when working with Marlene, whose development is traced in Chapter 6.

For this study, I selected two women from among adults who contacted the University of Nevada–Reno and the Truckee Meadows Community College remedial reading programs for assistance with their reading. Each of these institutions for higher education is located in Reno, a community in northwestern Nevada with a population of approximately one-quarter million. Two of the women who we introduced in Chapter 1, Gina and Marlene, worked separately with me in RMA sessions approximately once per week for twelve to sixteen weeks.

Gina and Marlene were selected on the basis of preliminary miscue analysis and reading attitude interviews. I used a version of the Reading Interview

BACKGROUND

RESEARCH DESIGN

51

(Y. Goodman et al. 1987) which had been adapted for use with older readers to help me identify individuals who needed to revalue themselves as readers—those who believed they had failed in reading. Gina and Marlene also demonstrated reading strategies which indicated they were non-proficient readers according to the guidelines proposed in the *Reading Miscue Inventory* (Y. Goodman et al. 1987, 146–147); that is, the comprehension profile showed that more than 40 percent of the miscues made by each reader resulted in some loss of comprehension.

RMA PROCEDURES

The following procedures were used with Gina and Marlene in order to conduct the research. I worked with Gina first, and then several months later I began working with Marlene.

1. At the outset of the investigation, the adapted reading interview was used to gather data on Gina's and Marlene's perceptions of the reading process and their perceptions of their own strengths and weaknesses as readers (see Appendix D).

2. At the conclusion of the investigation, selected questions from the adapted Reading Interview with additional open-ended questions were asked to assess whether their perceptions identified in the beginning had changed during the course of the study. This Closing Interview is shown in Appendix E.

3. During each session, Gina and Marlene were asked to read and retell a text they had not read previously. Approximately 70 percent of the reading material was self-selected by Gina and Marlene. The miscues produced by the two readers in each text were analyzed using Procedure I of the Reading Miscue Inventory (see Chapter 3) to identify their strengths and weaknesses at the outset of the study and to document the development of effective strategies throughout the study (Y. Goodman et al. 1987).

4. One to two weeks after the session held to tape-record the reading, an RMA session was held. During that session, the reader and I tape-recorded their discussion of the miscues made during the previous session. I selected for discussion a number of miscues which showed effective use of strategies, as well as miscues that showed a variety of ineffective strategies. Because confidence building is critical to the success of RMA as an instructional tool, the sessions tended, especially in the beginning, to focus on encouraging readers to revalue those strategies that are effective. Specifically, initial RMA sessions concentrated on having readers analyze miscues that showed "strength" or "partial strength" in controlling the syntactic relationships within the text, in addition to miscues that suggested "no loss" or "partial loss" of semantic information. Patterns of strength and weaknesses in controlling the semantic and syntactic systems of language were revealed in the Reading Miscue Inventory analysis after each reading (see Chapter 3). Through focusing first on miscues that showed reader strength, I hoped to help Gina and Marlene build confidence and begin to revalue their perceptions about the nature of error. Gradually, as the RMA sessions continued, more attention was given to exploring miscues that suggested less productive strategy use (i.e., those that showed "loss" of comprehension and "weakness" in controlling syntax).

Ten to fifteen miscues were selected in advance of the one-hour session, but the number of miscues actually considered during any one session varied. During the RMA session, Gina, for example, was presented with a typescript of the previous reading, marked with the miscues to be discussed. The appropriate excerpts from the tape recorded reading were played, and Gina had an opportunity to view the text and the marked miscues, as well as to hear the actual reading. Naturally, she made many more miscues than we had time to discuss, and she could hear these miscues on the tape recording as we replayed excerpts. However, I chose to mark the typescript only with the miscues we planned to discuss. This decision was related to my initial concerns that actually *seeing* evidence of her many miscues would be alarming and might simply confirm her perception of herself as a nonreader. Also, because of the ways miscues influence one another, particularly within a sentence, I frequently chose sentences where only one miscue had been made (even if it was a complex miscue) or opted to discuss each miscue within a targeted sentence.

I pointed on the typescript to the miscue selected for discussion and said, "We'll talk about this one." Then the portion of the tape containing that miscue was played, and I said, "What did you do here?" Gina then described the miscue (e.g., "I said *would* and the story said *could*."). After the miscue was identified, the following questions were asked, in an attempt to raise to a conscious level the strategies of confirming and correcting:

1. Does the miscue make sense?
2. a. Was the miscue corrected?
   b. Should it have been?

If the answer to Questions 1 and 2a was "No," then an attempt was made to reveal other cueing systems the reader may have used in making the miscue. These questions were then asked:

3. Does the miscue look like what was on the page?
4. Does the miscue sound like what was on the page?

In an attempt to raise the strategies of selecting and predicting to a conscious level, the following question was always asked:

5. Why do you think you made this miscue?

Finally, for each miscue, readers were asked to evaluate the extent to which they thought the miscue was detrimental to their understanding of the text.

6. Did that miscue affect your understanding of the text?

Each RMA session was also tape recorded, and I transcribed reader responses to trace the development of each reader's model of the reading process.

GINA

Forty-one-year-old Gina was referred to me by the University of Nevada–Reno Reading Department. On a clear, crisp October day, she arrived at my home for an initial interview and the tape-recorded reading. Dressed in an elegant leather skirt and silk blouse, she appeared by outward signs to be unlike the stereotypical adult illiterate who has suffered social and financial setbacks as a result of an inability to read well. In fact, at the conclusion of the session she drove away in a Mercedes-Benz sports car.

But Gina was representative of many adults who had less than satisfactory schooling experiences. She believed that as a child she had dyslexia and that she was in some sense the victim of educators who were ignorant of her disease and who lacked the appropriate means for curing her.

> My mother tried to get me to read and write, but they didn't know about this dyslexia. . . . Mainly, my dyslexia was with my writing. Somebody would say something and I would put it down wrong, mix up letters. I would get them all backwards. . . . I think I had dyslexia very bad [but] I think I have conquered it. I don't write things backwards so much now. I think that if I'd worked with it earlier, then I don't think I'd have this particular problem. . . . Don't forget, this was going back a long time when whatever I had, whether it was dyslexia or learning disabilities, they didn't really have. I had always appeared to be intelligent.

Perhaps also typical was her inclination ultimately to absolve others of the responsibility for her failures, while denigrating her own methods for surviving in a literate society.

> [In school] it was easier to read plays. I found that not too bad. If we did something like Shakespeare, you'd just have to read a little bit out loud. Which wasn't bad. Then I would get the story by listening to all the other pieces. I suppose I've worked around it. I've been cheating all my life. Well, I know I've been cheating all my life.

After our initial discussion, I explained both the nature of this research and the commitment that would be required of Gina if she chose to participate. Gina agreed, and I then interviewed her regarding her specific attitudes about the reading process and her ability to read. The adapted reading interview I used contains fourteen questions (Appendix D), which collectively probed Gina's sense of the contrast between "good" reading strategies and the strategies she used. It also probed the instructional techniques she believed would assist her in becoming a better reader.

Gina's Strategies

The following responses characterize Gina's perceptions of the reading strategies she employed at the beginning of the study:

Ann: When you are reading and you come to something that gives you trouble, what do you do?
Gina: I try and work it out, then I just carry on and see whether that word will go into the next sentence. If I don't understand it, I just close the book up. I don't want to read on if I don't think I can understand it. Now I would try and get a dictionary out, if I had one. But not very often, I must admit.

Although Gina claimed to utilize the kind of read-on strategy which would be compatible with transactional sociopsycholinguistic theory, it is clear that its usefulness was limited for her. She had not internalized the notion that seldom is any one word critical to the understanding of text—in fact, she would rather "close the book up" than continue reading when something is problematic.

> Like I could try to read out loud, which I do. I try to look up the words in the dictionary, but sometimes I still can't get it. The whole idea of what I'm reading is wrong if I get one word wrong.

She also appeared to have decided that looking words up in the dictionary is the proper strategy to use when encountering something difficult, although she admitted she seldom used this strategy.

Ann: Describe yourself as a reader. What kind of reader are you?
Gina: I'm very slow as a reader, even when I read by myself, inwardly. I would say I'm a nonreader.
Ann: You consider yourself a nonreader?
Gina: Nonreader. Yes. Even when I read the paper, which I hate reading because it gets me all dirty. I can read. I can read things if I like them. I like skating, and even with my skating magazines I find it quite hard to finish the paragraph I'm reading. I would rather skip it and make up my own thing. That's because I know what they are talking about. But I would really like to sit down and read it. Maybe I would learn more, especially names.

I doubted that she was a nonreader; rather, she didn't believe she read in either the style or the volume that in her mind characterizes successful readers.

According to Gina, good readers consult dictionaries when words are difficult, but what else characterizes their reading?

Ann: Who is a good reader that you know?
Gina: My second husband was a good reader. He used to read to me in bed.
Ann: What made him a good reader?
Gina: He made it interesting. I could understand what he was reading, and it made the story interesting. I don't really know what made him a good reader. My first husband read about six to seven books a week, but he wasn't a good reader out loud.

Ann: Your first husband read more than your second one, but you felt the second was a better reader?

Gina: Yes, I thought the second one was to me a better reader because he used to read to me and he could express more in his voice. The other one used to see how fast he could read. I suppose he was a better reader, but not out loud.

Gina apparently perceived a dichotomy between what she would characterize as good reading and what she suspected others (perhaps me, specifically) would characterize as good reading. In her view, good readers are able to read out loud with expression and are able to make those listening understand what they're reading—qualities exhibited by her second husband. Yet she acknowledged that the volume of reading done by her first husband ("six to seven books a week") may make him the better reader. We know that, when teachers ask follow-up questions after a student has given an answer, the student frequently assumes something was incorrect about her response. Perhaps this phenomenon was at work in this situation. When I asked Gina to explain why she believed the husband who read more was *not* the better reader, I may have prompted Gina to "suppose he was a better reader." She rather easily capitulated her opinion of what good reading is (reading with expression and understanding) in favor of what she thought the reading "authority" (me, in this case) would believe constituted good reading: speed and volume of reading.

Gina revealed her notions about the strategies good readers use in the following response:

Ann: What did your second husband do when he came to something he didn't know?

Gina: I don't really know what he would have done. He wouldn't have gone for the dictionary. Mike [the first husband, who read six to seven books a week] would have done that, I think. I don't think he [the second husband] didn't know anything, but then he might have. I don't know. I never noticed him to not know anything.

Though Gina "never noticed him to not know anything," it is possible that he was someone who read on when something was problematic, never giving outward signs that he had the occasional difficulties that all readers do. Yet she thought that her first husband, the high-volume reader, would have consulted a dictionary if he didn't understand something he was reading. In Gina's mind, perhaps, good readers either know it all or consult a dictionary; they are not likely to use her inferior strategies of reading on or closing the book.

Gina's Instructional Model

I have chosen the term *instructional model* to refer to a reader's view of what reading instruction should look like. Frequently, this model is based on the kinds of experiences adult readers remember from their own schooling, but it may be linked to more recent experiences as well—media influence, for example. At any rate, we have found it useful to explore readers' expectations about instruction, since it so frequently helps us understand what they currently *value* about reading. Recognizing the differences between her strategies and those of good readers, what kind of instructional techniques did Gina believe would be helpful to poor readers? How might that be compared with the instruction she had received thus far in her life?

Ann: How did you learn how to read?

Gina: We learned with the ABCs. Then I missed a lot of that because I was ill. I had whooping cough, so I missed quite a lot when I was six to seven years old. Then when we moved I went to another school and I couldn't pronounce *k* or whatever they do. I didn't know about the syllables or nouns or anything like that. Well I did but I didn't understand them. Then I think at school they had the new formula way you could look at a word and guess it instead of trying to spell it out. I think that's how I learned to read, by memorizing the words that I knew instead of trying to spell it out.

Gina recalled that her early instruction was word-oriented, perhaps an eclectic methodology, as opposed to a phonics-oriented approach where students would "spell it out." But how much confidence did she have in this methodology? Would Gina teach others in the way she was taught?

Ann: If you knew somebody who was having trouble reading, what would you do to help that person? What would you recommend?

Gina: I would let them read, and I would point out things. You know, "What does that word say?" All the time. Like you do when you're teaching a child. Say the word over and over again; maybe get them to write it down. Maybe just sounding it out and saying it to you. I think that's all.

Gina's responses in the reading interview revealed a dichotomy between what Gina did and what she thought she should be doing in several ways: Good readers either know every word or look words up in the dictionary; Gina tried to read on, and when that was unsuccessful, she stopped reading. Good readers probably read a great deal of material; Gina recalled having read only one book in her lifetime. Good oral readers make whatever they are reading interesting to the listener; Gina lacked the confidence to enjoy reading aloud.

It is clear from her responses that Gina initially perceived herself to be an inadequate reader—a "nonreader," in fact, who has spent a lifetime "cheating." These attitudes suggested she might benefit from a strategy designed to rebuild her confidence, and she agreed to participate.

The Retrospective Miscue Analysis Sessions

The development of Gina's model of the reading process can be traced through a description of her responses during the retrospective miscue analysis sessions. Each RMA session was tape-recorded, and excerpts from Gina's responses to the RMA questions were noted on the RMA response form (Appendix C). Gina's first and second RMA sessions confirm the model of the reading process Gina held at the outset of the study. Her word-oriented, text-reproduction emphasis began to shift to a meaning-construction focus in Session Number 3, and that trend was firmly in place during the final five RMA sessions.

RMA Session Number 1   Gina's first RMA session was conducted approximately three weeks after our first meeting when she read *The Wreck of the Zephyr* (Van Allsburg 1983). Following are responses typical of Gina's first answers to the RMA question, "Does the miscue make sense?"

                                                                even
It doesn't seem the waves could ever

get that high.

Gina: I make that mistake quite a lot. Those simple words I tried to memorize as a kid instead of sounding it out.

It doesn't seem the waves could ever

         the
get that high.

Gina: Doesn't make sense. I wasn't concentrating.

¢ ominous

One morning, under an ominous sky, he prepared

to take his boat, the Zephyr, out to sea.

Gina: I didn't know the word anyway, but I can still get the gist. I need to be aware of words I don't know.

¢ treachering

It was surrounded by a treacherous reef.

Gina: I would have to spell it out. (She found *each* in *treacherous* and tried to pronounce *treacherous* as though the *each* sounded like the word she knew.)

out of

He took the boy   to   his house, and the

sailor's wife fed them oyster stew.

Gina: I completely reversed it. That's what I do. I didn't read it word for word. I can handle those words.

He walked for a long time and was surprised

sealine

that he didn't recognize the shoreline.

Gina: Not really. You don't say sealine.

At this point in the study, Gina apparently believed she needed to concentrate more effectively on "simple" words, sound-out or spell-out the more difficult words, and try harder to read "word-for-word." Yet through her own example she proves that the method of pronouncing the little words (e.g., *each*) within the big words (e.g., *treacherous*) is unreliable. She did need to concentrate more effectively, though her efforts need to be directed toward concentrating on meaning, not on the accurate identification of simple words.

Several of Gina's comments, however, pointed to strategies which could be strengthened through the RMA process. For example, she recognized that even though she substituted a nonword for *ominous* she was able to understand the story. Also, her remark that "you don't say sealine" demonstrated she is aware that written language should resemble spoken language. In future sessions, I encouraged Gina to rely on her extensive oral vocabulary to make real word substitutions when printed words were unfamiliar to her.

The next RMA question asked during RMA Session Number 1 required Gina to consider whether each miscue should be corrected. Her comments revealed that she recognized some of her miscues made sense, and she did not insist that these miscues should have been corrected. She justified these determinations with such remarks as: "could have got away with that one" (her belief that she "cheats" is reflected in this comment); "it must've sounded okay self- consciously in my mind"; and "it's the same." When miscues did not make sense, however, she stated they should be corrected, and made comments such as: "wouldn't have made sense"; "not correct grammar"; and "could visualize it better with the author's word." Remarks like "not correct grammar" show Gina understood the need to consider the syntactic system of language simultaneously with the semantic system when evaluating whether miscues make sense and whether they should be corrected.

When Gina was asked why she made particular miscues, she responded with these reasons:

He invited me to have a seat and listen

this
to his strange tale.

Gina: I'm not careful enough.

dark
The sky grew black and the waves rose up

like mountains.

Gina: This b/d reversal is what I used to have trouble with.

He walked for a long time and was surprised

sealine
that he didn't recognize the shoreline.

Gina: I skipped the first part.

The
A fisherman warned the boy to stay in port.

Gina: They don't look alike but sometimes in a sentence they can act the same.

When responding to this substitution of *the* for *a*, Gina revealed some accurate perceptions about the functions of words. However, these notions were outnumbered by her perceptions that her reading difficulties were caused by not being careful enough, by skipping the first parts of words, and by lingering tendencies to make what she described as reversals. Note that she readily explained her *dark* for *black* substitution as a vestige of her problem with reversals, without any acknowledgment (or perhaps recognition) that the miscue was acceptable syntactically and semantically and was not a typical reversal.

Some of Gina's misconceptions about the reading process were most deeply rooted in her notions about word recognition itself and about the strategies she used to recognize and pronounce words. One might suspect that this aspect of reading—the accurate identification of words—had received the majority of her attention and the attention of others over the years. It is apparent that issues of meaning construction and of understanding what has been read have received less attention and are in some sense less contaminated by a word-oriented view of the reading process. It was when Gina was asked, "Did that miscue affect your understanding of the text?" that she was the least critical of her strategies for making sense. The following examples are typical of her responses.

even
It doesn't seem the waves could ever

get that high.

Gina: It sounds like slang. More or less means the same.

He invited me to have a seat and listen to

this
his strange tale.

Gina: It wouldn't have put me off understanding the story.

Then, suddenly, the boy felt the Zephyr

beginning
begin   to shake.

Gina: I expect I would have corrected it even if I wouldn't have gone back to it—just mentally thought it.

ⓒ *full of*
Then the air was⧵filled with the sound of

breaking branches and ripping sails.

Gina: It wouldn't have stopped me from understanding.

Gina apparently realized that some miscues do not interfere with understanding text and do not require correction. It was clear that RMA sessions with Gina needed to focus on the legitimacy of these strategies, so she would feel less like a "cheater" and more like an effective and efficient reader.

RMA Session Number 2   This RMA session was based on Gina's reading of a 658-word editorial she selected from her *Travel and Leisure* magazine. Following are examples of Gina's responses to three major RMA questions in this second session. When she responded to the question, "Does the miscue make sense?" she made these comments:

(uc) swamped
sar-
We|swarmed to Europe to sightsee and

shop (mostly the latter, it seemed).

Gina: First time I was guessing. Then I looked harder and saw the *m*. Not very good grammar. I know *sw*.

Despite the fact that air travel remains,

transport
by far, our safest form of transportation,

we asked, "Is it safe to fly?"

Gina: I would have said it right if I'd looked at it hard enough.

I've said this before, but never was it

Traveling
so true: travel is no longer a luxury;

it is essential to our lives.

Gina: I would say that [*traveling*] more. *Traveling* is more personal. *Travel* is so cold.

Here is where several *Travel and Leisure*

editors and contributors have recently

(c) with
traveled (and will be reporting on soon).

Gina: I was reading too slow to get the gist of the story, and I didn't know what the last three letters were. It could have been "and with . . ." but it wasn't.

These remarks were similar to those in the first RMA session, to the extent that they revealed Gina's preoccupation with concentrating, or "looking harder" at letters within words. She did justify her substitution of *traveling* for *travel*, asserting her own preference for the word *traveling*. She had also begun to acknowledge that prediction is a factor in reading, as demonstrated in her explanation about why she substituted *with* for *will*.

Gina hinted in her reading interview about the possible efficacy of "carrying on" when she encountered difficulty in reading; but this strategy was still outweighed by her certainty that she needed to focus more intensely on letters within words to ensure accuracy. She made these remarks when responding to the question, "Why do you think you made this miscue?": "Not reading very well." "Sightseeing reading, you know, not spelling it out." "Looking at first three letters." "Didn't read the word, really the letters."

As in RMA Session Number 1, Gina rather tenaciously argued that meaning is not often disrupted as a result of her miscues. Yet she remained convinced that her carelessness and failure to sound out or spell out words was leading to her difficulty in recognizing words. When asked whether miscues affected her understanding of the text, she made comments like: "No, not even if I hadn't corrected, because the meaning is more or less the same." "Yes, but I just carried on thinking." "Not really. It was in the same kind of context."

RMA Sessions Numbers 3 through 9 Information from these RMA sessions will be combined for the purposes of discussion. It is important to note that beginning with RMA Session Number 3 and continuing through the remaining sessions, Gina began to abandon her preoccupation with letter/word recognition and began to focus her attention on understanding text, including attempts to unravel the subtleties of written language. The following examples have been selected from the remaining seven RMA sessions, and are representative of the judgments Gina made throughout those sessions.

Ann: Does the miscue make sense?

My baby brother Andrew made a few silly

                 then

baby sounds and began to cry.

Gina: I put extra words in and it makes sense. I wouldn't speak like [the text].

Cry all you want (to)

Gina: I was a little cross with the baby. I was a bit more vicious.

After all, it wasn't Andrew's fault that I

    stayed

had to stay home with him.

Gina: It makes sense, since I left the *to* out.

You don't have to be a genius to win the

play

prize, just smart enough to plan something

really interesting and original.

Gina: Maybe I was thinking he had to play the game to win the prize . . .

"Yes, Miss, it's very important," I said ⓒ

ⓣⓞ the lady on the telephone.

Gina: Wouldn't have made sense. I had to fix it.
Ann: What do you have to pay attention to in order to fix it?
Gina: Whether it makes sense to me.

proud

There was pride in her voice.

Gina: They mean the same thing but not in that sentence.

He walked and walked, and it was almost

place

night when he reached the palace of the

North Wind.

Gina: I understood. I don't use the word *palace* very much.

The other guests in the inn were

wonderstruck, and the innkeeper's wife

demanded

immediately determined that the tablecloth

should belong to her.

Gina: *Demanded* is stronger—I like my word better than the author's. Nobody listening would stop me.

It worked once in the inn, but when I

reached home it had lost its magic.

Gina: I read a little bit further in my mind and it didn't make sense, so I corrected it.

Gina had become a reader who was willing to make judgments about both her reading strategies and the text itself, even to the point of suggesting that her word choices were often more meaningful than the author's. Further, the strategies of predicting, sampling, confirming, and correcting when necessary had become strategies Gina recognized as effective when reading for meaning. For example, when I asked: "Why do you think you made that miscue?" Gina responded: "I skipped the word completely, thinking about what he was going to say. My subconscious mind knew what he was going to say." "I was looking ahead at *classes* and thought it said *glasses*—so I predicted *some glasses*. I corrected it when it didn't work." "I was getting into the story . . ."

And her comments revealed a growing confidence in her ability to make judgments about the meanings of text when she responded to the question, "Did that miscue affect your understanding of the text?"

I sat looking down at Andrew.

Gina: No. I got a different picture, but as long as he's looking at him it's all right. It doesn't matter if he's looking *down* at him."

The old king looked out of the window and

saw the delicate, pretty little creature

standing in the courtyard, so he arranged

that she might help a little lad named

Conrad who looked after the geese.

Gina: Maybe a bit, but I think the princess could have been both delighted and delicate and it wouldn't have made much difference.

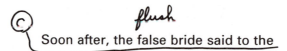

Soon after, the false bride said to the

husband-to-be, "Dear Prince, I pray you to

do me a favor."

Gina: Yeah. They mean something different. That's probably why I corrected it.

Discussion   The retrospective responses Gina made during nine sessions, across a period of four months, provide on-going evidence of her shifting view of the reading process. In the first two RMA sessions, the need for accuracy in word recognition dominated Gina's responses. Even when she admitted that meaning had probably not been disrupted, she persisted in her belief that she needed to concentrate and more closely examine the letters within words. The RMA sessions were designed to encourage her to decide that concentrating on making sense was the most effective and efficient strategy available to her, and, as the study progressed, her beliefs began to change.

I took an active role in organizing the RMA sessions so that Gina could discover for herself which strategies she was already using that were in fact efficient and effective. I also took advantage of so-called teachable moments during the retrospective sessions. As issues related to reading arose in the midst of discussions about miscues, I shared what I knew about reading, about readers, and about teaching, in much the same way that other professionals share what they know with their clients. Following are more detailed examples of the RMA discussions to give a sense of how I tried to capitalize on the many opportunities Gina and I had to extend her knowledge about reading.

Consider the following miscues and our exchanges:

I'll

"I'd be glad to," said the wife.

Ann: Any difference there?
Gina: *I'd* . . . *I'll* . . . isn't the same.
Ann: Some kind of funny tense difference between I would and I will.
Gina: *I'll be glad to* . . . I would say that more than I would say *I'd*. I don't use the word *I'd*.
Ann: So here again you're translating it into your own dialect, which is the right thing to do if you're paying attention to making sense.

to

All I have to do is sit here.

Gina: All I have to do is sit here. . . . Yes, I would say *to sit here*.
Ann: Do you need to correct it?
Gina: No.
Ann: Why do you think you are doing all of these? Why do you say *housekeeping* instead of *keeping house*? Why do you leave out *so*? Why do you say *I'll* instead of *I'd*?
Gina: I don't say *I'd*, that's why. Really what I am doing is taking this story into my hands a bit. Whether a school teacher would correct it or not I don't know.
Ann: A teacher who knew what she was doing would leave you alone. She would know that the best readers in her class do the same thing. You know what happens,

Gina? No one sits down and reads one-on-one with the best readers. If you've got it mastered by fourth grade, no one ever listens to you read again, except when they ask you to read a story or passage to the class. Usually no one else has copies of what you're reading, so they don't know when you insert a *to* that makes sense. Sometimes teachers have this whole bag of stuff they carry around, saying that bad readers make these mistakes, bad readers do this, and bad readers do that. They are spending all their recess time with the bad readers. They don't know that the good readers are also making mistakes, just different kinds.

Discussions like these about specific miscues often raised issues about reading in general, and I used these opportunities to redirect many of the misconceptions Gina possessed about reading (e.g., that good readers know all the words, never make mistakes, and remember everything they read; that poor readers like her need to pay closer attention to the letters within words).

The information provided in the final session further corroborates the changes in Gina's perceptions about the reading process. The shifts in attitude and reading strategies were mutually supportive, and she began to rely even more heavily on meaning-seeking as a primary reading strategy.

Changes in Strategies Utilized in the Reading Process

The change in Gina's attitude toward reading was accompanied by changes in the reading strategies she utilized. Those changes are documented through analyses of her reading using the Reading Miscue Inventory Procedure I.

Each of the texts for Gina's tape-recorded readings was selected either by her or by me with her approval. Gina indicated a desire at the outset to learn to read storybooks to children, commenting that she might like to work in a kindergarten. The majority of the texts she read reflected this interest in children's literature; in fact, several are from an anthology she purchased. On two occasions, she elected to read nonfiction articles from a newspaper and a magazine, respectively. I asked Gina to read *The Wreck of the Zephyr* at both the beginning and conclusion of the study, as a pre- and post-RMA indication of strategy use. I recognize that miscue analysis is seldom performed on a text that the reader knows well; however, this was a story neither Gina nor Marlene (the woman in the second case study) had ever read previously, and they did not read it for a second time until more than four months after their first readings.

Because Gina self-selected most of the texts (the exceptions are *Zephyr*, "Genius," and "Kept House"), the difficulty level is not arranged neatly from easier to more difficult over time. We believe that texts are easy or difficult to read according to how predictable they are for given readers. Predictability is influenced by such factors as the style, content, and complexity of the text, considered in light of the reader's background knowledge, interests, and purposes for reading. Since most texts were selected by the readers, reader interest and motivation is more evenly distributed across all texts. To compare her strategy use over time, I grouped the texts according to one measure of their difficulty, the Fry Readability Formula. Within each readability level grouping, the texts represent similar genre (i.e., Groups 1, 2, and 3 are fictional narratives; Group 4 texts are nonfiction articles). Trends are discernible within these groups over time, and these trends are discussed below. However, it is interesting to note that the data challenges a simplistic assumption that the group of texts rated at Grade 7 are harder than the Grade 5 texts. If that were true, we would expect Gina to be able to read the Grade 5 texts more proficiently. However, Gina read the Grade 7 text "North Wind" with 5.7 miscues per hundred words, and 75 percent of those miscues resulted in no loss of comprehension. Some two weeks later, she read the Grade 5 text "Palace" with 7.5 miscues per hundred words, with 78 percent of miscues resulting in no loss of comprehension. Clearly, factors other than word and sentence length, which underpin the Fry formula, influence the readability of a given text on any occasion.

Gina made a total of 743 miscues during the reading of these ten texts, which

Table 5-1   Gina's meaning construction and grammatical relationships

Title	Miscues per hundred words	Meaning construction			Grammatical relationships			
		No loss	Partial loss	Loss	Partial strength	Strength	Weakness	Over correction
Group 1 (Readability* = 3)								
Kept House (Session 8)	4.1	84%	3%	13%	65%	10%	6%	19%
Group 2 (Readability* = 5)								
Zephyr (#1) (Session 1)	10.2	55	11	34	56	16	21	7
Palace (Session 5)	7.5	78	10	12	67	13	8	12
Zephyr (#2) (Session 10)	5.5	80	3	17	74	6	13	7
Group 3 (Readability* = 7)								
Genius (Session 3)	6.2	57	7	36	50	17	24	9
North Wind (Session 4)	5.7	75	11	14	68	8	5	5
Goosegirl (Session 6)	9.9	47	8	45	45	16	37	2
Mouse (Session 9)	4.9	85	—	15	77	7	8	8
Group 4 (Readability* = College)								
Window Seat (Session 2)	11.7	39	8	53	37	23	36	4
Overfat (Session 7)	6.4	39	18	43	43	18	32	7

* Estimated using Fry Readability Formula.

were analyzed using Procedure I of the Reading Miscue Inventory. Summaries of the results of the miscue analysis are presented in Tables 5-1 and 5-2. The texts are grouped according to relative difficulty, and within each group the texts are presented in the order in which Gina read them. The actual session number is enclosed in parentheses beneath the title of the text.

Group 1   Only one text, "The Man Who Kept House," is included in Group 1 because Gina read only one story representing this level of difficulty. It was the eighth text she read, and it reveals many of the strengths Gina possessed at this point in the study. She made a modest 4.1 miscues per hundred words and retold the story quite thoroughly, as might be predicted with only 13 percent of her miscues potentially resulting in loss of meaning (Table 5-1). Only 6 percent of her miscues indicated weakness in controlling the syntactic relationships within the text (Table 5-1). Her reliance on graphophonic cues was moderate: 52 percent of her miscues were highly similar graphically, and 42 percent were highly similar in sound (Table 5-2). These percentages are typical of proficient readers. She exhibited overcorrection behavior in 19 percent of her miscues. This rather high percentage is possibly the result of her sense of control over this text—it was easy for her to read and she was able to correct miscues that were semantically and syntactically acceptable. Although this ability is indicative of her effectiveness in monitoring the construction of meaning, it suggests that she may be somewhat inefficient in processing this text. That is, the effort required to correct acceptable miscues may outweigh the benefits to the reader who is reading for meaning.

Group 2   The Group 2 texts include two readings of *The Wreck of the Zephyr*, once at the beginning of the study and a repeated reading four months later. The "Palace" text was selected by Gina from an anthology of short stories. Reflected

Table 5-2   Gina's graphic and sound similarity

Title	Graphic similarity			Sound similarity		
	High	Some	None	High	Some	None
Group 1						
Kept House	52%	32%	16%	42%	26%	32%
Group 2						
Zephyr (#1)	61	18	21	60	22	18
Palace	56	19	25	42	19	39
Zephyr (#2)	63	19	18	47	25	28
Group 3						
Genius	71	17	12	53	25	22
North Wind	60	28	12	47	30	23
Goosegirl	57	22	21	37	28	35
Mouse	53	21	26	31	37	32
Group 4						
Window Seat	72	23	5	57	32	11
Overfat	66	29	5	57	24	19

in this group of texts is Gina's dramatic reduction in miscues per hundred words (MPHW) from the beginning of the study until its end—a trend reflected in the other groups of texts as well. In her first reading of *Zephyr* she made 10.2 MPHW, and in her second reading she made 5.5 MPHW. In the "Palace" text, read midway through the study, she made 7.5 MPHW. Accompanying this reduction in MPHW is a marked increase in the percentage of miscues that suggest no loss in meaning—from 55 percent in *Zephyr* (#1), to 78 percent in "Palace," to 80 percent in *Zephyr* (#2). The percentage of miscues likely to result in a loss of meaning has concurrently declined from 34 percent in *Zephyr* (#1), to 12 percent in "Palace," and 17 percent in *Zephyr* (#2).

Gina's control over grammatical relationships also strengthened across time in the texts in Group 2 (Table 5-1). Miscues demonstrating weakness in controlling syntactic structures declined from 21 percent in *Zephyr* (#1) to 13 percent in *Zephyr* (#2). The interim "Palace" text shows weakness in only 8 percent of miscues. A steady increase across time in miscues demonstrating strength is also revealed in Table 5-1. Fifty-six percent of Gina's miscues in *Zephyr* (#1) reflected strength in controlling syntactic relationships. In "Palace" the percentage rose to 67 percent, and in *Zephyr* (#2) 74 percent of Gina's miscues reflected her ability to control the syntactic relationships within the text.

Gina's use of graphic cues remained stable across time in the Group 2 texts (Table 5-2). There was, however, a substantial lowering of her reliance on phonic cues. The percentage of miscues with high sound similarity between the text and the miscue declined from 60 percent in *Zephyr* (#1) to 47 percent in *Zephyr* (#2). In "Palace," only 42 percent of Gina's miscues were highly similar in sound to the text, and 39 percent of her miscues showed no sound similarity whatever.

Group 3   The texts in Group 3 contain one researcher-selected text, "My Brother is a Genius," and three reader-selected texts from an anthology of children's stories: "The Boy and the North Wind," "The Goosegirl," and "The City Mouse and the Country Mouse."

Before describing the miscue analysis findings for these four texts, it is important to describe the context in which one of the readings took place. "Goosegirl" was the sixth text read by Gina during this study, and it was the only reading performed under obviously stressful conditions. Gina and I typically met at Gina's house, and the readings and miscue analysis sessions were conducted at Gina's kitchen table. At the session during which "Goosegirl" was read, Gina's boyfriend, the airline pilot with whom she lived, was at home, rather boisterously preparing himself a late breakfast. He gave every indication that he resented the time Gina was spending at the table while he was preparing his own meal. Kitchen pots and pans slammed onto counter tops and stove burners as Gina attempted to read "Goosegirl" aloud into the tape recorder. Although I offered to leave and return at another time, Gina insisted that she would not "give in" to his childish behavior. The session was unpleasant, and Gina's reading of "Goosegirl" no doubt reflects the anxiety she was feeling: she made 9.9 MPHW and 45 percent of her miscues reflected a probable loss of meaning (Table 5-1). Thirty-seven percent of her miscues demonstrated a weakness in controlling syntactic relationships—the highest percentage of "weakness" she showed in any reading (Table 5-1). It is tempting to disregard this text, because there is a sense in which it is unrepresentative of Gina's usual reading style; but it serves as a reminder that the stress of everyday life will affect the success of any instructional technique.

The remaining three texts show a steady strengthening of strategies across time. In reading "Genius," Gina made 6.2 MPHW, declining to 5.7 MPHW in "North Wind," and further declining to 4.9 in "Mouse." Her ability to construct meaning as she reads also improved over time: 57 percent of the miscues in "Genius" resulted in no loss of comprehension; 75 percent of the "North Wind" miscues showed no loss of comprehension; and the "Mouse" no-loss percentage rose to 85 percent.

Strength in controlling syntax also reflected Gina's growing proficiency in reading. In "Genius," 50 percent of her miscues demonstrated "strength"; in "North Wind" and "Mouse" the percentages rose to 68 percent and 78 percent respectively. A scant 5 percent of miscues suggested weakness in "North Wind," and the weakness percentage was only 8 percent for "Mouse."

Reliance on graphophonic cues also reduced across time at this level of difficulty. Percentages of high graphic similarity were reduced from 71 percent in "Genius" to 60 percent in "North Wind," to 57 percent in "Goosegirl," and, finally, to 53 percent in "Mouse" (Table 5-2). The percentages of high sound similarity were reduced also, from 53 percent in "Genius" to 31 percent in "Mouse." These reductions in a focus on the graphophonic cueing system parallel the increases in her focus on semantic and syntactic cues, as described above. Gina's growing control over the reading process is obvious when these seventh-grade texts are compared over time.

Group 4 Both of the Group 4 texts were nonfiction articles selected by Gina; they were the second and seventh texts read by Gina during the study. Her growing competence is not as clearly demonstrated in these texts as in the Group 2 and 3 texts, but there are definite indications that she is becoming more proficient. For example, perhaps the most significant sign that her strategies are improving is the reduction in miscues per hundred words from 11.7 in "Window Seat" to 6.4 in "Overfat" (Table 5-1). Although the percentage of "no loss in meaning" miscues was the same for both readings (39 percent), Gina was in the second text able to reduce her percentage of loss from 53 percent to 43 percent. Keeping in mind that she was now making 5.3 fewer miscues per hundred words, she does indeed appear to be strengthening her strategies, even at this most difficult level. Her ability to control the grammatical relationships also demonstrates an increase in "strength" from 37 percent in "Window Seat" to 43 percent in "Overfat" (Table 5-1).

It is typical for readers to rely more heavily on graphophonic cues as reading material becomes more difficult, and Gina demonstrates a similar tendency. In "Window Seat" 72 percent of her miscues showed high graphic similarity, and 57 percent showed high sound similarity (Table 5-2). In "Overfat" high graphic similarity declined to 66 percent, while high sound similarity remained stable at 57 percent. However, there was an increase in the percentage of miscues which bore no sound similarity to the text, from 11 percent in "Window Seat" to 19 percent in "Overfat."

Discussion   In every grouping of texts, Gina displayed an improvement over time in the quality of her miscues, accompanied by a decline in the number of miscues she made. Her reading ability was strengthened as she moved from a text reproduction model of the reading process to a meaning construction model. But was retrospective miscue analysis responsible for these shifts in attitude and ability? At least two other factors may be cited as contributing to her success. First, Gina was extremely motivated in her desire to become a better reader. Second, she lived in a literate environment, and I recognize that any strategy which would encourage her to increase her reading of whole texts would contribute to an improvement in reading ability. However, during the course of this research, Gina was not participating in any other instructional setting, and no previous instruction had focused on encouraging her to develop her natural reading ability.

The Closing Interview

During the final session, a Closing Interview (see Appendix E) was used to ascertain whether there had been any changes in the way Gina perceived her strengths and weaknesses as a reader. In addition to the questions listed in the closing interview, appropriate questions were selected from the adapted reading interview conducted at the outset of the study. Gina was asked to respond to those questions as well. Following are relevant excerpts from the closing interview.

Ann: When you are reading and you come to something that gives you trouble, what do you do?

Gina: Well, now if I'm into the story I try to read on and I try and get the word later. I try to look at the next couple of words. The other day I actually went on, then I went back to it and I realized it was such a simple word—I should have got it really. Wasn't simple, but just because it was long I didn't get it. Then I went into the sentence and got it right. So that's what I try and do now.

In contrast with her initial answer to this question, Gina at the conclusion of the study seemed to value the strategy of reading on when encountering difficult text. There was a sense in her initial interview that although she used this strategy, she believed it was somehow substandard—that good readers looked words up in the dictionary.

Ann: How do you feel about yourself as a reader?

Gina: I feel a lot better since I've been with you. I felt like I was on the mend a little when I came to you. I still think reading is boring; I don't find it that exciting. I'd rather go out and do a lot of things and see it in action than I would to read it. But I do like it a little bit more than I did before. I mean I will pick up a paper now, and I will get into a book. But if the book has a boring paragraph, I can leave that paragraph and go on to the next. And so therefore short stories or short articles I find much more interesting than I did before. . . . If I want to read something, I might read it. If I find somebody that has the knowledge about it, then I would ask them.

Ann: Rather talk about it than read about it?

Gina: Yeah. But, as I say, I'm a lot better than I was.

In her own words, Gina has changed from someone who used to "close up the book" if she encountered a word she didn't know to someone who now is willing to skip entire paragraphs when they are boring. She wouldn't allow herself to skip words before—now she gives herself permission to skip chunks of text in order to suit her purposes for reading. She has assumed control of the reasons for reading; she has begun to own her own process. And in assuming that ownership she is free to admit, without apologizing, that she often finds reading boring and believes the information-gathering value of reading can frequently be replaced with conversation. Further indication of her growing sense of control is revealed in the next exchange.

Ann: Do you have any different attitudes about reading than you had at the beginning?

Gina: I find that now I am looking around for something to read. Used to be when I was in a doctor's waiting room, I would just sit there. And now I will try to find a paper or a book to read. Anything, rather than just sit there and be bored. Before I wouldn't touch a piece of paper with words on it. It would either be scary, or I knew I couldn't even read "the cat sat on the mat." Why would I want to read it if I couldn't understand it?

The lessening of fear about the reading process has no doubt contributed to her willingness to attempt reading. During her initial Reading Interview, Gina stated: "My whole life I've been scared of the word *read*." Reading is no longer something that frightens her.

Gina's perceptions about her strategies changed as well. In addition to acknowledging the value of reading on or skipping boring paragraphs, she had discovered that closing a book is not the only alternative available when she doesn't understand what she is reading:

Gina: Also, I find that if I'm reading without understanding, I'll either change the article or go back and read, and say to myself, "Now try and understand it." Whereas, before I didn't used to.
Ann: So you feel like you persevere more?
Gina: Yeah, I'm persevering more. I'm persevering a lot more.
Ann: Do you think that's related to the fact that you have more confidence in your reading now?
Gina: Yeah. I think I have a lot more confidence in my reading now. . . . Whether I'll sit down and read ten books a week is another story. . . . I find that it is quite interesting to read, I must admit. I am surprised that people write such a lot of rubbish, though. And I never knew that before.

Reading for meaning had become a focus in Gina's reading. She was attempting to be conscious of understanding text as she read and was aware that focusing on making sense will help her read more effectively. Interestingly, her growing control of the reading process had given her the confidence to make statements she would not have made at the beginning of this study: she was willing to acknowledge her own strengths, and she was also willing to read critically and decide that much written material is "rubbish."

In a follow-up line of questions related to reading strategies, Gina revealed her current model of the good reader.

Ann: Tell me what you think about clever readers. How are they different from you, and how are they just like you?
Gina: I think good readers want to improve themselves, even if they read novels. They want to improve their insight into the world.
Ann: Do they make mistakes?
Gina: Yeah. I think they make mistakes in their ordinary, everyday reading. I think good readers always want to understand what they are reading. I think they understand what they are reading, but there might be one word that they have never heard of. Then they will try to learn that word. Some of them will put it into their vocabulary, others will say "OK, that's what it is."
Ann: If you're reading for pleasure, is it as important to fuss with words?
Gina: No, just go on to the next sex, or murder, or whatever. In fact, the authors that write those books will not use those words so much, I find. They will try and not use as many big words.
Ann: What about other kinds of miscues? What about when you substitute *his horse* for *the horse*?
Gina: That really doesn't matter as much. If you make too many mistakes where it is the wrong person, then it could confuse the plot. If you make too many mistakes, you may get the wrong person playing the wrong part. Which you have got to realize.
Ann: You realize that by doing what?
Gina: Going over it again. You have to pay attention to the next paragraph, mainly. Then you might figure it out.
Ann: You can only do that if you're paying attention to what?
Gina: The story, I think, the story mainly. By getting into the story, by what makes sense more than anything.

In her own words, Gina confirmed that retrospective miscue analysis has contributed to her greater self-confidence and improved reading strategies.

6

Surviving Reading Instruction

Ann M. Marek

MARLENE WAS A CONTRAST TO Gina in nearly every respect. Her appearance contrasted dramatically—Gina was 41, blond, and glamorous. Marlene was 21, brunette, and heavy-set. Gina lived with an airline pilot in an exclusive foothills neighborhood in Reno. Marlene lived with her parents and two younger brothers in a modest dwelling in Sparks, Reno's lower- and middle-income residential suburb. More subtle differences between the two exist, however. At 41, Gina was just beginning to reveal herself as a "nonreader" to her friends and the world at large. For more than twenty years Gina had survived because, as she described it, she "faked it"—never allowing those with whom she worked and lived to realize the extent of her difficulties. Marlene had been in special education classes since junior high, and almost proudly boasted that she had had dyslexia since first grade, though she reported having begun to cure herself. Gina avoided applying for any kind of position which required her to complete an application—Marlene wrote on her applications that she had a reading disability. Gina was in the throes of deciding whether to pursue a "course" at a college—Marlene had been going to Truckee Meadows Community College for two years, taking classes in automotive mechanics and electronics.

Marlene worked two part-time jobs: one as a dishwasher for a nursing home and the other as a night-time janitor for a fabric store. She began her four-month participation in this study during July of 1986. Her English and reading instructor at Truckee Meadows Community College referred her as a possible subject, stating that Marlene was a "classic dyslexic" who had overcome some of her difficulties. Marlene's two courses in reading instruction at Truckee Meadows were comprised of individualized workbook activities, combined with remediation using a kinesthetic approach. She had discontinued her participation in these courses prior to beginning her work with me.

Like Gina, Marlene had vivid memories about her schooling. She related the following experience during her initial session:

Ann: Do you have any memories of being in junior high school and what you did about reading then?
Marlene: They had me read into a tape recorder to see if I had any feeling, and when I didn't the teacher stuck her fingernails in my leg. I got her back. I threw a desk at her.
Ann: What do you mean by "feeling"?
Marlene: It's like when you get to the end of a sentence you're supposed to go lower or higher, and with me it was all the same thing. When she listened to my tape she said, "This sounds like a broken person trying to read this."

And, also like Gina, Marlene felt victimized by an educational system which did not recognize nor properly treat her dyslexia. There was unmistakable bitterness in her voice as she shared her thoughts about her failure to learn to read well:

Marlene: Teachers were playing God, lawyer, doctor, everything, saying, "Oh, she's going to die when she's eighteen. You might as well take her out of school and put her in the state institution." I was healthy, it's just that they did not know what the word "dyslexia" was and they fought all the time with my mother when she said "She has dyslexia. It is a reading problem."

Ann: How do you feel about the dyslexia at this point in your life?

Marlene: It's hard to fill out an application to get a job when you put down you have a reading problem. "Oh, let's tell her we don't have any jobs." It is hard to get jobs. The only job that comes halfway decent to me is dishwashing. But what if I want enough money to live on? What if I want something else? It's hard to find a employer to take you. They won't hire me and give me a chance. That's the whole problem. Nobody gives you a chance.

Ann: Do you still feel plagued by dyslexia, or are you working through it?

Marlene: Part of me feels, "Why me?" The other part says, "Life's that way," I guess. I let it go.

The adapted reading interview (see Appendix D) was used to gather information about Marlene's perceptions of the reading process and her ability to read. Her responses to the following questions were tape recorded during her first session. In general, she was initially more reticent to discuss her reading than Gina had been.

Marlene describes the reading strategies she uses in the following way:

Ann: When you are reading and you come to something that gives you trouble, what do you do?

Marlene: Skip over it. Sometimes I write the word down and ask my parents what it means.

Marlene's Strategies

Her statement that she would ask others to provide meanings for words is indicative of a very dependent strategy. And it is clear in the following excerpt that although skipping words is a reading strategy one might recognize as a strength, it is merely one Marlene resorted to when she was unable to execute the strategy she believed was better—looking up words in the dictionary:

Ann: Who is a good reader that you know?

Marlene: My mom.

Ann: What makes her a good reader?

Marlene: She reads a lot. She helps me.

Ann: Does she ever come to something she doesn't know?

Marlene: Yeah.

Ann: What does she do?

Marlene: She looks up words in the dictionary.

Ann: Do you ever do that?

Marlene: Not really, because I can never find the words.

Marlene seemed completely immobilized by her difficulties with word recognition. She believed that consulting a dictionary was the right strategy to use—it's just that she could never find the words. Her only other apparent alternatives were to ask someone what the words meant—not very helpful when reading alone—or to skip them. She never claimed that when skipping words she could frequently discern their meanings from the contexts. Reading for meaning was not the primary focus of Marlene's reading.

Marlene's Instructional Model

Marlene recalled that she learned to read in first grade by memorizing words:

Ann: How did you learn to read?

Marlene: Going home to ask my parents to help me memorize the page. Then I could sit in class and if the teacher called on me I could read.

This recollection is clearly focused on the accurate rendition of text when called upon by the teacher. And in Marlene's mind, the reading had to be so accurate that, in fact, memorization was necessary. The instructional technique she would recommend for readers having difficulty is a familiar one:

Ann: If you knew someone who was having difficulty with reading, how would you help them?
Marlene: Tell them to practice.
Ann: How?
Marlene: Sit down and read a book with somebody.
Ann: How does that work?
Marlene: You sit down and read along with someone and if you get in trouble you have them say the word and keep going on. But if you keep missing that word, stop and spell the word, and say it, and go through that way.

Marlene seemed convinced that learning to be a better reader required the direct assistance of a teacher who would monitor and correct every word Marlene read. And I had the definite sense that Marlene would be reluctant to assume ownership of her reading—that a teacher who refused to "say the words" would once again be someone who was abdicating responsibility for truly helping her. Marlene did, however, possess the characteristics of a reader for whom retrospective miscue analysis might be useful, and so without undue concern about her reluctance to do so, I asked her to read *The Wreck of the Zephyr*, unaided, into a tape recorder. Despite her belief that teachers should help readers by "giving them the words," she willingly read this 1,270-word story without assistance from me. She made 77 miscues while reading *Zephyr*—an average of 6 miscues per hundred words. Her reading was analyzed using Procedure I of the Reading Miscue Inventory, and findings from that analysis are presented in Tables 6.1 and 6.2.

Marlene possessed many of the same strengths and weaknesses Gina did at the outset of the study. Her reading strategies were effective in only about half of her miscues, and her self-confidence about her reading ability was very low. In some ways, her negative attitudes were even more entrenched than Gina's—she almost seemed to say, "Try to help me. I dare you." But her motivation was high; indeed, she had contacted me about participating in the study. It was just that her defenses against another failure were firmly in place as she began the study.

The Retrospective Miscue Analysis Sessions

Marlene's developing model of the reading process is documented in this section. There is an important difference between the RMA sessions conducted with Gina and those conducted with Marlene. The difference is not in how the sessions were structured but, rather, in how each of the readers responded. Gina's responses to the RMA questions were largely predictable. She began by focusing on text features and moved toward exploring semantic and syntactic qualities of text. Seldom did she respond unpredictably to the question "Does the miscue make sense?" The extent to which her answers were predictable, of course, paralleled the extent to which they matched my judgments of what made sense (Page 1973).

Marlene, on the other hand, rather frequently made judgments which did not coincide with mine, and she vigorously and elaborately justified her evaluations of those miscues. In so doing, she caused me to reexamine my own model of the reading process, placing a premium on the reader's judgment of what makes sense and clarifying the role of the teacher in helping readers improve their reading. "Reflections on Revaluing" later in this chapter has a fuller discussion of this point.

RMA Session Number 1   Fifteen miscues were selected from Marlene's reading of *The Wreck of the Zephyr* for her first RMA session. Ten of them were selected as evidence of effective and efficient reading strategies; five were examples of ineffective strategies. Marlene was less tentative than Gina in asserting that her miscues made sense, but, in this initial RMA session, she frequently did not elaborate about her reasons for believing miscues made sense. When she did offer an explanation, it was usually to argue that the miscue made sense with the text leading up to it, even though subsequent text rendered the miscue untenable. Following are examples of these remarks:

©   *storm*
Already a strong wind was blowing.

Ann: Does the miscue make sense?
Marlene: Yeah. Until you get to the word *wind*.

When he was done with his song, the sailor

© *went*
sent the boy to bed.

Marlene: I was thinking about the sailor going to bed, but it falls apart at *went the boy to bed*.

Marlene quickly realized that prediction was a component of the reading process, although it was not yet clear whether she recognized the value of this strategy. She also, in this first session, invented the term "stopper" to refer to the point in the text which signaled to her that a miscue had been made and correction was necessary.

Despite frequent assertions that her miscues made sense, Marlene's belief that text should be flawlessly reproduced was revealed in her responses to the questions "Was the miscue corrected? Should it have been?" Consider the following comments:

He seemed to be reading my mind when he

old
said, "Odd, isn't it?"

Ann: Should it have been corrected?
Marlene: Yeah, because the way the guy wrote the book it said *odd* instead of *old*, and I switch small words like that.

When the boy opened his eyes, he found

the
himself lying on a beach.

Marlene: Yeah, because it's not the word the author put there. I usually, when it comes to small words, put in the one I want and not the one they write.

In response to the question "Why do you think you made the miscue?" Marlene frequently stated that she was "trying to rush through," or that she was "skipping words." She had not yet recognized that many of her miscues were the result of legitimate, but inaccurate, predictions, and that prediction was an essential component of proficient reading.

Like Gina, Marlene was able early in the RMA sessions to point out the redundancy in text, often stating that meaning was not affected, even by miscues which were not semantically acceptable and were not corrected. Consider these examples:

Ann: Did that miscue affect your understanding of the text?

$ orgreen
One morning, under an ominous sky, he prepared

to take his boat, the Zephyr, out to sea.

Marlene: No. Because I already knew what the sky was like.

$ cherous
It was surrounded by a treacherous reef.

Marlene: No. Because they keep bringing up the same thing through the story. If you don't get it there you'll get it later.

Marlene was beginning to understand that it is the varying quality of miscues that separates good readers from poor readers when she and I had a discussion about the following miscue:

ⓒ storm
Already a strong wind was blowing.

Ann: Did you need to correct that one?
Marlene: Yeah, to make the sentence come out right.
Ann: What else could you have done if you didn't want to correct it? Could you have made another miscue in order to make it work?
Marlene: Yeah.
Ann: What would it have been?
Marlene: Just left out *wind*.
Ann: So you could have done two different things there and kept it all intact, had it make sense, and go on. I want you to remember that, because there's a time or two later on when you do just that. One miscue gets you to a point, so you go ahead and commit another one in order to make it work for you, which is what good readers do. They make a lot of substitutions, which is one word for another, and a lot of omissions. But they do it in such a way that they leave a sentence that has made sense. So that's a good kind of strategy.

This example, again, shows the extent to which I took advantage of opportunities to share with Marlene what I knew about reading and about readers. It is in the midst of these discussions that teachers/researchers are able to be supportive of readers in the revaluing process; and it is this kind of discussion which is at the heart of retrospective miscue analysis.

RMA Session Number 2   This session was based on Marlene's reading of "My Brother is a Genius," a 1,873-word short story. In this session, Marlene began to strengthen her resolve that many of her miscues made sense. The miscues in this session were selected from the first two pages of the text because they demonstrated a chronological progression from low- to high-quality miscues. She offered the following rationalizations for why her miscues made sense:

Ann: Does the miscue make sense?

So

",Go ahead and cry! Cry all you want to!"

Marlene: Sounds better with *So*.

smoothing

I guess they do have a soothing sound.

Marlene: Yeah. The two words sorta seem like they're meaning the same thing at the time you're reading.

You don't have to be a genius to win

the prize, just smart enough to plan

organized

something really interesting and original.

Marlene: Yeah. You said earlier *original* but you also want a project that's organized and interesting.

Furthermore, she no longer insisted that all of her miscues should have been corrected:

Ann: Should the miscue have been corrected?

Andrew stopped crying and tried to take

my

hold of the dictionary.

Marlene: Didn't really matter.

I don't know about that, but I know we

schools

get a good education in our school.

Marlene: The kid could be saying "all the schools."

And Marlene continued to respond with the entire story in mind when asked the following question:

Ann: Did that miscue affect your understanding of the text?

brothers
"If it bothers you to think of it as

baby sitting," my father said, "then

don't think of it as baby sitting."

Marlene: Not that much because it goes on and tells what's happening in the story.

You just happen to do your studying in the room

where your (baby) brother is sleeping.

Marlene: Not that much because it talks more in the story about the baby brother.

RMA Sessions Numbers 3 through 11   Examples from later RMA sessions confirm Marlene's growing sense of ownership over the reading process. Beyond the second session, Marlene seldom insisted she needed to correct miscues which were fully semantically acceptable. Even when miscues initially seemed to have little apparent justification, Marlene frequently rationalized her judgments about making sense, and her rationalizations were usually convincing. For example:

Ann: Does the miscue make sense?

Wood accused his step-mother of duplicity

unauthorized
and unorthodox conduct as a married woman.

Marlene: Something that's *unorthodox* would probably also be *unauthorized*. It's saying the
            same thing.

decided
He looked across the room and discovered

that one of his students was dozing off

in his class.

Marlene: Yeah. The teacher could be looking at him and saying "I don't know if he's already asleep or if he's falling asleep," and then decide he's asleep . . .

What is important to note is that retrospective miscue analysis as an instructional technique was teaching Marlene that she is in control of what makes sense, and that it is her obligation to monitor understanding as she reads. Any attempt to dissuade her in her judgments about whether miscues made sense would have once again made her dependent upon someone else to determine whether what she was reading made sense to her. Retrospective miscue analysis was designed to make readers less, not more, dependent on others.

Even if a particular miscue didn't perfectly fit the sentence in which it was found, it was often conceptually in line with the text as a whole, and Marlene would justify it on those grounds. For example:

area

It's not fancy, but the arena was built for

rodeo and there isn't a bad seat in the place.

Ann: Does the miscue make sense?
Marlene: Yeah. The rodeo *arena* is in the rodeo *area* so they refer to the same place.

Several of Marlene's responses to the question "Does the miscue make sense?" reveal her ever-increasing confidence in reading. So sure of herself had Marlene become that she made the following comments in the midst of RMA sessions:

shot

He missed his first shot and (his) second.

Marlene: I didn't think it needed *his*. The author already said it in the first part. Hey! They oughta send their books to me first! I know how they should sound.

He was going to teach something to his

stubborn

stupid students.

Marlene: I think it sounded better with the students being *stubborn*.

kid

One child, in particular, Wrondel McMillian,

loved his Cabbage Patch doll and treated

his doll, Dexter Jones, like one of his

very own brothers.

Marlene: *Kid* makes more sense—more personal than *child*.

Discussion   Marlene had become very personally involved in analyzing her own reading and in making her own evaluations about which strategies were working well for her and which were ineffective. She invented the notion of "stoppers" and learned that if she were monitoring comprehension, the text itself would usually signal when a semantically or syntactically unacceptable miscue had been made (at which point the reader would "stop" to reprocess). Marlene's own evaluation of retrospective miscue analysis is presented in the final section of this chapter.

Changes in Strategies Utilized in the Reading Process

Marlene was able by the conclusion of this study to verbalize a model of the reading process which stresses that reading for meaning is the key to reading effectively. Miscue analysis data collected for the twelve texts she read during this research demonstrate how her changes in beliefs about the reading process were reflected in changes in her reading ability. During her initial interview, she stated that her favorite reading material (when she chose to read) was "Westerns"; consequently, several of the stories she selected to read were from her grandmother's copies of *Real West* magazine. A second group of stories she brought to read were contained in an anthology of stories written by a sophomore class from the high school her brother was attending. Four of the texts (*The Wreck of the Zephyr*, "My Brother is a Genius," "The Reno Rodeo," and "The Man Who Kept House") were selected by me. Like Gina, Marlene was asked to read *Zephyr* as both her first and last story.

Marlene made a total of 777 miscues during her reading of the twelve texts referred to above. Each of those miscues was analyzed using Procedure I of the Reading Miscue Inventory, and the results are summarized in the Tables 6-1 and 6-2. Though the texts are grouped according to one measure of relative difficulty, within each group the texts are listed in the order in which Marlene read them. See Chapter 5 for a discussion about the concept of readability.

Group 1   The eighth text read by Marlene during the course of this study was "The Man Who Kept House," estimated to be at a third-grade level according to the Fry Readability Formula. The miscue analysis data points to the ease with which Marlene was able to read this particular text. Her number of miscues per hundred words was 3.2, the lowest at any point in the study (Table 6-1). Ninety-two percent of her miscues were likely to result in no loss of comprehension (Table 6-1), and 84 percent of her miscues demonstrated strength in controlling the grammatical relationships in the text (Table 6-1). These two percentages are higher than any other percentages in their respective categories.

Fifty-eight percent of her miscues showed high graphic similarity to the text, and 21 percent were highly similar in sound (Table 6-2). These two percentages are among the lowest in their categories, demonstrating that as Marlene moved toward making miscues which make sense she also moved away from an overreliance on the graphophonic cueing system.

Group 2   The three texts in this group consist of two readings of *The Wreck of the Zephyr*, and a third text, a short story titled "The Clan Revisited." The "Clan" text, along with three others Marlene selected, is from an anthology of short stories written by a sophomore high school class. Across time within this group, Marlene reduced her miscues per hundred words from 6 in *Zephyr* (#1) to 5.4 in "Clan," and finally to 4.3 in *Zephyr* (#2). There was a steady increase in miscues which resulted in no loss in comprehension: 47 percent in *Zephyr* (#1); 70 percent in "Clan"; and 72 percent in *Zephyr* (#2); and a decrease in miscues likely to result in loss of comprehension: 45 percent in *Zephyr* (#1); 29 percent in "Clan"; and 22 percent in *Zephyr* (#2) (Table 6-1).

Table 6-1   Marlene's meaning construction and grammatical relationships

Title	Miscues per hundred words	Meaning construction			Grammatical relationships			
		No loss	Partial loss	Loss	Partial strength	Strength	Weakness	Over correction
Group 1 (Readability* = 3)								
Kept House (Session 8)	3.2	92%	—	8%	84%	8%	—	8%
Group 2 (Readability* = 5)								
Zephyr (#1) (Session 1)	6	47	8	45	51	22	27	—
Clan (Session 7)	5.4	70	1	29	71	9	20	—
Zephyr (#2) (Session 12)	4.3	72	6	22	72	13	13	2
Group 3 (Readability* = 7)								
Genius (Session 2)	7.7	59	10	31	64	19	14	3
Brain (Session 9)	4.9	58	8	35	58	14	23	5
Game (Session 10)	4.7	60	9	31	69	16	15	—
Group 4 (Readability* = 9)								
Rodeo (Session 3)	9.1	27	12	61	32	38	27	3
Gun (Session 4)	8.4	45	3	52	45	41	14	—
Cabbage (Session 11)	6.7	59	2	39	60	26	12	2
Group 5 (Readability* = College)								
Scandal (Session 5)	8.7	15	17	68	28	54	18	—
Mexico (Session 6)	8.6	32	4	64	36	38	26	—

* Estimated using Fry Readability Formula.

Concurrent with the increase in "meaning construction" strategies was an increase in miscues which reflect strength in maintaining structures that are syntactically acceptable: 51 percent in *Zephyr* (#1); 71 percent in "Clan"; and 72 percent in *Zephyr* (#2) (Table 6-1). Weakness in controlling syntactic relationships in text decreased from 27 percent in *Zephyr* (#1), to 20 percent in "Clan," to 13 percent in *Zephyr* (#2) (Table 6-2).

Marlene's declining reliance on the graphophonic cueing system is apparent in the percentages of high graphic and sound similarity. In *Zephyr* (#1) 83 percent of miscues showed high graphic similarity and 60 percent reflected a high sound similarity. Those percentages were lowered to 71 percent and 52 percent, respectively, in "Clan," and to 65 percent and 45 percent, respectively, in the second reading of *Zephyr*.

Group 3   The three texts in Group 3 contain one selected by me, "My Brother is a Genius," and two selected by Marlene from the high school short story anthology. Marlene reduced her level of miscues per hundred words from 7.7 in "Genius," to 4.9 and 4.7 in "Brain" and "Game," respectively (Table 6-1). This nearly 40 percent reduction in miscues was accompanied by only slight increases in miscues which reflect no loss of comprehension: 59 percent in "Genius"; 58 percent in "Brain"; and 60 percent in "Game" (Table 6-1). Slightly greater improvement in reading strategies was indicated in Marlene's control over grammatical relationships. Sixty-four percent of miscues showed "strength" in "Genius," 58 percent in "Brain," and 69 percent in "Game."

Table 6-2   Marlene's graphic and sound similarity

Title	Graphic similarity			Sound similarity		
	High	Some	None	High	Some	None
Group 1						
Kept House (Session 8)	58%	21%	21%	21%	36%	43%
Group 2						
Zephyr (#1) (Session 1)	83	11	6	60	36	4
Clan (Session 7)	71	23	6	52	37	1
Zephyr (#2) (Session 12)	65	27	8	45	37	18
Group 3						
Genius (Session 2)	73	21	6	58	31	11
Brain (Session 9)	68	27	5	52	38	10
Game (Session 10)	56	36	8	40	36	24
Group 4						
Rodeo (Session 3)	64	27	9	55	30	15
Gun (Session 4)	81	15	4	52	48	—
Cabbage (Session 11)	64	34	2	45	45	10
Group 5						
Scandal (Session 5)	75	21	4	56	40	4
Mexico (Session 6)	70	30	—	49	49	2

Marlene's focus on graphophonic cues declined in this group of texts. Graphic similarity was high for 73 percent of the miscues in "Genius," 68 percent in "Brain," and 56 percent in "Game." Sound similarity decreased as well, from 58 percent of miscues highly similar in "Genius," to 52 percent in "Brain," and 40 percent in "Game" (Table 6-2).

Group 4   This group of texts contains a magazine article titled "Reno Rodeo," a short story by Louis L'Amour titled "A Gun for Kilkenny," and a short story from the high school anthology, "Revenge of the Cabbage Patch Dolls." Each of these texts was chosen by Marlene.

More so than the Group 3 texts, this group provides solid evidence of improvement in Marlene's reading strategies. She made 9.1 miscues per hundred words in "Rodeo," lowering that rate to 8.4 in "Gun," and 6.7 in "Cabbage" (Table 6-1).

In the category of "Meaning Construction" Marlene increased the percentage of miscues likely to result in no loss of comprehension from 27 percent in "Rodeo" to 45 percent in "Gun" and 59 percent in "Cabbage" (Table 6-1). Miscues likely to result in a loss of comprehension declined from 61 percent to 39 percent in these same three texts.

The category of "Grammatical Relationships" shows an increase in miscues which demonstrate "strength" from 32 percent in "Rodeo," to 45 percent in "Gun," and, finally, to 60 percent in "Cabbage" (Table 6-1). Miscues which suggest "weakness" in controlling syntactical relationships in text declined from 27 percent in "Rodeo" to 14 percent and 12 percent in "Gun" and "Cabbage," respectively (Table 6-1).

Marlene's reliance on phonic cues also decreased—55 percent of miscues showed high sound similarity in "Rodeo," and 45 percent showed high similarity in "Cabbage." A particularly high percentage of miscues in "Gun" showed high graphic similarity to the text; the other two texts were stable at 64 percent (Table 6-1).

Group 5   "Jesse James in Mexico" and "The Missouri Scandal" were both selected by Marlene, and each was published in an early 1960s issue of *Real West* magazine. These stories, along with the "Reno Rodeo" article and "A Gun for Kilkenny" reflected Marlene's interest in reading Westerns. It is important to note that both "Mexico" and "Scandal" were estimated to be at the college level, and, indeed, they were particularly difficult. Archaic vocabulary and unpredictable syntax resulted in Marlene's relatively high 8.7 and 8.6 miscues per hundred words (Table 6-1), but she was able to improve the quality of those miscues over time—in this instance, a two-week span. A mere 15 percent of miscues in "Scandal" suggested no loss in meaning; that percentage rose to 32 percent in "Mexico." Only a slight decline in miscues resulting in loss of meaning was evident, from 68 percent in "Scandal" to 64 percent in "Mexico" (Table 6-1).

Marlene showed some improvement in her ability to control syntax. Twenty-eight percent of miscues in "Scandal" reflected strength in controlling grammatical relationships, rising to 36 percent in "Mexico." However, there was an accompanying increase in miscues which suggested "weakness," from 18 percent in "Scandal" to 26 percent in "Mexico" (Table 6-1).

Seventy-five percent of miscues in "Scandal" were highly similar in graphic features to the text; 70 percent were highly similar in "Mexico." Sound similarity was also reduced, from 56 percent in "Scandal" to 49 percent in "Mexico" (Table 6-2).

Discussion   In every group of texts, Marlene was able to demonstrate increasing effectiveness in at least one aspect of her reading. Miscues per hundred words frequently declined, while the numbers of high-quality miscues increased. The improvement in reading strategies was paralleled by her movement from a model of the reading process which emphasized accuracy in word recognition to one which focuses on the construction of meaning.

The Closing Interview

During the final session conducted with Marlene, she was interviewed extensively about her reactions to RMA used as an instructional strategy.

Ann: When you are reading and you come to something that gives you trouble, what do you do?
Marlene: Try to put a word I know into it.
Ann: Anything else?
Marlene: Skip it.
Ann: Are those helpful strategies, or not so helpful strategies?
Marlene: Some of it's good because if you skip one word you can pick up in the story what they're talking about and understand it.

Marlene has recognized that words can be understood from their context; not knowing an individual word is no longer a sufficient cause for her to stop reading. She does not stress the importance of consulting a dictionary when in trouble, as she did at the beginning of the study. By her own admission, Marlene felt more confident about her reading than she did in the beginning:

Ann: Is there anything you would like to change about your reading at this point?
Marlene: No. I'm better at it.
Ann: Describe yourself as a reader.

Marlene: Pretty good, getting better.
Ann: Have there been changes in how you read as a result of what we've been doing?
Marlene: I slow down on what I want to read and I try to understand. Before I used to read
           just to get to know the words. But now it's like "read this and try to understand it."
Ann: What kinds of miscues do you make now, as compared with the beginning?
Marlene: In the beginning I was making them with nonwords. Now I'm putting more
           words in which make the sentence sound better, or pretty close to what the
           author wanted.

These responses further confirm that Marlene has moved to a "meaning construction" model of the reading process. And it is clear that the "good reader" myth she has believed in has been somewhat disconfirmed. She no longer berates herself for failing to know all the words or for failing to look them up in a dictionary. Rather, she now concentrates on understanding what she reads and believes that a focus on meaning will hold the key to improving her reading:

Ann: How do you feel about your ability to continue to improve your reading?
Marlene: I can do it. It will take a lot of practice and reading a lot on my own.

Once again, the importance of "practice" has been emphasized, but not the kind of practice which requires assistance from a teacher.

At the outset of her participation in this study, Marlene stated that teachers never helped her very much as she tried to learn to read. There was apprehension on my part, since I suspected that Marlene might be resentful of yet another "teacher" who would not help—at least not in the ways Marlene would recognize as "help." As Marlene evaluated the usefulness of retrospective miscue analysis as an instructional strategy, she was clear in her differentiation between "teachers" and my role in this case.

Ann: In general, how do you feel about these kinds of sessions?
Marlene: I'm coming here and getting help. But if you said "Now, here's your homework,
           take it home and do it" it would be like "Oh gee, we're back in school with all
           this stuff." You'd be sort of turning them off because you'd be handing them a
           lot of homework. I think this way is a lot better because the person will feel like
           "Oh gee, I just read this and I won't have to be pressured by all the questions
           to answer." Here, you say "Well, read this and we will talk about it next week.
           Just remember what you read." Which to me is a little more personal, more fun.
           It's like she's getting you to learn something, but in a whole different way.
Ann: What I've really tried to do is not have me teach you anything, but have you
           learn something from doing your own analysis. You've decided for yourself for
           each miscue which things are positive about them and which things aren't useful.
Marlene: Your way is different from a schoolteacher's. Their way is "Okay, read Chapter
           1 and we'll talk about it tomorrow." But you only see me once a week. And I
           have a whole week to think about the story and the way it affected me when I
           was reading it, and the way I thought the author should have written it, or what
           I thought it should have sounded like. Then I come back the next time, and we
           get to talk about it. You come up with all these miscues, and I'm thinking, "Can
           we fix these or does this make sense?" If I was with a schoolteacher, she would
           say, "This is a miscue. This is wrong. Why don't you read what the author put
           there?" They automatically say, "This is what the author wrote and I want it said
           just this way."
Ann: The author's right. The reader's wrong.
Marlene: Yeah. The way your method goes, I think "This is what the reader wanted it to
           be, not what the teacher or the author wanted, but this is the way the reader is
           reading, and this is how the reader feels about it."
Ann: You are so articulate. It has taken me a long time to learn what you just said.
           No matter what anybody thinks, reading happens all alone, up inside our heads.
           There's nobody else in there. The text is only marginally in there. If we don't
           like it, we change it.
Marlene: We change it. I do it. Everybody does it.

Marlene has assumed ownership of her reading in the most complete sense. She places herself firmly among the community of readers ("I do it. Everybody does it."), no longer an outsider in a literate society.

Reflections on Revaluing

When Marlene pointed out the many ways in which the instruction she received from me was different from "what a schoolteacher" would do, I began to analyze my own role in the process of using retrospective miscue analysis as an instructional technique. I'm not certain how often research has a very powerful effect on the researcher, but the two women with whom I worked dramatically altered some of my previously held notions about the reading process, and helped me clarify what I believe about teaching, and, more importantly, learning. This section is devoted to sharing what I learned from two unsuspecting teachers: Gina and Marlene.

A number of years ago, my classroom at Toltec Elementary School in Eloy, Arizona, boasted a large yellow poster with bright orange print advising my students:

> A Tip for Toltec Tiger Readers: When you're reading and you come to something you don't know, read on and think about what would make sense. It usually works!

That advice was rooted in my belief that "making sense" was the ultimate reading strategy—if readers could focus on making sense of text, they would remediate for themselves much of the difficulty they often experienced. And a classroom rich with literature, drama, newspapers, and magazines would provide a natural incentive to read. I believed that language was easiest to learn when it was presented in "wholes," complete with beginnings, middles, and ends, and existing for some real purpose. These beliefs have not been mitigated by my work with Gina and Marlene. Rather, they have been strengthened.

My understanding of sociopsycholinguistic theory also led me to believe that for the reading process to be most accessible to students, they must be allowed the time and flexibility within a text to fully sample, predict, confirm, and self-correct. That meant I had a classroom where children were not allowed to "give one another the word" when plays were read and all had copies of the text (although they were allowed to give semantic clues). But when students were faced with something they didn't (apparently) know, I advised "Can you think of a word that would make sense?" and encouraged the substitution of words that made sense within the context. And when no words that made sense occurred to the reader, I said "Skip it. Go on." I knew from research that giving readers the words is an ineffective strategy—teachers find themselves giving the same word repeatedly throughout a text. The so-called remedial readers in my classroom were used to teachers who corrected every miscue and provided words when readers were unable to do so. Years of remediation had made many of them completely dependent upon their teachers, unwilling to take risks, and unsure of the purpose for reading.

I wanted to shatter these misconceptions. I wanted to remind them continually that reading for meaning was the only real reason for reading. I wanted them to assume control of making sense of text. But there was at least one flaw in my approach. I believed that I could control their judgments of what made sense; that my intrusion into their thought processes as they read was based on an accurate perception of what they were thinking. Let me share an example:

> It is 11:15 A.M. and third-grader Joe is spending fifteen minutes at the reading conference table with me. He is reading aloud from "Rumplestiltskin," and makes a miscue which apparently makes no sense. I allow him to finish the sentence before saying, "Hum . . . you said ____, does that make sense?" Joe looks up at me, thinks for a moment, and justifies his miscue. He continues reading.

Scenes like this were commonplace in my classroom. I felt justified in calling attention to miscues which didn't make sense, but what I failed to understand is that in so doing, I was continuing to impose *my* notion of what makes sense on the readers. My question "Does that make sense?" was merely a disguise for "That doesn't make sense to me. You need to reprocess the text and make a correction." My intention to help children focus on understanding was not at fault, but I needed to go one step further and help them internalize the question "Does this make sense *to me?*"

This realization became most clear to me in two consecutive RMA sessions with Marlene. RMA Session Number 2 focused on Marlene's miscues made in her previous week's reading of "My Brother is a Genius." At the conclusion of that session, I included in my notes the remark "I'm creating a Frankenstein," referring to her explanations for why many of her miscues made sense, even when they appeared to me to make little sense.

At the end of the second session, she read a magazine article called "The Reno Rodeo" into the tape recorder. Many of her miscues appeared likely to disrupt meaning (I calculated 61 percent probable "loss" of meaning). Her retelling score was 80 percent but it was clear she knew a great deal about local rodeo events from personal experience. I looked forward to the next session when we would discuss her miscues. Up to that point, she had been adamant in her insistence that most of her miscues made sense. I thought she would be forced to admit that the miscues in the "Rodeo" text did not make sense, and that she would begin to recognize the value of monitoring her comprehension. But Marlene did not react as I anticipated. Consider her justifications for the following miscues, each from the "Rodeo" text:

Happily, this outdoor rodeo is still

more down-home than uptown, and there isn't a

set
bad seat in the house.

Ann: Does the miscue make sense?
Marlene: Yeah. They could be talking about the way they run the show—what they're going to do and how they're going to do it—how they set it up.

But look, the indoors is for raising

hamstrings
hamsters, not cattle.

Ann: Does the miscue make sense?
Marlene: Yeah. Athletes are in indoor pavilions, doing stuff like strengthening their hamstrings.

Her unpredictable responses led me to realize that only the reader is in the position to judge whether miscues disrupt meaning. Further, a teacher attempting to control those determinations may only reinforce dependence on others to monitor understanding. Marlene's persistence in believing she was right helped me to see where I had been wrong.

Although reading is a vehicle for social interaction, its successful pursuit requires that readers be helped to become more independent than dependent in their transactions with texts. This may sound trivial, but much of what exists as remedial reading instruction encourages readers to rely on others to make sense for them. If they do this long enough, they forget that making sense was ever the purpose for reading. We cannot, in Gina's words, sit alongside the reader, point out the problems, and make the repairs. Instead, readers must learn to find the difficulties for themselves and resolve them in ways that make sense to them. Even Gina and Marlene, self-described nonreaders, used effective strategies, and when they were allowed to discover for themselves the worth and usefulness of those strategies, they incorporated more of them into their reading.

Ownership is the key to revaluing, but how can we foster the assumption of ownership of the process? Retrospective miscue analysis is one way we can take the mystique out of reading and let readers discover what researchers have discovered: that all readers make miscues, that the strategies they use are legitimate, that comprehending and comprehension are tentative, ever-shifting across a text, and shifting within the mind of a reader when the text is no longer present. We must engender a respect for the complexity of the process and their abilities relative to that process. The revaluing in this research has been twofold: Gina and Marlene were revaluing reading; I was revaluing readers.

7

Retrospective Miscue Analysis in Middle School

Yetta M. Goodman
Alan Flurkey

TAKING INTO ACCOUNT WHAT WE'D been learning about retrospective miscue analysis (RMA), Ann Marek and Yetta Goodman planned a study with seventh graders to verify our hypotheses, to extend our insights, and to raise new questions about how helping readers become conscious of the reading process supports them in revaluing themselves as readers. We were especially interested in discovering more about how readers, through RMA experiences: 1) revalue themselves as readers; 2) revalue the reading process; 3) talk and reflect about the reading process and their own reading proficiency; and 4) improve their actual reading strategies.

We planned to document middle school readers' abilities to talk and reflect on their own reading and the reading process. Although some researchers in the areas of metalinguistic and metacognitive awareness state that less able readers are not metalinguistically aware and that this lack is a probable cause for their problems in reading (Wong 1987), our work with RMA has led us to reject this conclusion. We wanted to extend the data with documentation about how adolescents talk about reading and the reading process and how this influences their reading proficiency.

In addition, most RMA research in classroom settings has generally focused on troubled readers. However, teachers report that proficient readers often make statements about the reading process and themselves as readers that are similar to statements made by those considered less proficient. We wondered if using RMA with proficient readers would reveal different kinds of responses to RMA procedures and whether the concept of revaluing has relevance for proficient readers as well. So the study was organized to discover whether readers labeled as "good" or "poor" on various measures respond differently to RMA procedures.

We formulated two research questions and a research design to gather and analyze the information necessary to answer the questions:

1. What does RMA reveal about the metalinguistic knowledge of good and poor readers in seventh grade?
   a. What beliefs do they articulate about the reading process?
   b. How do they make use of that knowledge?
   c. What do they do when their beliefs conflict with the evidence revealed through analyzing their own reading?
2. What effect does RMA have on the reading attitudes and abilities of poor readers in seventh grade?

a. How do their views about themselves as readers change?
b. How do their views about the reading process change?
c. How do their actual reading strategies change?

Selecting Students

This study, supported by the National Council of Teachers of English Research Foundation, involved sixteen students in seventh grade in a middle school in Tucson, Arizona. Using standardized test scores and other measures found in student records in addition to teacher judgment, nine readers were designated as poor readers, five students were designated as good readers, and two readers were in the middle range. However, reading test score data proved to be an unsatisfactory means for differentiating between good and poor readers. The stanine scores, ranging from first to seventh stanines, mislabeled students when compared with the reading strategy profiles generated from detailed miscue analysis. Some students who had low (second to fourth) to mid-range (fifth and sixth) stanine scores were actually quite effective and efficient in utilizing reading strategies. In other words, as they read, the patterns of their miscues resulted in sentences that were initially semantically and syntactically acceptable, or they self-corrected miscues that resulted in unacceptable structures. Some readers with mid-range scores demonstrated reading strategies that were inefficient and ineffective. These latter readers produced patterns of miscues that most often resulted in semantically and syntactically unacceptable sentences within the story context. In the last analysis, we used the standardized measures in conjunction with miscue analysis and the judgment of the classroom teacher to establish the designations.

In the conclusions of this research, we reject the notion of good and poor readers as general categories in favor of the concept of revaluing and explain our position concerning this issue in this chapter and throughout this book. However, since good reader/poor reader research is so prevalent in the reading field and since we used those terms in the NCTE research proposal, we maintain those labels in this chapter and use this opportunity to critique the use of those terms.

Figure 7-1 lists each student (they selected their own pseudonyms), the good/poor designation, the number of RMI and RMA sessions each participated in, and whether or not the closing and follow-up interviews were completed. Although we have done in-depth analyses on the students from whom we collected a complete set of data, we used transcripts from all the students to answer the research questions.

There was one factor that turned out to be fortuitous during the process of categorizing the students. Because of this factor, we stumbled onto data that provides unanticipated insights into middle school readers' responses concerning their beliefs and attitudes about the reading process and themselves as readers. In the middle school in which we worked, students designated as "academically talented" (because their reading scores were in the eighth and ninth stanines) were placed in separate classes and, therefore, not available for this study. Because of this unexpected population grouping, we discovered interesting issues about middle range (sixth and seven stanines) readers that have important implications for reading instruction. These issues will be discussed later.

Preparing for the Study

During August of 1989, we worked out specific procedures and adapted or designed data collection forms. We had meetings with the research team, including faculty, graduate students, and the classroom teacher (most have authored articles in this book). All members of the team were well versed in Reading Miscue Inventory (RMI) procedures, having taken classes focused on the reading process, applied linguistics, and miscue analysis. They all had completed many RMIs on students and had participated in RMA sessions. It is necessary that researchers who

Student Alias	Reader Designation	Reading Sessions	RMA Sessions	Closing Interview	Follow-Up Interview
Elizabeth	good	4 sessions	4 sessions	completed	completed
Jeannie	good	4 sessions	4 sessions	completed	completed
Kelly	good	4 sessions	4 sessions	completed	completed
Bernice	good	4 sessions	4 sessions	completed	completed
Hubert	good	4 sessions	4 sessions	completed	completed
Kari	middle (alternate)	15 sessions	15 sessions	completed	completed
Leon	middle (alternate)	4 sessions	4 sessions	completed	completed
Barry	poor	13 sessions	13 sessions	completed	completed
Edwin	poor	3 sessions	3 sessions	moved	moved
Joni	poor	11 sessions	11 sessions	completed	completed
Dave	poor	5 sessions	5 sessions	completed	completed
Guillermo	poor	3 sessions	2 sessions	moved	moved
Rudy	poor	12 sessions	12 sessions	completed	moved
Rolando	poor	13 sessions	13 sessions	completed	completed
Alfredo	poor	11 sessions	11 sessions	completed	completed
Felipe	poor	6 sessions	5 sessions	moved	moved

Figure 7-1   RMA Student Participants

use RMA have a strong foundation in miscue analysis, the theory and research that informs it, and its methodology and procedures.

The students selected for the study agreed to participate and got permission from their parents to do so. A Reading Interview (Y. Goodman et al. 1987) was administered to each of the students at the initial meeting in September, the following May at the end of the school year, and then again in the following September to establish the consistency of students' ideas about reading. This interview documents readers' stated beliefs about the reading process and about their reading ability. It establishes whether readers conceive of reading as a subskills, skills, or holistic model of reading (Harste & Burke 1977).

Researchers worked with the same students throughout the study as often as possible in order to establish a positive relationship between the researchers and the student. As shown in the above table, the poor readers met with the researchers approximately every week and the good readers about once a month. The students did get to know the other researchers because we often worked in teams, observing and critiquing each other's sessions. Each reader was tape-recorded individually reading a published text selected by the research team, then asked to retell the story. The student's reading and retelling were analyzed using RMI procedures. This analysis provided the opportunity to describe the relationship between actual reading strategies (as revealed through miscue analysis) and beliefs about the reading process (as indicated in interviews and RMA discussions).

After the initial RMI session, an RMA session was planned. RMA procedures began in September a week following the first RMI session and continued through May. The students designated as poor readers participated in almost twice as many sessions as the good readers because we assumed that we needed more time to help poor readers revalue reading and the reading process than we would need with good readers. Our assumption turned out to be valid.

RMA Procedures

The procedures during the sessions were similar to the RMA Session Outline described in Chapter 4 and followed by Ann with Gina and Marlene in Chapters 5 and 6. An initial session was planned with the reader to gather background information, establish rapport, and collect the first Reading Interview. In most cases the first reading and retelling for RMI analysis was done at this time. The materials needed for this session included a tape recorder, the background information sheet, a copy of the Reading Interview, the original published text to be read, and its typescript for RMI marking.

Next, the researcher prepared for the RMA session by double-checking the marking of the typescript from the initial RMI, coding the miscues using RMI Procedure III (see Chapter 3 and Y. Goodman et al. 1987), selecting miscues for the next RMA session, and preparing the RMA Session Organizer. The RMA Session Organizer helped the researcher remember the miscues to discuss with the reader. The line numbers on the typescript and the tape counter number were noted so the miscues could be found easily. The organizer also listed the miscues and any comments the researcher thought might be helpful during the RMA session. The example of the session organizer shown in Figure 7-2 was used with Rolando after he read "Pedro and Diablo," a story from *The Day It Snowed Tortillas*. The organizer shows that the purpose of the session was to help Rolando focus on the influence of his dialect and second language on his reading, his use of naming strategies, and his partially acceptable uncorrected miscues. As noted, the researcher planned to discuss Rolando's use of *y* in Spanish for *and* in English, as well as name substitutions for *Martinez*. Although the miscues are marked in advance and the comments are used to remind the researcher of possible issues to raise, the procedures are flexible and follow the reader's lead.

The materials needed during the RMA session included two tape recorders, a blank tape to record the RMA session, the tape of the previous reading, the published text with marked and unmarked typescripts, and the RMA Session Organizer. The researcher and the student listened to a segment of the original reading and marked the selected miscue on the blank typescript, evaluating the miscue by asking the RMA questions. Initially the researcher marked the miscues to demonstrate the procedures and marking system, but eventually the student marked all the miscues in the selected passages. The entire RMA session was tape recorded on the second tape recorder for further analysis. At the end of the sessions, a new reading was recorded to be marked and coded following RMI procedures, and also used to select miscues for the subsequent RMA session.

After each RMA session, the researcher listened to the RMA session tape recording and made notes on an adapted RMA Response Form (Appendix B). Other significant portions of the tape recording were transcribed and preparation began for the next RMA session. Although most of the procedures were usually followed quite consistently, the teachers/researchers took into consideration the students' responses and their own professional insights to adapt the procedures to capitalize on any particular critical teaching moments.

The RMA with Seventh Graders

Sometimes during this study, we scheduled additional sessions to obtain readings for RMI purposes if the RMA session went longer than expected. We also brought two students together at some sessions to gain insights into differences

RMA SESSION ORGANIZER

Rolando
_____   R1008:2-6/04 rma
(READER)   **(session)**

Day It Snowed Tortillas: Pedro and   **Session Focus:** Uncorrected partial
Diablo   acceptables/ influence of dialect/use of
_____   naming strategies
(TEXT)

M S Q #	Tape-Recorder Counter #	Line	Miscue	+/−	Notes:
				(Strength/weakness)	
1	(4)	title	ʸ Pedro and Diablo	+	What happened? Comment on Eng./Sp. pron.
2	(10)	107	El Diablo ⓓ	+	read "y friend…" Q? Can you read in Sp.
__	( )				
8	(11)	109	ⓒ In school if… ᵸᵉ	+	What was your prediction? Why self-cor.
			…leaning against the wall		
9	(39)	228	right over from.. ᵗʰᵉ	+	What was your prediction?
3	(19)	122	man's manzanita ...Old Man Martinez's tree..	+	Why did you substitute "manzanita" tree?
4	(22)	125	Manzanita ...Old Man Martinez…	+	Same question as above.
5	(26)	205	Manitonita ...Old Man Martinez…	+	Why substitute "Mantonita" here? Why did you change it? What was your strategy?
6	(30)	211	ⓤⓒ Compso- campso- We'll go to the camposanto..	−	What did you think it meant? Why change? What did you end up doing? Why?
			…dividing up the dead souls		
7	(47)	309	ꜱCampsotento in the camposanto…		What was your strategy for dealing with this word? Did it help you?
__	( )	__		__	
10	(60)	421	ⓒ ⓒ ⓤⓒ saw the f- ..and they say that from ⓒ ᵗʰᵉ that day on…		Who do the 'they's refer to in 421 & 423? Did you realize that when you made the miscue? If so, why didn't you self correct?
__	( )	__		__	

name { 3, 4, 5

noun { 6, 7

NOTES:
See retelling notes on page 1 of the typescript to add to the RMA transcription.

Form: 12/21/89   Session Date: _____

Figure 7-2   Rolando's RMA Session

between one-on-one sessions and the pairing of students. Because we wanted to make some comparisons between students, we selected most of the reading materials using similar published texts for the readers. There were occasions, though, when we asked readers to bring in school work or personal home reading materials to enhance our understanding about their reading.

Each RMA session was tape recorded and transcribed in order to provide a permanent record of the changes in perceptions about the reading process and in the strategies used during the reading. Students were often asked to read aloud the section in the published text selected by the researcher that would be the focus of the miscue discussion. In this way, we discovered whether they made similar miscues during this second reading. They then listened to the original reading and marked any miscues they heard on the blank typescript. Then a discussion about the nature of the miscue(s) began. The researcher and the student used an adapted RMA Response Form to help them analyze the reader's perceptions about the reading process and the ways those perceptions changed over time. The adapted form includes the following questions used to analyze each miscue selected for discussion:

1. Does the miscue make sense?
2. Does the miscue sound like language?
3. Was the miscue corrected? Should it have been?
4. Does the miscue look like/sound like the text item?
5. Why do you think you made this miscue?
6. Did that miscue affect your understanding of the text?

Through these questions and the discussion about what they mean for the reader, we were able to document, as subsequent examples show, answers to our research questions. This chapter is organized to answer the research questions in general while Chapters 8, 9, and 10 present in-depth case studies of some of the students.

METALINGUISTIC KNOWLEDGE OF GOOD AND POOR READERS

The first research question examines the metalinguistic knowledge of good and poor readers by considering: a) what beliefs readers articulate about the reading process; b) how readers make use of their beliefs; and c) what they do when their beliefs conflict with evidence from their own reading.

Beliefs Readers Articulate about the Reading Process

All the examples document the ability of readers to talk and think about language, and to articulate their knowledge and beliefs about language. Both good and poor readers expressed their beliefs about themselves as readers, describing various kinds of reading problems, especially at the beginning of the study. For example, Alfredo, who was designated as a poor reader in the study, expressed the belief that he was a slow reader. He maintained this belief in spite of evidence which demonstrated his use of effective and efficient reading strategies: "I would like to read faster. I think I read too slow. It don't sound good." Bernice, labeled a good reader, initially attributed her substitutions and omissions, which usually were semantically and syntactically acceptable, to being lazy. When her researcher asked her, "What did you do when your miscues didn't make sense?," she replied "Half of the time I went back." When the researcher showed her that she regressed and self-corrected over 80 percent of her miscues in a particular story, Bernice responded: "Some of them I just didn't go back. Lazy."

Probably the most significant finding of our study concerns the complexity of metalinguistic knowledge and its relationship to language use. We found that all the readers, regardless of proficiency or ability, even from the beginning of the study, were able to articulate not only beliefs about the reading process and about their strengths and weaknesses as readers but were able to make statements that reveal their concepts or knowledge about the reading process. All students were able to discuss the language cueing systems (pragmatic, semantic, syntactic, and graphophonic) as well as the reading strategies (predicting, confirming, and searching for meaning). They often used their own metaphors or terminology to talk about the systems and strategies, but there was no doubt that their terms related to the concepts.

For example, in his final Reading Interview, Rudy, one of the designated poor readers, showed evidence of his awareness of graphophonic as well as syntactic information. He expressed his knowledge of the linguistic units in his reading and an awareness of the confirmation process as well in his discussion with the researcher:

Alan: When you are reading and come to something you don't know, what do you do?
Rudy: I skip it and read on. Then I go back and see what the word says.
Alan: Do you ever do anything else?
Rudy: I sound it out before I go back.

During the fourth RMA session, Felipe, also labeled a poor reader, responded to the selected miscues in his reading of "Bill Evers and the Tigers" (1972) and revealed his knowledge of the language cueing systems and his reading strategies. He discussed his reaction to the following miscue:

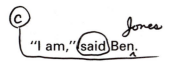

Felipe: Oh! *I am Ben.*
Alan: You took out the word *said*, right?
Felipe: Yeah.
Alan: Does that make sense to say, *I am Ben?*
Felipe: I don't know. You can say that on the phone but it's kinda weird.

As the researcher and Felipe talked more about this reading, the researcher suggested that Felipe's miscue was a "pretty good prediction." Then they focused on whether or not the miscue made sense.

Alan: It made sense, but you went back and corrected it. I wonder what you were thinking.
Felipe: I probably thought it didn't make any sense.

Discussion of a subsequent miscue provided more data about Felipe's language knowledge.

Evans

"Oh, hello," Ben said. "Is this Bill Evers?"

They listened to the tape two times without Felipe hearing the miscue.

Alan: I want you to listen to the last name that you give him.
Felipe: Evans.
Alan: Okay. What do you suppose happened there?
Felipe: God, I don't know.
Alan: Does *Evans* make sense?
Felipe: *Bill Evans?* Yeah, but . . .
Alan: Does it look like the word *Evers?*

Felipe: Yeah, well sort of . . . just the *ev*.
Alan: And by the way, *r* kind of looks like *n*, so they both kind of look the same. Um . . . It made sense?
Felipe: Bill Evers is a baseball player.

The conversation then focused on whether saying *Evans* instead of *Evers* made a difference to this story. The researcher explained how good readers substitute names in such settings and Felipe decided it was acceptable to substitute any name as long as "it fit the story." Felipe was able to articulate his knowledge of strategy use. He discussed the process he used to reject a prediction of a linguistic feature. He revealed his language knowledge in his discussion of proper nouns and was able to discuss his use of textual information to make clear his self-correction strategies. His comment about the kind of language acceptable during a phone conversation was evidence of his pragmatic knowledge.

The example of Rolando, another reader designated as poor, working out the pronunciation of the book title and name *Jumanji* provides insight into how his knowledge of language supported his reading strategy use.

Alan: Let's talk about what was going on in your mind as you were doing what you did.
Rolando: I guess 'cause I looked at it again. I was thinking that wasn't right 'cause the letters aren't right. If it had an *a* then it would be *Jumeenia*.
Alan: Okay. I have a bunch of questions . . . Is it okay for a reader to just settle on what they think the title is?
Rolando: Yeah, because if you have what the idea is, just go with what you think.
Alan: That's a great answer. That's a neat way of looking at it. I wish more kids adopted that stance. You said it could go either way. You said it could go *Hameena* because the *J* could sound like an *H*.
Rolando: Uh huh [yes].
Alan: Or it could be *Jumeenia*, right, 'cause it could sound like a *J*. When you said it could sound like an *H* what resource . . . what strength in your background were you drawing on?
Rolando: (interrupting) 'cause my brother's name is Juan and that's what the *J* starts with.
Alan: Right . . . in which language?
Rolando: Spanish.
Alan: So you're drawing on what you know about another language, right?
Rolando: Yeah.
Alan: But you decided . . .
Rolando: (*interrupting*) Like *p* and *h* phone. I heard the *p* and I guess 'cause *Humeenia*. It might be I guess 'cause some *J* words start with an *H* . . . sometimes, the *h* sound. And *Jumania* . . . I think (settled) on *Jumania* because that's the best thing.
Alan: You eventually decide on *Jumania* and I'm wondering why you went with a *J* sound instead of an *H* sound.
Rolando: Well, I got more background on the *J* sound than the *H* sound.
Alan: I have no idea really how to pronounce that word. I can pronounce it a few different ways. . . . I'm wondering do you have any thoughts on . . . is that an English word or what language?
Rolando: It's almost like a German word, kind of. I don't know . . . like a German, or I guess German.
Alan: Could you predict safely that it was a Spanish word?
Rolando: No.
Alan: Why not?
Rolando: Well, maybe. Cause *Hameenia*, that's a Spanish . . . I can . . . *Hamennia* . . . that's how you could say it in Spanish maybe.

It is notable that this reader was well aware of the influences of other languages and the effect of their phonological patterns on English. The ability to draw on what they know about language and bring it to the reading act is a hallmark of efficient readers. The clarity of Rolando's articulation, a so-called poor reader, of what he knows about language was striking.

It is important to recognize the role of social interaction or conversation in this process. Discussing their reading with an interested and serious teacher/researcher whose purpose was to show the readers the strengths revealed in their miscues provided each reader with a context in which language became the focus. In such contexts it was necessary that readers use language to talk about language. They were comfortable doing so and participated easily with the researchers. In order to make the statements that they did in exploring their uses of the reading process, it became evident that the readers were thinking about their language processes. The role of the teacher/researcher in such conversations was crucial.

How Readers Make Use of Their Beliefs about Reading

However, it appears that the relationship between a reader's articulated knowledge about language and the reading process is complex. Interestingly, all readers, despite their proficiency level, initially articulated models of the reading process that were phonics- or skills-oriented. That is, they believed, as Rudy showed in his interview above, that during reading "I sound it out before I go back."

We were especially surprised that those categorized as good readers had a skills views of the reading process as well. This was contrary to our previous experiences with proficient readers. Although they did use reading strategies proficiently, all the good readers in this study described themselves as "not very good" readers initially. In discussing reading strategies for coping with "something they did not know" good and poor readers mentioned "sound it out"; "look it up in the dictionary"; and "ask somebody to tell me." The importance of this response is discovering what the reader considers the *it* to be. Proficient readers tend to describe the *it* as chunks of texts such as sentences, ideas, or paragraphs. However, less proficient readers consider the *it* to be a word. Their focus is on word recognition such as attacking and sounding out. This skills model of the reading process seems to be heavily influenced by the instructional orientations in their previous reading programs. For example, when asked how they would help another student who was having reading difficulty, several responded that they would help that student using the same technique that they had been taught. One student said: "Probably pronounce it or something and sound it out." When he was encouraged to suggest any other ways he might help the student, he said: "Have them turn the pages to see if they ran over it before . . . go back and see if they read it before, or say the word. Probably tell them the word."

But as we have said, these designated good readers were not the top readers according to test score data, and we hypothesize that readers who are in the middle range according to stanine scores may be there because of their attitudes about themselves as readers. Although the readers we designated as good were proficient readers according to miscue analysis, they believed that they were not good readers and seemed to hold a skills model of reading for themselves. Since all the readers in this group showed dramatic changes in views about themselves as readers, we conclude that many efficient and effective readers would benefit from retrospective miscue analysis.

When proficient readers hold a negative view of themselves as readers and a skills model of the reading process, it affects their self confidence in the same way that it does for troubled readers. These middle range readers read well for school and home purposes but still didn't value themselves as readers nor were they consciously aware of what they knew about reading and the reading process. We believe that test score data and teacher's responses to students' reading abilities based on test scores influence these readers' views about themselves as readers regardless of evidence from their reading to the contrary. Through RMA, by having them consider the qualitative nature of their reading, we began to change their views, and this resulted in greater confidence about their reading. Therefore, we conclude that most readers benefit from revaluing themselves as readers and gaining greater insight into their own knowledge about language and the reading process. Retrospective miscue analysis provides that opportunity.

When Readers' Beliefs Conflict with What They Do as Readers

Readers began to revalue themselves in a number of ways through the RMA sessions. But there were a number of ideas about readers and authors that they had to reconsider. Many of the students knew that authors have a right to their language choice in composing their texts. Early in the study most believed that as readers they did not have the right to change words or even punctuation as they read. Authority for these students resided in the language of the author. It took time to convince them that reading is a transactional process and that authors and readers have various roles in composing and interpreting texts. Eventually they came to believe that it was acceptable for them to construct their own meanings as they read. Through the process of evaluating the quality of their miscues, all the readers, to various degrees, began to revalue themselves as readers.

A second consideration that showed rather quickly in the revaluing process was a belief in the importance of constructing meaning rather than strictly rendering the surface features of the text. The concept of miscues and the relevation that all readers produce miscues was a third reconsideration that the students had to make.

Bernice, whose standardized test scores ranged in the middle stanines, articulated a somewhat holistic model of the reading process in her initial interview (see Chapter 10). For her, the RMA sessions seemed to strengthen and validate this orientation. In the following exchange Bernice reveals her willingness to be in control of the language of the published text as she constructs meaning as early as the first RMA session. Although Bernice did not view herself as a good reader at that time, she could conceptualize high-quality miscues during her discussions with Sarah Costello.

                                          doing
The husband stayed home and began to do

his wife's work.

Sarah: What did you do there?
Bernice: I didn't say *to do*.
Sarah: What did you say?
Bernice: I said *doing*. I don't know why, but I said *doing*.
Sarah: Can you make any guess about why you might have said *doing*?
Bernice: I must have missed *to* and looked at *do* and I quickly thought *doing* sounds better.
           I do that a lot. I miss little words that don't look that important.
Sarah: So what do you think? Do you think you have to read every word as it's written?
Bernice: No, I think you can leave out a couple words if it makes sense in your mind . . .
           in your own mind.

Even after accepting their right to construct meaning and the importance of meaning making as the central feature of reading, readers showed the influence of a schooling system in which errors are evidence of ignorance or laziness. Rolando was able to describe the power of errors as well as the pressure of adolescent society on students' views of themselves as readers (Chapter 8).

That's this guy . . . um . . . he combs his hair back. He's like a . . . he's a good friend of mine. He has trouble reading. He's like: "the lit-tle" [speaks haltingly like a syllable-by-syllable reader] like that, you know. There's those people that, you know, laugh and I . . . 'cause it's getting hard for a person not reading and people laugh, then it makes them, like "Oh this is stupid. I ain't gonna do this no more."

    . . . I only say that because if you're doing something, like, and they make fun of you doing it, you don't want nobody making fun of you. You want everybody to be, "Oh, he's cool" and that. So I guess like if other people . . . if the other person who thinks like: "Oh, he has that kind of tennis shoes on. I want those kind of tennis shoes because he has them . . . everybody else has them." And you hardly will be happy because you always want to do what other people want to do. And I think: "Oh, man, look at him. He don't even know how to read." And that person don't want people making fun of him, so he won't even try to read for people will make fun of him.

Toward the end of the study, Rolando articulated another view of the role of miscues when asked whether good readers ever come to something that they do not know in their reading:

Yes, because I guess nobody has ever explored all the words. Maybe, it's only someone that's very smart knows all the words, but still if they're real smart, read all fast, they'll make a mistake . . . no doubt about it. Everybody has to probably make a mistake. Nobody's perfect.

The second research question focuses on the seventh-grade poor readers and examines: a) how their views about themselves as readers change; b) how their views about the reading process changes; and c) how their actual reading strategies change.

As readers began to value their own problem-solving abilities in producing and explaining their miscues and their predicting and confirming strategies, positive views about themselves as readers increased. Readers who initially made it abundantly clear that they were not very good readers changed considerably in their ability to state that they were better readers or even good readers in some instances. They also became more confident about their right to edit the author's text as they read. Although all the students shifted in their articulated views of the reading process, each student had a somewhat different response to the RMA sessions.

Felipe initially held a subskills model of the reading process (almost as though that was what we as teachers/researchers wanted to hear), but quickly shifted his orientation when he learned that he would not be penalized for asserting that his miscues "made sense and didn't need to be corrected." His reading of "Bill Evers and the Tigers" during his fourth RMA session provided more examples of this phenomenon.

EFFECT OF RMA ON READING ATTITUDE AND ABILITIES

How Poor Readers' Views about Themselves as Readers Changed; How Poor Readers' Views about the Reading Process Changed

So the Tigers and the Red ~~Birds~~ *Reds* went on

with the game.

Felipe: (laughs with gusto after listening to the tape)
Alan: What was going on there, do you think?
Felipe: I was probably thinking of the Reds . . . the pro team.
Alan: Does that make your miscue make sense?
Felipe: Yeah.
Alan: Did you correct it?
Felipe: No.
Alan: Should you have?

Felipe: Yeah . . . Well, no, 'cause it made sense.
Alan: Well, that's an important thing you just said, Felipe, because every time I've asked
           you this before, you said. "Yeah, I should have corrected it," but now you said,
           "no, 'cause it made sense."
Felipe: Yeah . . . It made . . . 'cause this one made sense.

Felipe understood that the meaning he constructed is affected by his schema: his background and experiences. Felipe was a star athlete in his school. He was thinking about what he knew and was able to articulate his awareness of his ability as a reader to direct his construction of meaning. He realized that the miscue did not need correcting because it did not disrupt the meaning of the story.

Felipe previously believed that good reading was characterized by a flawless reproduction of the text. This view was first articulated during his initial Reading Interview.

Alan: What do you do when you come to something you don't know?
Felipe: Oh, I probably just try to sound it out.
Alan: Anything else?
Felipe: No, I just keep trying it, or I'll probably go and ask the teacher.
Alan: When I just said that "something you don't know," what did you think I meant?
           I mean what did you think the *something* was?
Felipe: Oh, a word. You see, when there's a word I don't know I just try to sound it out.

Felipe's view of the reading process focused on the word level. This contention was supported by the observation that Felipe did not identify any additional strategies to use other than asking the teacher. His resources for help in reading were dependent on others, not on his own problem-solving abilities. By the time the project had reached its midway point, Felipe began to articulate a meaning construction view.

Rudy, on the other hand, remained text-bound even at the conclusion of the study. Consider the following discussion:

I'll light *the* a fire in the fireplace.

Alan: Did that miscue make sense?
Rudy: Yes.
Alan: Why did you miscue?
Rudy: I was probably nervous or something.
Alan: Did the miscue affect the understanding?
Rudy: No.
Alan: Should you have corrected it?
Rudy: Yes, 'cause this was the right way and that was the wrong way.
Alan: But you said it made sense. If it makes sense, is it important that you change it?
Rudy: If it was this way (*points to* a), then I should put [read] it with the *a*.

Even after Rudy provided a rather complete retelling and good understanding of the story, he still clung to the belief that "good reading" was demonstrated by exact reproduction of the published text. At various times, throughout the project, there were glimmers that Rudy was grasping some concepts that support a meaning construction view. However, he never entirely rejected his text bound view. Follow-up interviews conducted during September revealed Rudy shifting totally back to valuing perfection in reading. His teacher in eighth grade believed that reading should be an errorless rendition of text and Rudy easily returned to his established beliefs. Rudy helps us keep in mind the power of context and the attitude of students toward authority figures in the attitudes they hold about reading. One year of RMA and a new view of reading was not sufficient for Rudy. This suggests the importance of all teachers in a school seriously discussing the views of reading that are demonstrated to students.

Alfredo shifted from a text-bound view to a meaning construction view as seen by the following discussion of a miscue during his eleventh RMA session.

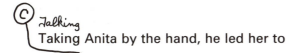

Taking Anita by the hand, he led her to

the street.

Alan:	Let's talk about what was happening here.
Alfredo:	I started with *talking* but changed it to *taking*.
Alan:	Right. Why do you suppose you did that?
Alfredo:	I thought it was going to say something like: *He was talking to his little sister, Anita.*
Alan:	And how do you know that it couldn't have been *talking*?
Alfredo:	Well, *Talking Anita* doesn't make sense.
Alan:	Anything else?
Alfredo:	I saw it and I read right here, *Anita by the hand*, and I went back and I saw *Taking*.

Alfredo showed his awareness of his use of several strategies which allowed him to control the reading process: predictions (he predicted a structure based on prior knowledge of the text); confirming and disconfirming (he rejected his initial choice because it doesn't make sense); sampling (he returned to the text to gather additional cues to help him understand) and appropriate self-correction.

Although each reader had varying views of the reading process and articulated their changes over time in different ways and to varying degrees, there is abundant evidence in the transcripts that each reader was less critical of his or her reading ability and more likely to take risks as a reader toward the end of the study.

Rolando, in his follow-up Reading Interview after the summer holidays, maintained a strong holistic stance in contrast with his stance at the beginning of the study.

Alan:	Who is a good reader you know?
Rolando:	I don't know. I can't be the judge. That person who reads himself can be the judge, cause I might not know . . . like . . . nobody can make a mistake, like miscues . . . everybody makes a miscue. So you can't say he reads better or he reads better. I mean everybody reads their own way.
Alan:	Let's suppose there is a hypothetical good reader and it could be you. What would make that person a good reader?
Rolando:	The way he understands the story, the words, the way he talks about it, the way he reads it, and his point of view.
Alan:	Do you think you are a good reader?
Rolando:	Yeah, I'm an okay reader. Pretty good.
Alan:	Why?
Rolando:	'Cause I'm pretty much able to understand what I read. And I like to read by myself . . . like when I'm home alone.

Bernice, one of the middle range readers according to reading test scores, discussed how the RMA sessions supported her belief in herself as a reader.

Sarah:	Has there been any change in your reading during the RMA sessions?
Bernice:	Yeah. I've read more smoothly and I haven't read word by word and letter by letter.
Sarah:	How do you feel about your ability to continue reading?
Bernice:	Oh, I'll read forever.

Sarah: Do you think you'll always improve?
Bernice: Yeah. You know, if you read something more you always improve.

There are various influences on readers' models of the reading process, and the ways in which those models affect reading proficiency. The influences that are most important include instructional experiences, teacher response and beliefs concerning accuracy, home influences, setting/context, and the specific material being read. It would help to understand, through additional research, how these various influences impact a reader's processing of written information at any particular point in time. In other words, we do not claim that the RMA sessions were the only influence on the changes in the students' reading, and their views about the reading process and about their reading ability. There is also evidence from retrospective miscue analysis done by Richard Coles (1981) of adolescents articulating different views about reading and themselves as readers depending on whether their responses were in home or school settings.

**How Poor Readers'
Reading Strategies
Changed**

Each of the poor readers became more effective and more efficient in their use of reading strategies throughout the course of the study, as documented in the case study chapters that follow. In the following excerpt Rolando discusses the semantically acceptable insertion miscue. Note that his sense of control over the reading process is such that he tenaciously defends his miscue.

"Not really," said Peter. "I'm sure somebody

~~so~~

left it here because it's boring."

Rolando: It's *so* boring.
Alan: You said, it's *so* boring, yeah. Oh, you put the word *so* in, right?
Rolando: Yeah.
Alan: Okay. That's a miscue that I didn't catch. Let's talk about that one first. Then, there's another one I want you to hear.
Rolando: . . . because it's so boring . . . it's boring . . . It sounds better because *so* . . . it puts the word like, . . . it's so boring. It's boring . . . more expression with so boring. 'Cause if you put, it's boring, you don't know what's boring, reading. But if you say it like: "I don't want to do this, this is boring," but the person knows like, oh, he's bored but not bored. But if you say *so* then he must be really bored . . . so it sounds better.
Alan: Did that miscue change the meaning of the sentence?
Rolando: No, it made it better I think.

There is evidence for all the readers that as readers shift in their conscious models of the reading process toward a meaning construction view, parallel shifts occur in their reading as measured by RMI. In other words, their miscues became more semantically and syntactically acceptable or they self-corrected more of the unacceptable miscues.

Even Rudy, with whom we were least successful, provides evidence of a shift. At the first and last session of the study, Rudy read "The Man Who Kept House." In the first session, he persevered, working hard (as shown on lines 102 and 103) to render a sensible text. However, the result of his sounding out and persevering strategies result in sentences that are syntactically and semantically unacceptable (see NN– coding). He finger-pointed and he had high graphic and sound similarity substitutions (see H above word substitutions).

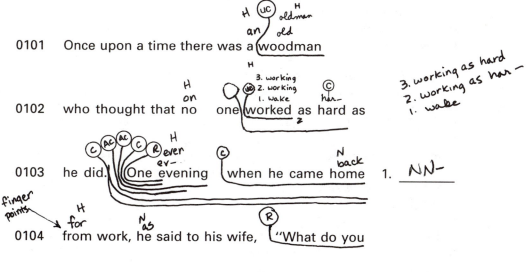

```
0101    Once upon a time there was a woodman
0102    who thought that no one worked as hard as
0103    he did. One evening when he came home    1. NN—
0104    from work, he said to his wife, "What do you
0105    do all day while I am away cutting wood?"    2. NN—
```

During his second reading more than nine months later, Rudy self-corrected with fewer regressions, and he produced a contraction and an omission which resulted in the second sentence being semantically and syntactically acceptable with no meaning change (see YYN coding). His prediction of *woman* for *woodman* is read as expected the third time *woodman* appears in the story, and is read as expected for the eight subsequent occurrences of *woodman* in the story.

```
0101    Once upon a time there was a woodman
0102    who thought that no one worked as hard as
0103    he did. One evening when he came home    1. YN—
0104    from work, he said to his wife, "What do you
0105    do all day while I am away cutting wood?"    2. YYN
```

All of our readers showed similar patterns of change. With the exception of Rudy, the shifts made by the poor readers were dramatic. However, we have no way of discovering whether these students would have become good readers anyway, or if the shift in their views about themselves as readers was the major influence in these changes. In other words, we are not willing to take credit for teaching these seventh graders to read. Rather, we believe that we have helped these students revalue their own abilities and that such revaluing is significant in order for reading proficiency to continue to expand and develop.

Major issues have emerged from this study as we used the research questions to frame this chapter. They relate to the terminology used for conceptualizing metalinguistic awareness and good and poor reader designations. We address these issues based on the conclusions from this study as well as previous RMA research and reports by teachers using RMA in instructional settings.

METALINGUISTIC OR CONSCIOUS KNOWLEDGE

All readers have conscious knowledge about reading. The readers we've worked with make comments on whether or not they are good readers and provide evidence to support their beliefs based on their stance toward the reading process. They state what good readers are capable of and they make statements about what could help them become better readers. In response to their miscues, they explain why they think they made the miscues and they talk about meaning, whether what they are reading sounds like language (syntactic acceptability), and the ways in which phonics works. Although their statements may represent misconceptions of the reading process, they show that they are consciously aware of language cueing systems and reading strategies. But their myths or misconceptions about language and the reading process should be kept in proper perspective. Many psychologists, teachers, and other researchers also make similar statements about the nature of the reading process, what readers need to be able to do to learn to read, and how readers can improve. In fact, even scholars in the field of reading theory and research disagree about the reading process and are in a quest to understand how reading works so the concepts in the field are still open to interpretation by experts and novices alike.

The issues of metalinguistic and metacognitive awareness are often related to what good and poor readers do and the notion that if poor readers are specifically instructed in particular skills, they will become better readers. Brown et al. suggest that

> if learners can be made aware of (a) basic strategies for reading and remembering, (b) simple rules of text construction, (c) differing demands of a variety of texts to which their information may be put, and (d) the importance of activating any background knowledge they may have, they cannot help but become more effective learners. Such self-awareness is prerequisite for self-regulation, the ability to orchestrate, monitor and check one's own cognitive activities (Brown et al. 1980, 20).

These concerns have led a large number of researchers in education to conclude that metalinguistic and metacognitive awareness is a prerequisite to becoming readers and writers. The implication that good readers are metalinguistically aware of their language processes while poor readers are not (though they can be taught to be "aware" and lessons to teach awareness abound) is simply not corroborated by RMA research. On the contrary, during retrospective miscue analysis readers talk about and examine their personal reading process, and have much to say about the nature of reading, the nature of language, and themselves as readers. When students participate in nonthreatening settings where they have reasons and opportunities to engage in conversations about reading as language users, then students talk about language and reveal their thinking about language. The RMA session is organized to help students take their own reading seriously, to respect their reading ability, and to recognize the strengths on which they need to capitalize. In such settings, readers are comfortable in revealing knowledge rarely activated in typical clinical settings.

All students we work with comment on their reading and writing processes. In other words, so-called poor as well as good readers possess what is described in the literature as metalinguistic knowledge and awareness. As prior examples in this chapter and throughout this book document, readers can and do articulate what they believe the reading process to be, which parts of the process they fail to control, and how they can improve their reading. Students make statements about how they read and what they are supposed to do as readers; they talk about the nature of texts; how they try various strategies; how they remember aspects of what they have read; ways in which they relate what they read to what they know. However, many readers believe that these kinds of strategies prove to themselves and to the world that they are not particularly good readers. Rather than assuming that good readers have metalinguistic knowledge and poor readers do not, it is more useful to discover what any reader, regardless of proficiency label, believes about the reading process, how they make use of that knowledge, and what they do when their beliefs conflict with what they do as they read.

As a result of this study, we do not find the terms metacognitive and metalinguistic awareness very useful for school settings or as a label for students' reading proficiencies. We prefer more direct and clear terminology. We simply state that engaging students in talking and thinking about language is one important part of reading instruction. This is something all language users do. It is not something esoteric that needs to be taught through direct lessons on metacognition or metalinguistics. Given opportunities to talk and think about language, teachers and students discover that as they read, they think, write, draw, wonder, and question. As students and teachers begin to inquire into the process, it is also probable that they will want to find out what other people think and what other people know (or think they know). This is how knowledge is generated and these are the ways in which we should be helping readers talk and think about the reading process.

Distinctions between good and poor readers are not well defined and are usually based on standardized tests or simplistic pre- and post-test comparisons. Comparison studies of good and poor readers dominate a good deal of reading research. Such studies "surprisingly" discover that the readers who are designated as poor readers are not as successful as good readers at whatever particular task they are set to do. Based on such studies, mythologies about good and poor readers have infiltrated teaching practices and the minds of teachers. So it is not surprising that studies have shown that good and poor readers are often treated differently by classroom teachers. Good readers spend more time reading silently whole authentic texts in class while poor readers spend more time doing skills worksheets and reading orally. Instruction supports good readers' focus on meaning and they are not interrupted by teachers in response to miscues, while poor readers are often interrupted and focused on surface text accuracy (Allington 1983; Haynes & Jenkins 1986; Hoffman & Clements 1981).

GOOD AND POOR READERS

Through miscue analysis, we have come to understand that no one is a good reader in general. All readers are more or less proficient depending on the purpose of the reading, the nature of the reading task, and the nature of the text being read. We identify readers as having degrees of efficiency and effectiveness based on their ability to produce miscues within a whole text. Readers whose patterns of miscues result in sentences that are semantically and syntactically accepted, or if unacceptable are corrected, we consider to be effective readers. In addition to being effective, if readers also show that they make non-deliberate substitutions, omissions, and insertions of function words, have high-quality substitution miscues, shift grammatical units of text without disruption to meaning, and have a good percent of substitution miscues that show only some or no graphic and sound similarity, we consider these readers to be efficient. We have defined readers as proficient if they show both effective and efficient reading strategies. We use retellings to corroborate the proficiency of the readers as revealed through miscue analysis.

Proficient readers are in control of the reading process. They read in order to make meaning; they manipulate text as shown by their miscues; they decide when reprocessing is necessary as shown by their overt regressions and self-corrections; they know when they understand and when they don't; they decide what's important or unimportant by determining what aspects of the text need more attention and what aspects need little or none. All proficient readers, however, come to texts they do not understand, and with these texts they are not proficient readers.

On the other hand, all readers are proficient readers in some settings, with some materials. Therefore, terms such as good or poor in relation to a reader is never a helpful designation. Proficiency is related to the reading of a specific text within a particular literacy event such as the reading of particular kinds of novels; research reports; maps; street signs; legal contracts; recipes; or the covers of compact disks or video games.

However, in the zeal to produce errorless oral readers in typical reading instruction settings, classroom teachers are faced with a large group of students who have come to believe that they are not good readers and so they often respond, especially in diagnostic and testing settings, as troubled readers. In addition, reading materials are often difficult because they are uninteresting, the concepts are not within the experience of the readers, the syntax is overly complex, or they are decontextualized from any authentic reading experience. In these situations, readers believe that in order to be successful it is better for them to show that they value careful examination of the surface features of the text more highly than their interpretations. They believe they need more skills instruction even though they are already over-reliant on the graphophonic cueing system. They work too hard as they read because they try to focus on making sense while also trying to remember all the rules of language. They are swimming in a sea of information. We believe that these readers are instruction dependent, a term used by Peter Board (1982) to suggest that these readers are trying to do what they believe they have been taught.

Regardless of the strategies readers use, their personal views of the reading process and of their own abilities influence the degree of confidence they exhibit during oral reading. We believe that this influences reading test scores and silent reading, especially in situations that readers believe are difficult for them.

In this study, we wanted to learn more about the ways RMA influences how middle-school students revalue themselves as readers; how they revalue the reading process; how they talk and reflect about the reading process and their own reading proficiency; and whether the RMA procedure improves their actual reading strategies. We conclude that RMA has the potential to help all readers, including proficient readers, revalue themselves as readers:

- Through RMA readers have the opportunity to discover and document their own views of the reading process as they talk about their own and other people's miscues with the support of a knowledgeable teacher/researcher.
- Through RMA readers become consciously aware of what they can do as a reader and what they know about language and in this way build confidence in their own reading ability.
- Through RMA readers have an opportunity to listen to themselves and talk about themselves in the process of becoming more effective and efficient as readers.
- Through RMA readers begin to evaluate miscues qualitatively rather than quantitatively and to see many miscues as supportive and necessary to the reading process.
- Through RMA readers begin to build a transactional view of the reading process and demythify a narrow skills-based view of reading.

Information about the reading process coupled with personal awareness can (but may not necessarily) lead to personal control over the reading process. Readers make intuitive decisions to assume or give up their responsibility as readers. RMA supports readers in making informed decisions about their reading development rather than capitulating to institutionalized definitions of readers and the reading process. Through assuming responsibility and taking a role in their reading instruction, students come to value themselves as readers and value reading as a way of developing power in their own lives.

8

Revaluing and Revelations

Alan Flurkey

RETROSPECTIVE MISCUE ANALYSIS IS A powerful tool not only for what it can do for readers in helping them to revalue themselves, but for what it can do for teachers, researchers, and parents to illuminate the marvelous and complex process of reading. This chapter addresses how RMA aids readers in revaluing themselves, and how RMA helps expand our understanding of the reading process. In addition, I wish to focus on what I found most intriguing about RMA, readers, and reading—insights that took me by genuine surprise, the wholly unanticipated.

RMA AND REVALUING

I remember vividly the community in Tucson, Arizona, where we conducted the RMA middle school study. The school was located in an older working class neighborhood of the city. Most of the homes were small, brick ranch houses with natural desert landscaping: cactus, native brush, and decorative gravel. Many other homes were surrounded by chain-link fences enclosing a dirt or sand yard, the resting place of an old car, or featuring a ball diamond or a swing set and a scrubby Palo Verde tree or huge flowering bougainvilleas. The attendance boundary also included a hilly, rural neighborhood in which several large expensive houses stood on multi-acre desert lots. The student body was composed of Euro- and Mexican-Americans in roughly equal proportions. The halls of the school were wide, clean, and well-lit, and hung with pep banners on game days. It was not uncommon to hear students conversing in Spanish in the dash between classes. The display cases which periodically interrupted rows of student lockers were decorated with student art or athletic trophies.

Over the period of a year, I conducted weekly RMA sessions with four students from Sarah Costello's seventh-grade language arts classes. Sarah, who was also a research colleague, made arrangements to release study participants from class once a week to conduct our sessions in a nearby storage room or an empty classroom down the hall. Most of our sessions were conducted one-on-one with one researcher and one participant; however, toward the end of the study, students had the opportunity to collaborate with each other in addition to working with the researchers.

ROLANDO

Rolando, age twelve, was one of the students with whom I worked. If I were inclined to speak in broad generalities, like the text of televised educational documentaries, I would consider Rolando a student *at risk* (Flores et al. 1991). Of medium height and with a somewhat heavy build, Rolando had thick wavy black hair. He wore thick glasses with silver metal frames which seemed to sit lightly on his roundish face. He frequently wore a black Raiders' baseball cap, brim forward, and a black and silver satin baseball jacket. He always seemed to have a friendly, easy manner about him—an outgoing personality.

Rolando's academic standing and his school behavior were what may have caused some to consider him at risk. On his ITBS (Iowa Test of Basic Skills) test the previous year, he scored in the third stanine, an interval which placed his score in the lowest 11–23% (a score on the ITBS which incidentally qualified him as a participant in the RMA study). Rolando was also frequently in trouble with school authorities. He had been suspended several times for different infractions: talking back to teachers; selling candy which he brought back from his visits to relatives in Hermosillo; fighting. Sometimes he was sent home, and occasionally I needed to retrieve him from in-school suspension to conduct our RMA sessions. Rolando's academic standing and the record of his school behavior made for an uneasy comparison with the laid-back, thoughtful person I came to know. This was only one of the contradictions that I uncovered in the course of this research.

My first impression of Rolando as a reader came from listening to his oral reading. The first text he read was the folk tale, "The Man Who Kept House," a story which would not be considered challenging to the typical seventh grader. On the surface, one might be tempted to describe his reading as plodding—unfolding at a laborious, painstaking pace, with substitution, insertion, and omission miscues, as the following examples suggest:

$\emptyset$ *repiled* - (RM)

"I can do all that," replied the husband.

Well

"We'll do it tomorrow!"   RM = *repeated miscue*

• • •

He began to make some butter. As he put

$ *cern*

(UC) $ *cern*   *pronounced: Kern*

the cream into the churn, he said, "This is

not going to be hard work. All I have to do

(C) *re-*

is sit here and move this stick up and down.

to

Soon the cream will turn into butter."

UC = *repeated but uncorrected*

• • •

woodman

It was not very long before the woodman's

(C)(C)   (AC)

the C-   4. *As she came near the house*

wife came home. As she came near the   3. *Came the house*

                                              2. *as she came near the house*

                                         3   1. *as the C-*

                                        4

house, she could hear the cow mooing, the

```
    ———3
  ‿‿‿‿——4
```

baby crying, and her husband shouting for help.

AC = abandoned correct

Classifying Rolando as a reader "at risk" would be a superficial appraisal on several counts, however. A miscue analysis (Y. Goodman et al. 1987) of Rolando's performance reveals a pattern of miscues that reflect a concern for meaning. Structures which contain semantically unacceptable miscues are corrected and most of his substitutions either reflect a grammatical strength or are completely acceptable within the context of the story (see Table 8-1). The following example from Rolando's initial reading is typical in revealing his focus on language structure and meaning. On line 501, he transforms the adverb *then* into a dependent clause marker. To reconcile this transformation, he substitutes a comma for a period on line 502, effectively combining two sentences into one. This reorganization of clauses was made obvious by his intonation. He also omits the noun modifier *left* on line 504, but goes back and corrects, and the tape shows that he was laughing out loud as he did so.

501   *When*
      Then he climbed down from the roof and

502   *, he*
      went into the house. He pulled the end of the

503   rope out of the fireplace and put it around

504   his left leg.
      3. his left leg
      2. his (uh)
      1. his leg

In addition to generating a miscue analysis profile that indicates a proficient reader, Rolando's complete retelling of the story also depicts a command of comprehension.

Hence, another contradiction: On the surface, Rolando's performance might suggest a reader who painstakingly and unsuccessfully was trying to reproduce a copy of the written text. But from the beginning of the study, miscue analysis, his story retelling, and his responses to interview questions suggested that he viewed reading as a meaning-centered process. Rolando's response to question 1 of the Reading Interview (Y. Goodman et al. 1987) supports this contention:

Alan: When you are reading and come to something you don't know, what do you do?

Rolando: I try to figure it out at first, you know, real hard? And, if I keep on not trying to understand it, I'll go get some help from the teacher.

Alan: What were you talking about? What did you think of when I said, "something you don't know"?

Rolando: Like when I'm reading a story, like if it's a mystery or a problem and I don't understand it, I'll go up there (skips text) or avoid it if I can, if I don't know what it is.

Alan: Could *it* be anything else?

Rolando: I don't know.
Alan: Do you ever do anything else?
Rolando: I guess ask a friend, or sometimes I skip it or keep on reading.

In the above excerpt, Rolando makes reference to skipping something that he doesn't know. A reader who subscribes to a word-centered or text production view of the reading process (or who thinks this is what the interviewer wants to hear and so tries to accommodate him or her) typically responds with something like, "I sound it out" (the *it* being a word). Rolando never mentions "words" and instead maintains a focus on meaning by referring to things larger than words: mysteries and problems. Even when pressed with the follow-up question, "Do you ever do anything else?" Rolando makes only what could be interpreted as a veiled reference to "words": a reader would probably "ask a friend" about or "skip" a word. It is also just as plausible that Rolando would ask a friend about or skip something conceptually larger than a word. And even if we were to assume that Rolando is referring to skipping words in the follow-up response, it is notable that he was referring to a "keep reading" or deliberate omission strategy—a meaning-centered strategy that every proficient reader uses when necessary.

So here is a twelve-year-old student who is considered an academic and behavioral liability by the educational system and whose reading is characterized by a labored performance. Yet he is also a pleasant individual who, as a reader, comprehends as he reads and comprehends what he reads (K. Goodman 1976).

Over the course of the study, the RMA sessions contributed to Rolando's growth as a reader. By employing miscue analysis, a comparison of the two oral readings of "The Man Who Kept House" spaced one calendar year apart reveals that the number of miscues per hundred words dropped from 6.6 to 3.0 (Table 8-1).

But more important than the quantity of miscues is the comparison that shows an increase in the number of syntactically and semantically acceptable sentences as well as an increase in the number of sentences that did not produce a meaning change. These changes are indicative of an increased focus on meaning construction during the act of reading. Rolando's change in miscue patterns is accompanied by a shift away from concerns for surface features of text as a comparison of the graphic similarity of his miscues indicates. This shift, to a larger percentage of miscues that bear no similarity to the text, suggests a decrease in concern for text reproduction. Hence, a side-by-side comparison of Rolando's initial and final readings clearly show that, while he was a proficient reader to begin with, he has become a more efficient reader over time, i.e., constructing meaning using the fewest necessary visual cues.

Table 8-1   Comparison of Rolando's initial and final readings*

Title	Miscues per hundred words	Sentences with syntactic acceptability		Sentences with semantic acceptability		Sentences with meaning change			Graphic similarity of 1:1 substitutions			Total time
		Yes	No	Yes	No	Yes	Partial	No	High	Some	None	
Kept House (Session 1)*	6.6	96%	4%	85%	15%	3%	7%	90%	76%	10%	14%	5m 52s
Kept House (Session 13)*	3.0	100%	0%	97%	3%	0%	1%	99%	62%	15%	23%	5m 24s

  * Analysis using Procedure III (Y. Goodman et al. 1987).
 ** Estimated readability = 3 using Fry Readability Formula.

The concept of revaluing is an important companion to RMA. Kenneth Good-man (Chapter 2, K. Goodman 1982, 1986) writes that when readers revalue them-selves, they take a fresh look at themselves by recognizing the linguistic strengths and personal experiences they bring to an act of reading. Readers also revalue the reading process as they begin to view reading as a constructive, personally meaningful, transactive process, rather than an act in which the goal is to produce a faithful reproduction of the text.

Yetta Goodman and Ann Marek state that the power of retrospective miscue analysis lies in enabling readers to rethink about themselves as readers and to revalue the reading process itself (Chapter 1). The comparison of Rolando's reader profiles in Table 8-1 demonstrate a shift away from reading as an act of text repro-duction and supports this contention. But this is not the only piece of evidence; Rolando's comments similarly disclose a shift in thinking.

As stated earlier, Rolando's response to Reading Interview question 1 reveals that he held a holistic view of reading from the beginning. Other responses from that interview support this interpretation. When asked how a person becomes a good reader, his response takes a naturalistic, developmental cast in his focus on learning to read by reading:

Alan: Let's go back to thinking about this kid in class that you know is a good reader. You said, "studying and practice a lot" makes a good reader. What did you mean by that?

Rolando: Well, since probably kindergarten he read real good. And I guess his mom made him read [unintelligible]. And he started reading and reading until he got to probably third grade, then he started reading more and more and I guess it's like a plant. If you keep on watering it, it will grow and grow. And that's how if you keep on practicing, you get better and better. So I guess that's how he got to be a good reader.

In the next question, Rolando shows that while he may be unaware of the universal-ity of the reading process or unclear about how the reading process works, he understands it to be an internal process that each person must work out individ-ually.

Alan: Do you think [that good reader in class] ever comes to something he doesn't know?

Rolando: Yeah.

Alan: Okay. What do you think that they do when they come to something they don't know?

Rolando: (laughs at the naiveté or incredulity of the question) Well I'm not sure because I'm not them and I'm not with them all the time. But sometimes, like last year, José-Miguel, he was in sixth grade, and he had some trouble. And sometimes he wouldn't even ask me and he's smarter than me. So sometimes he asked me. And I would tell him and I would try to understand. And I would go to the teacher and ask 'em. So he went to the teacher.

Alan: Well, I don't see how he could be much smarter than you. You've got this all figured out. So you say he did ask you . . . ?

Rolando: Yeah, I told him to go to the teacher because I didn't know really. Probably in the book.

Alan: Is there anything that he does when he comes to something he doesn't know or he might do?

Rolando: Well, he might skip it. I know him real good. [He'd say], "Just forget it," and go on to the next thing and come back and do it again.

In the above response, Rolando indicates that even good readers encounter unknowns when reading. This implies a belief that "knowing all the words" is not what makes a good reader. However, Rolando also reveals his belief in appealing to the authority of a more knowledgeable reader (in this case, the teacher) when dealing with an unknown. This can be interpreted as an adaptive strategy—after all, if someone who you perceive to be more knowledgeable than yourself is stuck with a problem, it is reasonable to advise him to seek more knowledgeable counsel. This last admission contrasts with what Rolando reveals about his beliefs in future sessions, however; that the authority in dealing with text rests with himself. This is the only time that he mentions appealing to the teacher as a source of help. This suggests that, while appealing to a teacher for help in solving a problem is one possible solution, it is not one that he uses. He also mentions the strategy of deliberately omitting and returning to the problem if more information resulted in a solution, a strategy he mentioned earlier in the interview.

Rolando's RMA sessions allowed him to confirm and validate his holistic views of the reading process. As the sessions unfolded, he seemed to grasp the concepts and language of miscue analysis as if giving shape to thoughts he had already been flirting with. A readministration of the Reading Interview one year later portrayed Rolando as reflexive and philosophical on the topics of himself as a reader and the reading process. His thinking is mature and reasoned:

Alan: Who is a good reader you know?
Rolando: I don't know. I can't be the judge. That person who reads itself can be the judge, 'cause I might not know, like—nobody can make a mistake, like, miscues—everybody makes a miscue. So you can't say he reads better or he reads better. I mean everybody reads their own way.
Alan: Let's suppose there is a hypothetical good reader and it could be you. What would make that person a good reader?
Rolando: The way he understands the story, the words, the way he talks about it, the way he reads it, and his point of view.
Alan: If that hypothetical reader came to something that they didn't know? Okay. First of all let me back up. Get this hypothetical reader that's good. Do you think they ever come to something they don't know?
Rolando: Always, yeah.
Alan: What do you think they'd do?
Rolando: I don't know.
Alan: You said, "Always, yeah." Like that, real quick. How come?
Rolando: Why?
Alan: You were just so sure. I said, "Let's say there's this hypothetical good reader. Do you think they ever come to something they don't know?" You said, "Always."
Rolando: Yes, because I guess nobody has ever explored all the words. Maybe it's only someone that's very smart knows all the words, but still if they're real smart, read all fast, they'll make a miscue—no doubt about it. Everybody has to probably make a miscue. Nobody's perfect.
Alan: If that person came to something they didn't know, what do you think they'd do?
Rolando: Again, I don't know. That matters who was reading. For me, I would just—the only thing I can answer is me, 'cause I know me. If you're going to answer that question you gotta ask every single person in the world about—if you want to find that. Well, and then for me, I have to, you know, think about it, look it up or something, or just pass it and read another story. Or just make a prediction.

Rolando shows us that he thinks of reading as a meaning-centered process. For example, he understands that the mark of good readers is that they are able to make meaning for themselves. In his response to "What makes a good reader," he identifies the following as critical attributes: quality of comprehension, quality of presenting what has been comprehended, quality of processing, and the reader's perspective. His focus on the quality of the attribute is conveyed by his use of the word "way"—"The way he understands the story, the words. The way he talks about it, the way he reads it, and his point of view." It is clear from this response that Rolando's conception of the reading process is considered and sophisticated. It is interesting that each of the attributes that he has identified has a close parallel in sociopsycholinguistic theory: ideating, perceiving, and presenting (K. Goodman et al. 1987). He does mention "words," but he does so in connection with under-standing the story—perhaps referring to the extent of a reader's vocabulary as a linguistic resource in understanding a story or using the term "words" to refer to text in the collective sense. It is also plausible that he is simultaneously entertaining both a word-oriented and a meaning-oriented focus on reading; however, this is not reconciled with the spirit of his other responses.

Rolando recognizes both the universal and special aspects of the reading pro-cess. Regarding universality, he knows that every reader, even the hypothetical good reader, will eventually encounter an unknown because "nobody has ever explored all the words." He also knows that the production of miscues is an inevita-ble consequence of engaging in the reading process: "No doubt about it. Everybody has to probably make a miscue. Nobody's perfect."

Even though Rolando recognizes certain universal aspects of the reading pro-cess, he takes care to point out that each reader has a set of unique experiences and resources that they bring to the process. When asked, "Who is a good reader?" his initial response is to hedge at answering the question directly. Instead, he address a problematic aspect of the question itself. He recognizes that to answer the question would require the dubious act of judging the competence of a reader based on his or her performance. He recognizes this as a trap for the unwary, so he wisely refuses to make a judgment.

Rolando is also careful to point out that the particular strategies that a specific reader chooses are unique to each person. When asked, "What do you think a good reader would do when they come to something they don't know?" again he deftly sidesteps a direct answer, choosing instead to cast doubt on the validity of the question. He does this by stating that he can't know how others specifically carry forth their mental processes and that such a thing would vary from person to person with as many configurations as there are people. Rolando is willing and able to articulate the strategies that he would use, but he makes it clear that he is unable to speak for another reader.

To this point we have seen how Rolando, a reader "at risk," was actually a proficient reader with thoughtful views about reading and the world. By helping to revalue the reading process and himself as a reader, the RMA sessions provided a forum for confirming and extending his thinking and provided an opportunity for him to become a more efficient reader.

REVELATIONS

Retrospective miscue analysis consists of several sessions that provide opportu-nities for a reader to revalue himself or herself as a reader, and to revalue the reading process. I have provided the preceding profile of Rolando to support that contention. But of even greater interest were the unanticipated disclosures, observations, and conversations that I encountered during the course of this study. These occasions made RMA a fascinating and engaging endeavor. The unantici-pated findings generally took three forms: information about the reader; informa-tion that explains how the reading process works; and information that supports a transactional sociopsycholinguistic theory of the reading process.

The Reader

As teachers, we often express regret that there is too little time to get to know our students as well as we would like. A single year goes quickly and we work with many students in a given day. In a departmentalized middle school or high school, these concerns are compounded by the way schooling is organized. In the course of this study I came to know things about Rolando, the student and the person out of school, that I doubt other teachers would have the time to learn. I was not probing or searching the way one might if one were going about constructing a detailed case study. Rather, things came up incidentally in the context of our conversations about reading. The content of a passage or the way a particular passage was read would spark a discussion about something else which we would discuss for a while before returning to the point before the digression. Even though each of the RMA sessions was organized with a particular focus in mind, our conversations would meander among topics the way relaxed conversations tend to do. It was in this manner that I discovered the depth, thoughtfulness, and intelligence that this at-risk, suspension-prone student had to offer.

Rolando had many sides, and many perceptions of himself. On one occasion he talked about himself as a movie critic, and he talked of his experiences as horseman on another. I became acquainted with his entrepreneurial spirit and the family background that fed his thinking. Still on other occasions he talked about his Mexican heritage, his love of reading, or his journalistic aspirations. On one occasion, a discussion about good readers sparked a memorable conversation about comparing the merits and disadvantages of books and movies as media for telling stories.

Rolando: Well, a lot of people I know are good readers, but they don't usually express them, they just read.
Alan: How did you know they were good readers?
Rolando: Well a lot of years [I've been with them]. At the end of the year they give awards for good readers. A lot of my friends say, "I read twenty books this year" and stuff. And sometimes a friend of mine will tell me, "I read this book; this is a really good book." They'll tell me about the book that they read.
Alan: They get awards for the books they read; they tell you about good books. Anything else that tells you they're a good reader?
Rolando: A's in the reading. That's all.
Alan: Anything else? Let's see how long we can make the list.
Rolando: Or probably when I'm watching a movie . . . 'Cause a lot of times when they make movies, they make books before the movie. Uh, I'm a real critic about movies. So that's how I mostly know. Like my friends will read the books before the movies. Like *The Outsiders*.
Alan: That's a smart way to look at how you know about stories. There's a whole issue there, like what's better, the story or the book? You say you're a critic—do you ever kind of get into that, what's better, the book or the movie?
Rolando: Well, not really. There's two things best about them both, 'cause in the movies like, you just have to sit down and relax. Don't do nothing, just look at it; that's relaxing. But in a book you can do whatever you want—you're in your own space. And you can read it, like you know, when to stop or if you don't want to. And sometimes it has more things to say than it did in the movie. Like express more in the book. Then again in the movie you just sit down and watch it and enjoy it.

It is unlikely that many would disagree with Rolando's analysis of different qualities of personal response and the role of the imagination in transaction with print versus cinema. Later, he talked about when his habits began to change—the point at which he began to value himself as a reader. He credits a caring sixth-grade teacher with nurturing his interest in books.

Rolando: [I learned to read in] kindergarten I guess. Well, back then I wasn't really into books. I didn't really like books. The truth, "Oh, it was so boring, I would really rather watch the movie." And then I got into sixth grade and I started liking books. "Oh, these are pretty cool books." So I started reading math papers—that was my best subject—you know like, "What's this problem, math?" Then I started reading library books, war books, little books, and around. I started reading from the library. That's where I started learning how to read.

In a subsequent disclosure, Rolando stated that the watershed in his life as a reader came when he discovered books about the Civil War. The adventure and drama that he found in both fiction and nonfiction books propelled him into other works of fiction. From these discussions, there was no doubt that Rolando saw himself as a reader.

Findings derived from RMA sessions have led to insights about how the reading process works for an individual. These findings have also helped me understand how the process works in the broader sense. Rolando's miscues and his reflections about the processing that resulted in their production allow us to see how linguistic cueing systems and one's life experiences work in symphony as one reads efficiently.

On one occasion, a discussion about a pair of substitution miscues led us to talk about how Rolando goes about constructing a visual meaning as he reads—again comparing the meaning constructing process to watching a movie. The miscues occurred during the reading of an Appalachian folk tale in which the main character mounts his mule and calls out a thank-you to another character.

The Process

He jumped on the mule in a hip and hurry.

Then he remembered his manners.

"Mighty much obliged for the favor," he called

as he headed up the trail toward home.

Alan:	Did you hear what you said? . . . *headed. .*
Rolando:	*. . . from the trail toward home.*
Alan:	Okay . . . *headed from*
Rolando:	Uh huh. . . . *the trail* . . . That makes sense.
Alan:	Okay. Let's listen again because I want to make sure you got it all because I'm not sure that's exactly—I heard the front part—

I thought that Rolando did not detect the first of the two substitutions, so I replayed this portion of the tape. We listened to the passage again.

Rolando:	*. . . the rail . . .*
Alan:	Okay. Let's look at that.
Rolando:	There's a *tr*—, a rail can be a railroad. It can . . . can't it be like a barbed-wire fence? A rail . . . ? Like, you could hold onto something. Maybe I got mixed up. Maybe I was really getting into the story and I was imagining stuff, you know, when you're reading you're supposed to, huh? When you're reading, you imagine stuff how it is in the book. Like, "One snowy afternoon . . ." You imagine it. Then it's like a movie, but you're filming it and you're reading off the parts. So I guess that's what I did. Instead of *trail*, I put *rail* and *toward* used *the rail*—he was walking toward home—*from the rail toward home.*

At first, Rolando attributes the production of his miscues to "getting mixed up." This is an ostensible reference to focusing on surface level cues, the letters and words of print. This attribution of a miscue to reckless reading is often a knee-jerk reaction that readers (especially those who subscribe to a text reproduction view of the reading process) give before thinking about the meaning-related reasons for the production of a miscue. And indeed, Rolando immediately abandons careless reading as a reason, and instead regards the miscue as a consequence of his focusing on the meaning of the story. He compares using his imagination as he reads for meaning to the filming of a movie. Although he offers no certain reason for his prediction of *rail* instead of *trail*, he clearly articulates the process he employs in visualizing a story.

The exchange continues and leads to a discussion about Rolando's involvement with raising horses.

Alan: Do you have any experience with horses?
Rolando: Yeah. I have one.
Alan: Tell me about it a little bit.
Rolando: I have one. Yeah, my dad has three. We keep them over there by—you know the airport over there? There's like an airport that way. About—airport there and from over here, half—there's like a bunch of homes—desert. I don't know what's the name of it, but that's where we keep them. My dad has about five acres.
Alan: I'm dying to ask you what you do with them.
Rolando: I ride them. I feed them most of the time. My dad, he buys the food and I feed them. Well sometimes—I don't feed them always because I'm hardly over there. I'm here, you know, with my aunt. So he buys the food and he tells me go, you know, a pail of hay? A bail? And then some grain. We just feed them. But then, it's in the open desert so when I go over there I saddle them up and ride them.
Alan: We could talk about this for a long time. (Both laugh.) You're really lucky. Um, talk to me about corrals. What are they made out of? As far as the fence goes?
Rolando: It's just like (points) some of this; poles. (Points to hollow aluminum tubing, 2-inch diameter, on the utility closet wall which is used to encase electrical/telephone wires.) Like, exactly like that separate pole right there, except thicker. I mean, it's hollow—you know, nothing inside, but rounder. And my dad, he's a welder too, and he welds them and he makes a cage. (I pointed to the word *rail*.) A *rail*! Yeah.
Alan: . . . *headed from the rail toward home.*
Rolando: Um hum. Yeah.
Alan: If I was making a movie, I could see a guy hop on his horse—you know, taking up the reins from the rail, hopping on his horse, and turning around.
Rolando: Yeah, *toward home*.

By examining the above exchange closely, one can see that the reflective discussion of a miscue can reveal how language and thought work together in the production of meaning during reading. Through RMA, teacher and student have exposed how the use of linguistic cueing systems and background experiences work together to construct Rolando's unique interpretation of the story. It is here that the complexities of the reading process are laid open. As Rolando reads, he visualizes the story as the director of his own "film." In addition, his experience as a horseman who has ridden in corrals fashioned by his father from steel poles contributes to the construction of a completely acceptable linguistic structure in which the horseman in the story has "headed from the rail toward home," as opposed to the text version in which the horseman has "headed up the trail toward home." Rolando's construction can then be viewed in the context of his grammatical competence and his ability to make predictions based on his personal experiences. It offers a look through the window on the reading process (K. Goodman 1973).

It should be well noted that as Rolando compares his use of imagination as he reads to the filming of a movie, he is addressing the parallels between his experiences of constructing meaning in two different sign systems. It is through this forum that Rolando is expressing his thoughts on how he thinks while he reads. Such a demonstration of metacognitive processing would not be expected if one subscribed to the belief that less skilled readers lack the ability to engage in metacognitive processing. Remember that Rolando would most likely be considered among less skilled readers by traditional measures of achievement.

Retrospective miscue analysis has provided valuable insights which support a transactional sociopsycholinguistic view of the reading process. Miscue research has demonstrated that miscues occur more frequently in the beginning of a text than in the middle (K. Goodman & Y. Goodman 1977; Menosky 1971). This is consistent with a theoretical view of the reading process in which readers are more prone to make less acceptable first guesses when sampling at the beginning of a text because they do not have as large an informational reservoir at the beginning of a story as they do farther on. As readers continue with a story, they develop a richer context and are thus able to make better and more acceptable predictions.

RMA data adds support to this theoretical view. In the following exchange about a miscue that occurs in the first sentence of a story, Rolando addresses this phenomenon and discusses it in the context of strategy use. His comments support what sociopsycholinguistic theory predicts. The exchange occurred during the sixth RMA session.

To the best of my knowledge, there's never

$regultion

been a regulation that forbids one to keep

pets in a space station.

Rolando read the sentence and produced no miscues. Then he listened to the tape of the original reading and laughed when he heard his miscue.

Alan: What did you say?
Rolando: *Regultion?*
Alan: Yeah, could you write that down however you think it should be spelled?
Rolando: Ah, *regulations?* That's something—regulations? I guess I didn't understand it, or I wasn't really interested in reading that day. Something that happens if I don't feel like reading, I don't really pay attention to the words and trying to figure them out as much as I do. But right now, I'm in the mood, so it's *regulation.*
Alan: Okay. Also, you know what the story's about. You've read it once. So that might help, too. But how did you deal with it the first time? You said . . .
Rolando: *Re-, re-, regultion?* That's what I said?
Alan: Yeah.
Rolando: Uh, I don't know—when I was reading, that's what it sounds like. The *u* and *tion. Gultion*—right here. If the *r-e*'s gone, it's *gul, g-u-l,* /shun/, *t-i-o-n.*
Alan: Why didn't you go back and self-correct?
Rolando: Well, there I just wanted to read through the—in the beginning, you want to get to the "what happens" more. In the beginnings, hardly something never really happens this time, so I just try to really skip that, I guess, and keep on reading and when it comes, maybe figure it out. Just one word ain't gonna be the whole story importance. Might not. May might, then again.

As before, Rolando initially excuses the miscue as a result of "not paying attention," but further discussion reveals the purpose and intelligence behind his actions. Not only was he making use of available graphophonic cues, he also made use of a "keep reading" strategy. He knew that although his miscue was not meaningful, a good way to deal with the unknown was to keep reading to get more information. He knew that if the word turned out to be important to the story, it was likely to come up again, at which time he would have gained more information on which to base a prediction. He also knew that the understanding of a story does not hinge on the understanding of any one word.

CONCLUSION

There is much more to be said about Rolando's complex literacy configuration (Taylor 1993). The picture I have presented here is far from complete. Missing are examples which illustrate how his linguistic competence in Spanish influences his construction of English texts, or examples which detail how the influence of previously encountered texts influence the construction of current texts.

I hasten to add that Rolando would probably not strike the casual observer as a particularly verbally skilled student. His speech is filled with half-sentences and false starts. He frequently appears to change thoughts in mid-utterance. But to this we must pose the question of, "How closely can a casual observer listen?" And the related question, "What is it about RMA sessions that allows us to listen so closely?" I must also add that I do not think that Rolando's participation in the RMA sessions accounted for his display of sophisticated thinking; rather, RMA simply provided a forum for its visibility. Are there *any* assumptions we can make when considering the characteristics of less proficient readers?

Yetta and Ann write of two stances that can be taken with respect to organizing RMA sessions: the research stance and the instructional stance (see Chapter 4). I have found both to provide important and intriguing information. As an instructional technique, RMA continues to show its effectiveness in providing opportunities for readers to revalue themselves. As a research tool, RMA uses readers' reflections on how they use the reading process to inform us about themselves, the process, and reading theory.

Ken Goodman has said that miscue analysis gives us a window on the reading process. By providing a venue for listening very closely to what readers tell us, retrospective miscue analysis has helped to open that window even wider.

9

Strategies and Metaphors

Joel Brown

WORKING WITH MISCUE ANALYSIS HAS been an engaging learning experience for me for the past several years. It has caused me to think about language and reading as something which possesses an infinite number of nuances and shades of meaning. Teachers cannot use miscue analysis without learning more about the readers with whom they work. There are always questions and ideas which draw attention to the social relationships of the classroom and the home, and to the experience students have had with other teachers. Working with retrospective miscue analysis (RMA) has helped me learn not just about the reading process but also about the essence of making meaning. I learned about the students, but I also learned about myself. Assumptions that previously went unchallenged and assessments I had been making about students' reading were being pushed further—even though I viewed reading as a transactional sociopsycholinguistic process.

In this chapter I focus on one student in particular, Kari, who helped me grow as a learner. She was a seventh grader who had red hair, shining eyes, and a special sensitivity to the world. She was verbally expressive, and our schedules matched well during the project, so we increased the number of planned readings and sessions. Her Iowa Test of Basic Skills (ITBS) scores placed her in the fourth stanine. She stated that she was not a good reader, and that she would just like to pronounce her words better. During our first meeting she commented on what improvement she'd like to make in her reading: "Like if I come to a word then I'll read—like if it's a word I can't pronounce then I kind of like stutter or something. Kind of like to make that a little bit better, so I don't stutter that much when I read." During our final interview I asked about a good reader who Kari might know. Her response: "Who's a good reader? Umm. Who's a good reader that I know? Well, I don't mean to be conceited but I think I have become a good reader."

Kari was one of the designated "poor" readers included in the National Council of Teachers of English study discussed in Chapter 7. When we first met, Kari read the standard piece for the project which all the kids read both in the beginning and then again a year and a half later. The piece was a Norwegian tale called "The Man Who Kept House." Over time she read other material: a newspaper article, a book, and chapters from books she was reading on her own, though we returned to stories at the end. Through just thirteen texts and the discussion of just over 100 miscues in a year and a half, she and I both discovered her to be a bright, productive reader, aware of what school and reading were all about.

KARI

Joel Brown acknowledges the support of his colleague, Geane Hanson, who provided valuable insights and recommendations in the development of this chapter. Geane also worked closely with Kari in her dissertation research about daydreaming (Hanson 1992).

Kari's Awareness of Her Reading Strategies

Kari's awareness and use of reading strategies was clear from the start. In the initial reading interview, one strategy she talked about was omitting or skipping words. As sessions continued, she began to have less respect for skipping words, preferring to substitute, or "figure it out from the contexts." At the end of the first year, she still did not accept that omitting words could be a positive strategy in some instances. Her mistrust of this strategy was also revealed in her description of her cousin, someone she considered a good reader. When asked what he would do if he came to something he didn't know when he was reading she responded, "He would probably just go on. But if it's a word he would probably look it up in the dictionary. 'Cause that 'wanting-to-know' bothers him if he just skips it." This early concern for precise replication of text on Kari's part shifted somewhat over time, and during the final interview conducted after the summer break, she stated that skipping words could be acceptable. She also surprised me during that interview with her answer to the question regarding what a good reader, her cousin, does when he comes to something he doesn't know:

Kari: Well, I think that in terms of reading, I think he would discover something new. He wouldn't think of it as "not knowing." He'd put it as . . . he's discovered something.
Joel: Humm. Interesting.
Kari: So instead of "not knowing," he's "discovered."
Joel: So he wouldn't think of himself as not knowing something when he came to it.
Kari: Yeah.
Joel: It would be more of . . .
Kari: A discovery.

At this point in time, her view of a good reader shows a concern for meaning beyond even what I had considered. She shows this by rejecting the notion that the reader must think of it as "not knowing" something. Her characterization of reading as open-ended and exploratory suggests a perspective of suspended judgment[1] or tentativeness which could well be an important consideration for a reader, one which contributes to the lifelong experience of adventure in learning through reading.

More often than not, Kari explained her miscues by saying that the miscues "made sense" or "sound better" than the text. Through our discussions, I found evidence that she understood each of the reading strategies recognized in miscue analysis (Y. Goodman et al. 1987), even though, of course, she did not know the technical terms for those strategies. The following examples from our conversations demonstrate Kari's awareness of her reading strategies.

Predicting

In predicting strategies, she used the word "guessing" and explained what she thought the author was going to say:

Ⓡ He could not leave a note for his wife if

Ⓒ could
she was out picking berries and he was . . .

---

[1] "Suspended disbelief" is an understood and critical component in visual media theory. See Lindgren (1970).

Joel: Why do you suppose you did that?
Kari: Guessing. I thought it was going to say *He could not leave a note for his wife if she was out picking berries*, and he *could* go hunting if he left a note.

Her knowledge of sampling strategies is revealed in the following remarks made by Kari as she discussed her strategies during the second reading interview, conducted six months after the start of the study. She looked at a page to illustrate her comments:

Sampling

Kari: 'Cause you know, you're looking, you don't know it, but I mean you can see ahead down the page. Like I'm looking at *comes* . . . . And I can see *to come* right below it.

Kari articulates ways of monitoring the text as she discusses miscues. She relates correction strategies to her confirmation strategies as well. Consider the following examples from two different sessions:

Confirming/ Disconfirming and Correcting

It's a real beauty even with a bent handlebar.

I'm sure sorry about that.

Kari: And when I saw *sure sorry*, [I] must've said, "Here, wait a minute, this doesn't make sense." And then looked back to see what my mistake is. And then picked up the *I'm* and put it there. Well, maybe I thought it wasn't going to make sense.
Joel: How would you know that?
Kari: Because when I first read it, I thought that it didn't sound right.

He could not leave a note for his wife if

she was out picking berries and he was . . .

Kari: *She was out picking berries and* . . . (subvocalized reading.) That wouldn't make sense, so I'm glad I corrected it. You can't say that, because it just doesn't make sense.
Joel: If you were reading by yourself would you correct it?
Kari: Well, knowing me, it's hard to tell because sometimes I do and sometimes I don't.
Joel: Huh. Okay.
Kari: But it just depends if I'm in the mood or: "Oh, I'd better correct it." And it depends on my mood or I'm lazy and say: "Oh, it makes sense, why should I?" (laughs) You know.

Kari reveals the inferencing process in reading when she shares her thinking about the book *Jumanji*:

Inferencing

Joel: Would you want to try this one (referring to *Jumanji*)? Take a look and see what you think.
Kari: Is this a Japanese name?

The following miscue provides another example:

Peter and Judy covered their ears as sounds

the

of splintering wood and breaking china
^
fell on

filled the house.

Kari: You know when I first read this through—*splintering wood*—and not down here—I got a picture of—after I read this, I kind of got a picture of not the china, I had a picture of wood, you know, b-i-i-i-g pieces of wood that are tall, falling on this house, just you know, and then china, just like little rain or something just coming down.

Terminating

She discusses her options to read or not, based on personal preferences. She was reflecting on termination strategies in the following discussion:

Kari: I like it when I get a book that I like, but if I don't find a book that I like then I don't like it very much you know. . . . If I get a book that I like, I won't want to stop reading it. . . . And the reading isn't that pleasureful if I don't get a book that I like. So it's kind of weird.

Kari: I picked 'em up and barely read one paragraph. I was dissatisfied with the *Sweet Valley High* book.

Strategy Use

During our third and final closing interview I began a review of the strategies to see what she thought about what we had "learned" through the work in the project. As I wrote down each of the strategy names she proceeded to copy them and interpret each one in her own words, even inventing and explaining them with miscue examples. A copy of her written notes is shown in Figure 9-1.

SAmpleing : cooking all arouwd ~~to~~ page / reading small portion to decide.

checking Notalwayis needed to be corrected

                    cow
The cat eats chicken

sound correction: to makes something better ~~than~~.

inferrensing – useing what you know to predict

perdicting = guessing about something w/ the gathered information to help.

termination: to stop Reading

Figure 9-1   Kari's Definitions of Reading Strategies

Of course, underlying her awareness of the strategies she used in reading was her focus on the cueing systems. The demands she placed upon herself shifted from a concern for precise replication of the graphophonics or surface text features to a concern for understanding meaning. Comparing the first and last RMA sessions illustrates this shift.

For the first RMA session after her reading of "The Man Who Kept House" I selected five miscues for us to evaluate together. For each miscue I asked some form of the question: "Why do you think you said (miscue)?" Of her answers for the five selected miscues, two were meaning-based and three were based on graphophonics cues. However, two things are important to note. First, with just the encouragement that there were no "right" answers, her response regarding the very first miscue we discussed was, "I guess it did—'cause it made sense!" This remark was made before either I or her classroom teacher began any instruction about the reading process. Second, her graphophonic-based reasoning was simply that she "didn't see" the words or parts of words in question.

During the last RMA session we discussed a story about cave paintings. Her reasons for making seven selected miscues reflected four meaning-based, two graphics-based, and one which included meaning and syntactic reasoning. Meaning-based reasons included reference to how her miscue did or did not make sense. Reasons related to the surface features of the text included "not paying attention" and a substitution of *one* for *on* because they looked alike.

Kari: Because *one* and *on* kind of are the same thing when it comes to word terms.
Joel: How do you mean?
Kari: Well, like, they're only one letter difference.

The miscue which reflected both meaning and syntactic awareness was an instance of her use of a contraction, *that's* for *that is*. When asked why she made this miscue, she responded: "'Cause *that's* sounds better than *that is* 'cause I hardly ever do that. I always am using contractions."

It should be noted that the statistical analysis of her miscues reflected a continual shift toward proficient reading. Early in the study she was reading narratives such as "The Man Who Kept House" selected from a basal reader. Her reading of this folk tale revealed abilities beyond her standardized test scores. She made fewer than three miscues per hundred words, and her miscues resulted in syntactic acceptability scores of over 98 percent and semantic acceptability over 97 percent. At the end of the study, eighteen months later, she read the same tale with 100 percent syntactic and semantic acceptability, and made 4.3 miscues per hundred words. Her retellings were thorough for both readings.

As the sessions continued, she selected some of her own reading material, and I made some selections based upon her interests. These texts were more complex than the first one, but her RMI statistics revealed a proficient reader when the texts were appropriately selected. The range of miscues per hundred words was from 2.7 to 8.9, but all her readings resulted in syntactic and semantic acceptability scores of over 90 percent. Her retellings showed knowledge of the plot, theme, and major events. Her reading of nonfiction texts showed that she needed more experience reading a range of genre.

One of the first impressions from Kari's transcripts was the considerable value she gave to the authority of text. During the first session, we discussed substituting *in* for *into* for the phrase *putting the water into a pot*. She insisted that this miscue should be corrected: "Because you should always—if you notice it, correct a word." In this session we began our continuous discussion of whether an author would rewrite a story exactly the same, word for word, if all copies of it were lost and the

INSTRUCTIONAL PRACTICES AND PERSONAL INTERPRETATIONS
The Authority of the Text

author were asked to write it again. And if the author is forced in that circumstance to change the text, we discussed whether readers also have permission to change the text. Kari remained convinced that each word the author selected was extremely important. When discussing a nonword substitution for *antimacassar* I asked: "Is that word necessary to the story do you think?" Kari: "Well, undoubtedly to the author it was." I didn't know what this word was myself and so we discussed whether we should look it up because it really didn't interfere with our understanding of the story. The term appears only once in a description of a chair. I was willing to pass it over but Kari very politely brought up one of her reasons for looking it up.

Kari: Are you getting grades?
Joel: Not for the project. This isn't for class, it's just a project. I'm a research assistant. But I'm also taking classes.
Kari: I was going to say if it's for your class, then you should [look up the word], 'cause it would get you a better grade.
Joel: Oh yeah? To look up the word?
Kari: Yeah.
Joel: Uhhh. (laughs)
Kari: If you're in class and doing this, you should because it gets you a better grade.

Even after several examples of agreeing that she had indeed improved upon what the author of a piece had written, she felt that writing a letter to an author talking about possible changes to a text would not be a good idea. Kari: "I was thinking at first, well I don't know if that would be a good idea because you know she might think—take it as an insult or something." Kari continued to express a verbal concern for sticking to the text, even though her experience of altering and at times improving it increased. Beyond getting a good grade, she voiced concerns for how teachers, as early as in first grade, had told her that if she didn't correct a miscue it would be "wrong." And that this was a way to become a good reader.

However, the written word was important to Kari for yet another reason. She herself was an author. She liked to write and had several stories underway which we talked about throughout the meetings. During a discussion of one of her poems, she talked about a teacher's criticism in a very indignant tone. She felt her teacher's suggestion about how she should depict a waterfall in a poem was inappropriate.

Kari: I wrote a poem called "Waterfalls." And they said: "Clean and crisp!" Waterfalls are not clean and crisp! They're not crisp. They're not like a butterfly.
Joel: Humm.
Kari: They're not beautiful like a butterfly, as my ending . . . . I have my way of writing.

I began to wonder if her concern for text was an empathy for authors prompted by how her writing was treated in school. If this is the case, how writing was taught could play an important part in readers' views of text, and consequently influence their views of reading.

Schooling

The influence of Kari's school experience left its mark on her attitudes as well. This is reflected through her concern for grades, getting things "right," and her definition of a good reader at the beginning of the sessions. The issue of grades arose again after we discussed her improvement of one part of the text.

so

"You were gone a long (time)," he said.

She was quite positive about this miscue:

Kari: I think the one with the *so* sounds better. 'Cause it gives you more strong effect, of how the family was feeling. I mean, if you just say: *You were gone a long time,* but if you say: *You were gone so long,* then you can tell how they really felt more.

But after I attempted to tie this into her ideas about reading in general by suggesting that she could be more lenient, for example, with reading to her little sister or small children, her response changed:

Joel: So if you were reading that to little kids that you were babysitting, would you go back and correct it?
Kari: Especially little kids when they're young. Because if you like to read, then I think you would get better grades because you would learn more than a person that didn't want to learn.

Interestingly, she tied reading text precisely as written with the idea of learning. She, like other readers in the study, also tied the notion of learning to the presence of "big words" in the text. Regarding the nonword substitution for *antimacassar,* Kari commented: "Big words are almost always important. 'Cause a lot of authors that are writing for young children, I think, sometimes they put big words in there to make them learn bigger words and get onto, um, more, higher level."

During the spring interview at the end of year one in the study, she provided a critique of her experiences in school. Early in her school career, Kari had been relegated to a low ability reading group. Interestingly, the reasons she still uses to explain this grouping are not particularly related to her learning to read.

Kari: She always had me in the lowest group in reading . . . . And she treated us different 'cause she had four groups of reading. And she always treated the low group the worst, and I was in the "B" group. In first grade I wasn't too smart, you know.
Joel: You were in the low group of reading.
Kari: The low group of reading and plus the low group of your studies.
Joel: Oh. And that's the "B" group.
Kari: Yeah. "A" is "you're good"; "B" is "you're not."
Joel: So that was only divided into two.
Kari: And when I was in sixth grade, they did it again, except they did it into three groups. And it was totally backwards. It was "C" is the really really smart people. And "B" is the people who aren't dumb, they're almost smart, but they're average kind of. And then "A" group was you know where you're dumb, or you're something like that. And I wasn't dumb. I deserved to be in "B" group as far as I was concerned, cause I was average.
Joel: And where were you?
Kari: I was in the last group.
Joel: Again in the sixth grade?
Kari: Yep. But this teacher didn't like me. I think that was the whole point. I know he didn't like me.

During her final interview, Kari talked extensively about where her attitudes toward her own reading came from, how she felt, and what recommendations she had for teachers in their questioning strategies, grading, and grouping:

Joel: Do you have any different attitudes towards reading than you had at the beginning?
Kari: Oh, yeah. I used to hate reading.
Joel: Oh, yeah. How come?

Kari: When school started they made you read the *Crystal Kingdom* books and had to answer the questions. That's when I began to hate reading. 'Cause I figure all my life I'm going to be given reading and I'm going to have to answer these dumb questions . . . . Why can't we just read the story? That's what reading's all about. To read, not answer questions.

Joel: Yeah.

Kari: They want to know if you're paying attention—that's why I hated reading. Up until about now.

Joel: Humm. So you're enjoying reading now?

Kari: Yeah. And I don't mind answering questions now.

Joel: Yeah. How come? I was going to ask you that, how come those questions were "dumb?" Are those questions different from the questions we've gone through?

Kari: It made me feel uptight . . . . I hate these questions because they're just so dumb and I'm not good at reading, the way I used to be. I didn't mean I wasn't good at reading, I meant I wasn't good at answering the reading questions.

Joel: And what about our questions?

Kari: They're okay, 'cause I feel comfortable because I don't have to worry about a grade, or getting in trouble from my parents because they're wrong. . . . I'm not going to get graded on it or nothing.

Joel: Do you still feel that there's a right and a wrong?

Kari: No. But in school, yeah.

Joel: Do you think reading should be in first grade then?

Kari: Yeah.

Joel: Even if it's like what you had?

Kari: Well, no. I don't think that there should be groups. Everyone should be treated equally. I don't care if they're smarter than the others. That's just—that's just too young, I mean, sure it's nice for them to get a head start, but I don't think it's right for them to have to be compared with the other kids. 'Cause then the other kids get to hating them.

Joel: So everyone should be treated equally. Why should they be treated equally?

Kari: 'Cause it makes everybody feel like, "Oh well, man, I can do better." You don't have to worry about who's ahead of you.

Joel: Is that distracting, in terms of learning?

Kari: Yeah . . . . 'Cause you're always worried about "God, how am I ever going to pass this level?" And you're worried about how those people are ahead of me, and I'll never be able to get that high.

Joel: And what does that do for your interest in reading?

Kari: I think it makes you not want to read.

While Kari was not quite aware enough to talk about the differences between the questions at the end of the basal reader she had experienced and the open ended questions we worked on during our sessions, one of her comments might provide grounds for a comparison. When she comments that basal questions were to see "if you're paying attention," the issue separated for me. Children are always paying attention to something, the question is *what*. For the basal readers, the demand was for attention to the surface features of the text on the page. For our sessions, it was for what was going on in her mind. This recent recognition of her participation in the reading process allowed her to say " . . . that's why I hated reading. Up until about now." It separated the curricular "learning to read" from the active process of always "reading to learn."

Her last recommendation for schooling and her reasoning speak clearly:

Kari: First of all: Reading class is, I think, you should be able to pick your own book and give a report on it. There shouldn't be this big ol' thick book like *Sun Spray* that you're supposed to know about. I don't think that's good. I don't like that type of reading 'cause you can't read free.

Joel: Humm.

Kari: Pick you own book. 'Cause if I were a reading teacher I would let the kid choose their own book. Just make sure it was on their own level. Unless they were really smart and they want to get on with it. And let them choose their own book, have them read it, do a report on it, give it to me. I don't think that's fun not to be able to choose your own.

Joel: Nice. Anything else?

Kari: I don't think that our teacher understands that we don't like the stories that are in the book . . . . We like our own type of thing. We're all different. She gives us all the same thing. We're different people. So we're not like machines, you know, where we all like the same thing. It's undoubtedly what she thinks, or the school thinks, because we don't all like the same thing. What they need is just to get rid of the *Sun Spray* and give us more library books.

Joel: Yeah. Get rid of that and go use library books. Is that your own idea?

Kari: Yeah.

Joel: Okay. When did you think of this?

Kari: Uh. Just now.

Joel: Just now?

Kari: When I was talking about the *Sun Spray* 'cause *Sun Spray* is just so boring.

As Kari reveals, her new appreciation of reading is a result of our mutual recognition of her active participation in the reading process not only because of the open-ended RMA questions, but also because in our discussions we looked at what she actually does when she reads. Her intimate understanding of this is found in how she accepted changes to text if they made sense or sounded better, and in how she would use terms such as "sounds better" and "sound it out." "Makes sense" and "sounds better" for Kari involved everything from syntactic transformations to dialect difference, each time involving a preference for her own response to the text.

For example, Kari inserts *a* before *while* in the sentence: They stopped while Pablo looked the situation over. The insertion of *a* cues her to insert a stop between what are now two independent clauses. Never noticing the insertion of *a*, she provides a rationale for inserting the stop, which she refers to as a comma.

Kari: It sounded weird. Doesn't this sound better with a comma? Watch: They read it like this first: *They stopped a while Pablo looked the situation over. They stopped a while* [comma] *Pablo looked the situation over.* 'Cause it sounds better.

Joel: Why does it sound better?

Kari: Sounds like he's madder.

When Kari mentioned the strategy of "sounding it out," I pursued her meaning. She said it meant "Take a little bit at a time." "Gotta look at the words you got, the parts of the word . . ." Kari's concept of "sound it out" is not simply a letter-by-letter strategy, but rather a form of word search. When reading a newspaper article about Nelson Mandela, she came to the word *apartheid* and spent 38 seconds trying variations of possible readings for various clusters of letters under her breath. During that time, she tried a substitution, the word *authority*. Clearly, she did not go letter-by-letter, but rather tested possible solutions for various selected parts of the word and the possible sounds that the parts could represent. Her final check was again best determined by sense. Indeed, her substitution of *authority* for *apartheid*, which made sense, demonstrates viable phonological knowledge, since "p's" can be silent as in *psyched*, and "d's" can sound like "t's," as in *walked*. When considering the value of phonics it is important for teachers to understand that there are innumerable potential sound-letter relationships in the real work of reading.

> Scissors is one way of spelling *sizurz*. One other way is *psozzyrrhzz*, which is justified by *ps* in *psalm*; *o* in *women*; *z* in *buzz*; *yrrh* in *myrrh*. There are 81,997,919 other justifiable ways (Pitman, as cited in Barnitz 1980, 320).

I am suggesting that what Kari terms "sound it out" represents a more involved process than what is usually considered when "sounding out" is taught, or learned.

Sound and Sense

Use of Metaphors

Kari's mind was always actively processing information while reading, and for her own purposes. In her discussion of reading, she invented her own metaphors relating what she was doing as a reader with her knowledge of the real world. For example, she compared her use of words to ingredients of a recipe:

Kari: It's supposed to sound—well I mean it just is supposed to fit in, I guess is what I'm trying to say.
Joel: Fit it where?
Kari: Like, just the right amount of this, and just the right . . . like a recipe. You need just the right amount of everything.
Joel: Neat. Yeah. And then if you have everything that's just what you need then it sounds . . .
Kari: Yeah. And if you add something that you really don't need, then it's going to turn out wrong.
Joel: If you add something do you think it will always turn out wrong?
Kari: Not necessarily, I mean because, of course, over there with the *the* it didn't matter. . . . I mean, 'cause that's just like saying "Well, I'm adding extra ingredients 'cause I want to make a better type of cookie." Or I want more cookie dough and stuff.

This is important cognitively for more reasons than that it shows an active learner. It underlines the importance of how readers must see for themselves the process of reading as something which they actually do. If they are to take control of their reading it must be through how they themselves think about how reading works. Not that their metaphors would be the most conventional ones, but that these may be necessary touchstones for a reader's developing awareness and self-regulatory behavior. Kari's metaphors lay the groundwork for her personalization of conventional knowledge.

Kari: Comma's just a little bit more grown though.
Joel: Think so?
Kari: It's like "and" [as a conjunction] is like a baby or something and comma is like "I'm the big adult," you know. And people respect me more, like I'm better or something you know. And the "and" is like it's used for little things [that aren't] important.
Joel: Yeah. Are there any other marks that have those kinds of . . .
Kari: Attitu—
Joel: Yeah, attitudes?
Kari: They can give you that type of wondering-like attitude. Well, exclamation. Exclamation is very, you know, noticeable. And it's like, HURRY UP, it takes over when there's an emergency. It's like the ambulance or something. Like the police or . . .
Joel: Would that go with the "and" or the comma?
Kari: Neither one, cause . . . it probably falls into the comma category but the exclamation is the type that is like an ambulance. Or something's happened and it's alerting, you know. It's like a fire alarm at the school. It alerts you to get out of the school quick, you know. That's what the exclamation is, kind of. Sometimes it's happy, sometimes it's serious, and sometimes it's sad. And the period is kind of that, that sadness. It kind of falls into the "and" situation, because period isn't anything. Period is just for normal everyday things, it's a nothing.
Joel: Is it a pause at all?
Kari: No. Just the ending.

In retrospective miscue analysis the reader is the informant for the reader through the processes of self-reflection and revaluing. The reader's constructions take precedence over those of the researcher or teacher. Readers' constructions show us what students do and how they think, and consequently help teachers provide a flexible and appropriate environment for their growth. Kari helps teachers be careful. Too often instructional ideas fail to be as alive to students as teachers think. School has traditionally imposed its style of activity over the students' style of activity in ways that can be arresting to their development. This has been partly the result in the turning of early *descriptive* linguistic knowledge into *prescriptive* programs and basal texts, as Kenneth Goodman recognized so long ago (K. Goodman 1964, 1969; see also K. Goodman 1993).

Kari's attitudes toward the RMA questions suggest that there are ways to help students focus on meaning, and to see themselves as meaning makers. Retrospective miscue analysis works to help Kari explain her own reading activity and explore her own meaning. The RMA framework supports her as she continues her development, finds new challenges, and confronts new ideas. Without the arbitrary imposition of authority, Kari can value and experience her knowledge, which gives substance to her development. Without the preeminence of right and wrong textbook answers, there can be, as Kari said about her cousin's reading, "discovery." For teachers and researchers, the failure to attend to the actual activity of students' minds risks the perpetuation of the adult metaphor that young people's minds are *tabula rasa* (blank slates) and risks the institution of what Kari herself termed classroom "death work."

THE COLLABORATIVE NATURE OF READING INSTRUCTION

A friend of mine, a professional diagnostician, once gave an exam to Navajo children. One of the questions asked which building materials were better suited for the construction of a house: wood or stone. She noticed that many of the children answered that stone was much better and due to the confines of the test she had to mark that answer as incorrect. However, she was curious and asked one of the kids why they had marked "stone." "Well," the student said, "if you used wood, first you would have to plant the trees." In the same way that the test developer did not appreciate the complexity of children's learning, I found this research experience helped me reconsider my own misunderstandings, misinterpretations, and miscues. I miscued on what I heard on the tape recordings. I missed miscues which were on tape, and I miscued on what Kari said in sessions. More often than I expected, I got answers that I did not anticipate. Piaget taught us that children think differently than adults, yet there has been little exploration of this phenomenon in daily classroom practice. Kari herself seemed intimately aware and at ease with this distinction when she talked about adults or teachers simply being "different people."

The discovery for myself was that as much as the reader is involved in the process of reading, so am I. While she reads, I am reading along. While she miscues, so do I. Many researchers have explored the problems of talking to students, some of whom have considered observers' biases which are known to exist for a multitude of reasons (see Bridges 1985 and Hill & Larsen 1983 for more cognitively based discussions). It was William Page (1973), however, who first outlined the difficulties in view of miscue research and reading. He termed it "the observation process," and pointed out that if readers are engaged in a process, so also is the observer. Indeed, understanding the shared nature of the reading process equalizes the relationship between teachers and students. And the reflective nature of retrospective miscue analysis provides countless opportunities for teachers and readers to share what they know about reading, and about discovering themselves as readers. As Kari summed it up nicely: "Everyone actually loves to read, they just don't know it."

10

Building Confidence in a Proficient Reader

Sarah Costello

THE PURPOSE OF THIS CASE study is to discern the impact of retrospective miscue analysis on a successful reader. My interest is based on practical application. By using retrospective miscue analysis (RMA) in a collaborative setting in my seventh- and eighth-grade classrooms and reading related research (Worsnop 1977; Stephensen 1980; Marek 1987), I recognized the value of RMA with non-proficient readers, but I questioned the validity of doing RMA with proficient readers. They were already successful as readers. Would talking about reading on a conscious level confuse the reading process? What benefit would a proficient reader get from participating in RMA sessions? Looking for answers to these questions was my rationale for doing an in-depth case study on Bernice, a proficient reader who was part of the NCTE study discussed in Chapter 7. I hoped to discover what this proficient reader believes about the reading process, how she makes use of that knowledge, and what happens when her beliefs are in conflict with what she is doing when reading.

Our interactions with Bernice consisted of three reading interviews, five reading sessions, and five RMA sessions. The RMA sessions followed procedures outlined in Chapters 4 and 7. The sessions consisted of collecting a taped reading and a retelling during one week, and then following up with an RMA session and discussion during the next sessions. Before the RMA session, a miscue analysis was done using Procedure III of the Reading Miscue Inventory (Y. Goodman et al. 1987). During each RMA session, Bernice was presented with a typescript of the previous reading marked with the miscues to be discussed. The appropriate excerpts from the tape-recorded reading were played, and Bernice had the opportunity to view the text and the marked miscues, as well as to hear her actual reading. Sessions would last approximately forty-five minutes, constrained by class schedules.

The texts Bernice read varied in difficulty and genre to obtain a variety of reading strategies which are documented through miscue analysis. This analysis gave me an opportunity to understand the relationship between Bernice's actual reading strategies as revealed through the RMI and her beliefs about the reading process as indicated in interviews and RMA discussions.

Bernice was a twelve-year-old girl attending a seventh grade in a middle school when she became one of the participants in our NCTE study. She was successful in school, maintaining Honor Society status throughout the year. On the California

Achievement Test she scored in the seventh stanine in reading, and her teacher recommended her as a good student who does well in her classes.

At the beginning of the study during the Reading Interview, Bernice voiced a simplistic model of the reading process, asserting that a good reader provides an unabridged rendering of the text:

Sarah: Who is a good reader that you know?
Bernice: My mom, definitely.
Sarah: What makes her a good reader?
Bernice: We have a whole bunch of books at home. She reads them aloud. She studies the questions at the bottom of the page and when she reads she never stumbles on a long word and she knows how to pronounce it and everything.
Sarah: Do you think she ever comes to something she doesn't know when reading?
Bernice: Well, I don't think so.
Sarah: If your mom did come to something she didn't know, what do you think she would do?
Bernice: She would probably do the same thing I do. She'd probably ask questions about it to us or say, "Bernice, go get the dictionary."

Bernice believed that a good reader reads every word on a page correctly and does not stumble on words. In discussing her school experiences, Bernice revealed a myriad of techniques used to "help her learn to read."

Sarah: How did you learn to read?
Bernice: First they took my pencil and put it in my hand and they drew lines with me. They made me write sentences and they made me read it back again. Then I was in a remedial class where you had to write out a sentence and put your periods in red and your question marks in green and then write out the special word that you find there that is really hard to understand in yellow. It was a little confusing. I don't think we ever used a pencil.
Sarah: So you were in remedial reading and they helped you learn to read by marking all these different things. Did that help you or confuse you?
Bernice: They helped me a lot because next year I went into basic reading. Then the next time I went up a little. I've just been going up up up.

As our interview progressed Bernice shared other school experiences about how she learned to read.

Sarah: Were the remedial teachers in your school or special teachers who came to help you?
Bernice: Regular teachers but some had to teach remedial class. Ms. Jones was really nice. She would always have us put our hand down here and go syllable by syllable, and every time your chin would hit your hand you know that meant you had one. Then they put me in the high group. Then they said "Oh good. Now you are out of this place." It made me happy.
Sarah: I bet. Did knowing what a syllable was help you in reading?
Bernice: Yes (emphatically). I used to just pronounce words without syllables like *maybe*. I'd go *ma . . . da*. I couldn't do syllables right.
Sarah: What would you like to do better as a reader now?
Bernice: I'd like to quit stumbling on words. I'd like to know all the words and then quit stumbling.

I became intrigued with Bernice. Here was a reader who began as a remedial reader but was characterized as a very good reader in middle school. Her notions about reading were directed toward getting every word right, sounding out words, looking all words up in the dictionary. Not once during the interview did she mention reading for meaning or understanding the story.

Bernice's focus on the graphophonic cueing system was evident during the first RMA session using "The Man Who Kept House." The session focus was on self-correcting when there was a meaning loss. Although she employed good self-correction strategies, her discussion focused entirely on graphophonic information. Bernice's perfectionist view of the reading process was apparent in the following dialogue:

Once upon a time there was a woodman
(handwritten: © wooden man)

who thought that no one worked as hard as

he did.

Sarah:	What did you do?
Bernice:	I went *wooden man* because I saw the *n* before I saw the rest of the word. Sometimes I do that. I look at the next letter and just say the word.
Sarah:	What makes you do that?
Bernice:	I don't know.
Sarah:	Tell me this. If it says, *Once upon a time there was a wooden man who thought that no one worked as hard as he did*, does that miscue make sense?
Bernice:	No.
Sarah:	Why not?
Bernice:	Well, it's hard to explain. *That no one* doesn't make sense.
Sarah:	I'm talking about the miscue with the wooden man. Does that miscue make sense in the story?
Bernice:	No.
Sarah:	Why not?
Bernice:	Because they were talking about a man who cut wood.
Sarah:	So the word you miscued—*the wooden man*—didn't make sense because you were talking about a person that cut wood. Do you think you should have gone back and corrected that?
Bernice:	Yes.
Sarah:	And did you?
Bernice:	Yes.
Sarah:	Why?
Bernice:	Because if I didn't correct I would never be able to read it again. My grandma always tells me you have to go back and say the word again until you get it right.

Bernice's comment that if she didn't correct the miscue she would read it wrong every time reflected her belief that reading should be an accurate rendition of the text. There was no room for error in her model of the reading process.

Bernice was frustrated with her miscues and annoyed that she continued to make them. The first session was the most difficult because although I tried to focus on her strengths, she continued to see miscues as mistakes—mistakes that she shouldn't be making.

When he got back to the house he saw a
(handwritten: © said)

big pig inside with its nose in the churn.

Sarah:	Did your miscue make sense?
Bernice:	No.
Sarah:	Why not?

Bernice: (reading) *he said a pig* . . .
Sarah: Okay. It didn't make sense. What did you do?
Bernice: I think the thing we did in the beginning with the wooden man. 'Cause I saw the *s* and the *a* and I saw the *w*.
Sarah: What did you do there?
Bernice: I looked at the *s* and *a* and maybe the *w* looked like an *i*. And I did a mistake. A very large mistake.

Whenever Bernice discussed a miscue she went to extreme lengths to rationalize her miscue, examining the text intently to decide why she created a certain miscue. But throughout the RMA sessions, when confronted with inconsistencies in her reading and what she said she was doing when reading, Bernice was pushed into a state of disequilibrium. In a lengthy discussion concerning a substitution of *the* for *a* Bernice was contradictory in her contention that it affected the meaning of the text. Interestingly enough, there was no graphic similarity for her to refer to when discussing the miscue.

I'll light ~~a~~ *the* fire in the fireplace.

Sarah: Does that miscue make sense?
Bernice: No, because in this sentence where they have it, *the fire* means there is already a fire.
Sarah: Do you get two different meanings for what I'm going to do?
Bernice: Yes. Because I was thinking there already is a fire and he's going to light the fire again. That's what I thought. But when you read, *I'll light "a" fire* that means there is no fire there but you are going to light it.
Sarah: So you see two different meanings. I'll light *the* fire, I'll light *a* fire.
Bernice: Yes.
Sarah: What you are saying when you said *I'll light the fire* you meant, "light a fire that is already lit"?
Bernice: If it said "I'll put something on *the* fire" you wouldn't put something on *a* fire. I'm getting you confused, aren't I? I'm getting me confused.
Sarah: Read the two sentences.
Bernice: It makes more sense saying *a* instead of *the*.
Sarah: Should you have corrected that miscue?
Bernice: Yeah.
Sarah: Why?
Bernice: Because, to me, it would affect the meaning of the story. To me it did if there was already a fire.
Sarah: Bernice, do you feel like every time you read you should read exactly every word that is on the page?
Bernice: No.
Sarah: Sometimes you can substitute words but this isn't one of those times?
Bernice: Yeah. Even though it's a little word, like *a*, or you substitute *a* for something and it won't make sense, but sometimes you can leave it out and it will make sense.
Sarah: That's right. But if I substitute *the* for *a* in this sentence, *I'll light a fire in the fireplace*, it won't make sense.
Bernice: It wouldn't make sense to me.
Sarah: Why do you think you didn't correct that then?
Bernice: Because *the* is a common word, I guess. You see *the* a lot. Plus I probably didn't notice it.
Sarah: Why wouldn't you notice it?
Bernice: Because it wasn't that big of a mistake for me to have it affect the meaning.
Sarah: Here you didn't notice it and here you did. What is the difference in these two?
Bernice: This one affects more of the meaning to it.
Sarah: So it has a different meaning but it didn't affect it that much that you would have to go back and correct it. But you said you should have gone back and corrected it.
Bernice: I think I should have!

In the process of analyzing miscues and reflecting on her own reading strategies she began to recognize her very significant role in understanding the text. At the same time it gave me insights into Bernice's understanding of the English determiner system. Participation in RMA sessions justified and gave credence to the repertoire of strategies that Bernice incorporated to construct meaning from the text as she read. As the sessions continued, Bernice began to look at miscues and reading from a different perspective. She began to look inward to herself and at times beyond the text to the author, questioning his or her use of words or understandings about the world. Consider these miscues in her reading of "Anita's Gift" (Morgan 1955):

No one was there looking up at their apartment.

Bernice:	I know why I made that miscue. You know. Picture an apartment. You don't just see one apartment. You see a whole bunch of apartments.
Sarah:	Okay. So what you know about apartments made you miscue. Did you self-correct?
Bernice:	I'm not sure. I think I did. I did it again. I said *the* apartment instead of *their* apartment.
Sarah:	And that's the miscue I wanted to talk about. Not the *apartments*. That's a good reason why you said *apartments* and you went back and self-corrected. Did you need to self-correct the *s*?
Bernice:	I don't know.
Sarah:	Let's read the sentence. *No one was there looking at the apartments.* Did it change the meaning of the story?
Bernice:	No.
Sarah:	Let's go back to this miscue, *the* for *their*. Did that miscue disrupt the meaning?
Bernice:	No. It didn't hurt it at all.
Sarah:	So the miscue makes sense. Didn't hurt the meaning. Did you self-correct that one?
Bernice:	No.
Sarah:	Did you need to?
Bernice:	No.
Sarah:	Why not?
Bernice:	Because *their* and *the* would make sense either way.

In discussing miscues in "Anita's Gift," Bernice looked to her own background experience to understand her miscues. She began to look for the logic of her miscues and to question authors and their expertise.

"And we have flowers all year in the beautiful

gardens of our beloved island, don't we

children?"

Sarah:	What did you do there?
Bernice:	I said *islands* instead of *island*.
Sarah:	Did that make sense?
Bernice:	I think it did. I've always imagined Puerto Rico as having a lot of islands. It makes sense.
Sarah:	So with the knowledge or information you already had in your head about Puerto Rico that works.

Bernice: Yeah.
Sarah: That's another point, Bernice. When you are reading you are always pulling from your background knowledge. What you already know in your head, bringing that to the text. Maybe someone who never heard of Puerto Rico before . . .
Bernice: They would have said "beloved island."
Sarah: They may have, right. So your idea in your head was that Puerto Rico had many islands so that fit. Did you self-correct that?
Bernice: No.
Sarah: Did you need to?
Bernice: No.
Sarah: Is that a good miscue then?
Bernice: Yeah.

At this point Bernice justified her miscue because it made sense to her. The following example is from her reading of *Jumanji*.

When his sister caught up with him, he was

front

kneeling at the foot of the tree looking at a

long thin box.

Sarah: Did you see your miscue?
Bernice: Yeah. I said *front* instead of *foot*.
Sarah: Does your miscue make sense?
Bernice: Well, it does if you don't know what the foot of a tree is. I wasn't familiar with that. So, then I figured out what the foot of the tree meant, so I said *front*.
Sarah: So, you are saying the front of the tree made more sense. Did you correct that one?
Bernice: No.
Sarah: And why not?
Bernice: Because *foot* and *front* meant the same thing in this text.
Sarah: You miscued why?
Bernice: Because *foot* to me didn't look right. It looked better if it said *front*.
Sarah: What do you think made you pick that word?
Bernice: Because if you are thinking of a foot of a tree. Okay. A tree has all front because it is circular. When you are thinking the front of something the foot and the front . . . mainly because they begin with an *f*.

As the sessions continued Bernice became more relaxed. Instead of blaming herself, she looked at her miscues inquisitively, trying to recreate what was happening for her when she miscued.

Bernice discussed a fine semantic point in explaining why *grasping* is a better word than *grabbing*. She is comfortable defending her position, recognizing her power as a reader to choose, select, and reject the text in her quest for meaning. The following miscue was made during her reading of *Jumanji*:

She grabbed the dice and moved to a blank.

Sarah: What was your miscue?
Bernice: I said *grasped* at the dice.
Sarah: Did your miscue make sense?
Bernice: Yes. Because when you are thinking you are grasping for all it's worth in this story.

Sarah:	Did you self-correct?
Bernice:	No. I started out saying the right thing by saying *grab*, but then I thought that don't make sense and I said *grasped*. Because grasping is more like, you know, you are ready to get on with this and you are ready to have Peter wake up.
Sarah:	Did your miscue look like what is on the page?
Bernice:	Yes.
Sarah:	Very similar, aren't they?
Bernice:	Here's how I think grabbing and grasping are different. When you grab something, you are taking it and not giving it back. When you grasp something you are grasping it and then you are giving it back. That's what it sounds like. And he was grasping the dice because he was going to roll them again.
Sarah:	Did that miscue affect your understanding?
Bernice:	No.
Sarah:	Do you think that is a good miscue?
Bernice:	Yes. It doesn't hurt the story at all.

"Gender Benders" was the last text Bernice read during the school year. It is a science essay discussing various types of fish. When her most verbalized strategy, sounding out, didn't work, she read on, stating that she understood the meaning from the context of the story, and more significantly, it didn't matter if she didn't know the word, she understood the meaning.

Hermaphratrites

Many are hermaphrodites, which means that they

can be both male and female.

Sarah:	What did you do there?
Bernice:	I said *hermaphratrites*.
Sarah:	Why do you think you did that?
Bernice:	'Cause I never saw that word before.
Sarah:	When you came to that word how did you try to figure it out?
Bernice:	I tried to sound it out and then I tried to look ahead and see what it means. Finally, I found out what it meant, but I still don't know how to pronounce it.
Sarah:	Does it matter if you pronounce it *hermaphrodites* or *hermaphratrites* in getting the meaning of the story?
Bernice:	Not much.

In this closing interview, Bernice discussed what she had learned about the strategies she uses as a reader, complete with references to previous miscues we talked about.

Sarah:	Okay. How do you feel about your ability to improve your reading?
Bernice:	Oh. I'm dying to. I want to improve my reading.
Sarah:	The things we talked about, the strategies, do you think that is going to help you improve your reading?
Bernice:	Yes.
Sarah:	What are the strategies?
Bernice:	Self-predicting and background knowledge is really good 'cause then you don't get stuck on it 'cause if I have the title (and I'm thinking of *Jumanji*—I never heard of that before), I didn't have any knowledge but then I got flowing through it 'cause I had a little bit of knowledge. The other one about Pablo, I knew a lot about Mexico and Puerto Rico and Spanish so it was easier for me to understand.
Sarah:	How did that affect your miscues?
Bernice:	It made them better, like when they said Puerto Rico island when actually there are many islands so it made it—the story—have more sense. Don't tell the author that.

Bernice even shared one of her special survival strategies that helped her in reading.

Sarah: Can you tell me about self-prediction?
Bernice: In Ohio I learned it one way and in Florida they told me a different way.
Sarah: Tell me what you mean by that.
Bernice: Well, in Ohio they said you need to memorize the word before you read it. They were saying to look ahead, remember what the word is, and look ahead and read like that. Finally I caught on to it, but then we moved down to Florida they told me to memorize behind it and read forward. So I got all confused from Florida to Ohio, so I just made up my own way. I just read directly on to the story and then if something exciting came up I would think about what would happen next. It would change the story, some of the words some of the times, and some of the times it wouldn't. So it just depends.
Sarah: And you think self-predicting is going to help you?
Bernice: It will help you go smoother. So you don't have to go like a robot pronouncing every word. Working-like-this.
Sarah: So you think you realized you were doing this self-predicting before we got to-gether and talked about it? Did you consciously start doing that? Or when we started looking at miscues and talking about predicting did you realize that was a strategy you made up?
Bernice: I really didn't start paying much attention to it until we got into it in miscue sessions. Before I just never paid attention to it. I was just reading.

One significant outcome resulting from RMA sessions was the confidence Bernice exhibited in her reading, which led to more risk-taking in the classroom. This risk-taking is shown by her comment during the interview about her willing-ness to volunteer in class to read aloud:

Bernice: It can be fun, or hard reading like social studies. I learned to like reading, even social studies. I've even started to read out loud in class in social studies. I had reading [class] before I had social studies [in the semester] and in reading I would not read out loud. I would not do it unless she called on me without me raising my hand because I got too embarrassed that I sounded like a robot.

Bernice became more confident in her reading, which led to more risk-taking behavior in the classroom. This was one significant outcome resulting from RMA sessions. At the beginning of the study, Bernice referred to her mother and brother and commented on how they stopped her all the time, correcting her reading and telling her she had to get every word correct. According to the initial Reading Interview, her mother was one of the better readers she knew, a reader who doesn't come to any words she doesn't know. In the closing interview, seven months later, Bernice questioned her superiors (by her admission) in reading—her mother and her brother:

Bernice: Don't you just hate when you are reading out loud and you mess up on a little word like *then* or *and* and they go *the*.
Sarah: It doesn't really matter.
Bernice: I can't stand when I'm reading with my mom or my brother and they always go *the* or *and* or when I just barely mispronounce a word my mom or my brother will always pronounce it for me.
Sarah: It seems you may have more understanding of the reading process than they do now. Understanding that that doesn't disrupt the meaning.
Bernice: Yeah.
Sarah: To get the meaning of the story you don't have to get every exact word.
Bernice: It's not like you have to read like a robot like my mom and my brother. They always read like a robot. Every single solitary word. If they miss it I don't do that to them.
Sarah: That's what happens when you focus on the word instead of predicting like you were saying.
Bernice: Yeah.

Sarah: Like you were saying, you read a lot smoother.
Bernice: It's like when you read every solitary word you are going to mess up more . . .
            than when you read for the meaning of the story.

Bernice became a confident enough reader to volunteer to read in class. And though she stated that she never thought about reading before, she now questioned others and their assertions about reading.

Toward the final session Bernice verbalized a variety of strategies that she may have been using when miscueing. She talked about what she was thinking when she produced certain miscues. It's not that her strategies changed dramatically when reading—she was always an efficient, effective reader. The difference was that now she had the language and opportunity to discuss what she was doing when reading, and she was able to expand and enrich her interpretations of miscues. Often, Bernice had two or three hypotheses about why she might have miscued. Consider this example from her reading of "Western Gladiators."

of shank

Sometimes the numbers shrank to as few as 40

or 50.

Sarah: What was your miscue?
Bernice: *Shank* instead of *shrank*. (laughing) Don't ask me why I did that. I don't know. I
            guess I just messed up a letter or something.
Sarah: Okay. There we go again. Focusing on the letters instead of the meaning. We
            talked about if you just look at the letters on the page you mess up a lot unless
            you are using all your cueing systems. Meaning! Your background knowledge,
            the way language sounds. Did you self-correct that one?
Bernice: I don't think I did. (listens) I know what I did. I put *of shank*. I put *of* in there.
            Maybe I was thinking the number of rattlers shrank.
Sarah: You were predicting what you expected to see. Sometimes the number of . . .
Bernice: I thought *shank* was one of those fancy words for a group of rattlers.
Sarah: You were predicting, reading along, constructing meaning.
Bernice: Even though *shank* probably isn't even a word in the English language.
Sarah: What I care about is why you may have made that miscue, not so much if it's a
            word or not. I'm not so caught in the rightness or wrongness of the miscue. I
            just say "I wonder why she made that miscue. I wonder what she was doing. She
            substituted and put *of* in." It's interesting that you were saying that you thought
            it might have been another word for a group of rattlers that you didn't know
            about. Good. Interesting. See, I find that very interesting as a researcher.
Bernice: Yeah. And that night I was talking to a neighbor and their last name is Shank.
            Maybe I had it on the mind.

The tenor of the sessions changed slowly over time. The first time this was noted was during *Anita's Gift* when Bernice took over the session, turning on me and quizzing me about what I do when I'm reading. During the final session Bernice looked at the typescript and made observations and discussed miscues that she felt were significant. Her sophistication in discussing and analyzing her miscues became evident:

Bernice: (laughing, looking at the typescript of "Western Gladiators" with miscues
            marked) Notice these are all at the beginning.
Sarah: That's true. Towards the end it starts flowing a lot easier.
Bernice: That's because I'm getting more information from the beginning of it. I'm kind
            of anxious to see what happened in the story.

Bernice put all the discussions we had on miscues and reading into perspective when she explained the world of reading instruction through the eyes of a student:

Sarah: You are a good strong reader. Sometimes you rely too much on the letters on the page, which sometimes messes up the meaning, but you go back and correct those miscues. So I just want to make the point again, because when I first met you, you said that that was all you did when you read. You had to get every word that was on the page.

Bernice: That's what I was taught my entire life. I guess they divide the world in half, then one half teaches one way and then the other half teaches the other way.

There was a definite shift from the beginning of the study to the end, reflected in Bernice's comments made during our last RMA session. Her rationalizations reflected what she was actually doing when reading. It was acceptable to substitute words and omit words as long it made sense.

Sarah: So tell me what you think about what I'm telling you.

Bernice: This makes sense. Not reading it word for word. Because if you are reading it word for word then you are concentrating on the word and you are forgetting the rest of what you read. It's meaningless.

By the final reading interview Bernice has assimilated some of the ideas we discussed about reading during the year.

Sarah: Bernice, when you are reading and you come to something you don't know what do you do?

Bernice: Usually, I try to sound it out and try to figure out what it is from what I already know. And if I have no idea what it is and I look at the words surrounding it, I'll just use a word that I think would go in there.

When asked about how she would help someone who was having trouble with reading, she said she would let them read it sentence by sentence.

Bernice: I wouldn't get annoyed. Now if it was something like *a* for *the* I would let it go.

Sarah: So you would stop them if it was a meaning change.

Bernice: Yes. If they read it perfectly, the first sentence, I would go to the second sentence.

Sarah: What does perfect mean?

Bernice: Kind of smoothly and still have the meaning of the sentence.

Sarah: So you are saying perfectly means smoothly and the same meaning of the story. Does that mean you have to say every word?

Bernice: No. Just to get the gist of it. And kind of let it go.

When asked how a teacher would help that person, Bernice suggested innocently that a teacher would probably get a tutor.

Sarah: And what would the tutor do for that person?

Bernice: Well, go over . . . probably do what you do. Make them read a story and they write down all the things and then a week later you would say "Now listen to this." They would say "Now does that sound right to you?" And they would say "No, it doesn't sound quite right." I would kind of make them try to figure it out. I think a tutor would take the time to let them discover for themselves.

Her comment, "a tutor would take the time to let them discover for themselves," is a powerful statement. Not only does it provide a rationale for RMA, but it also speaks to the empowerment of the reader. Students are in charge, discovering the reading process and their reading strategies.

When asked to discuss any changes in her reading since these RMA sessions, Bernice felt that she had improved as a reader.

Sarah: Have there been any changes in your reading during these RMA sessions?

Bernice: I've read more smoothly and I haven't read word-by-word-by-word and letter-by-letter.

Sarah: Anything else?

Bernice: How do I feel . . . You don't have to read word-for-word.

And, finally, when asked about how she felt about her ability to improve as a reader, Bernice stated confidently, "Oh, I'll read forever."

In answer to my question, "Would talking about reading on a conscious level confuse the reading process?," I think not. Rather than confuse Bernice, the sessions validated strategies that she had internalized intuitively. There is a tendency to think that because students are successful in reading they view reading from a holistic perspective. That was not the case for Bernice.

When Bernice's beliefs conflicted with the evidence revealed through analyzing her own miscues she didn't simply acquiesce. We had many long and intense discussions about whether it was permissible to substitute *a* for *the* in a sentence or if rereading a segment of text was a good strategy. Often she would hold fast to her contention that the miscue changed the text semantically. Bernice wasn't always ready to change her belief structures and found herself in a state of disequilibrium as she tried to connect what she believed with what she saw and heard on the tape recorder. I was impressed during the sessions when Bernice came up with comments from discussions we had engaged in months before to make her point. Bernice stated that she never really thought about what she was doing when she was reading. It appears she has done a lot of thinking about it since then. Perhaps there needs to be an incubation period during which these ideas can be thought about, assimilated, or thrown out, whichever the case may be.

In answer to my question, "What benefit does a proficient reader get out of participating in a RMA session?," it appears this reader became more confident in her reading abilities, beginning to question those around her. She focused on meaning and what made sense to her rather than trying to reproduce the text exactly, even to the point of questioning the author, as in the case of "Anita's Gift," suggesting maybe she knew a little bit more about Puerto Rico than the author did.

She seemed to be transferring the session experiences to the classroom setting, as evidenced by her admission that she had the courage to get up and read in class because, due to her predicting strategies, she didn't read like a robot.

I find it significant that all the RMA research mentions an increased level of self-confidence and self-assurance in the readers themselves. The same is true of Bernice. If nothing else, this experience led Bernice to a more realistic view of the reading process, one that allowed for trust and belief in herself as a reader.

After collecting this data I have answered some of my questions concerning the appropriateness of involving proficient students in RMA sessions. Successful readers do gain insights into their reading strategies.

A more subtle, but no less important, transformation occurs as well. Good readers who hold a text-reproduction model of the reading process can be intolerant and judgmental in their evaluation of others' reading abilities. Believing that accuracy is of paramount importance in reading, they are quick to correct their friends and siblings when reading aloud, rather than appreciating the process of self-correction and allowing that process to be used naturally. They revel in "giving words" when another reader hesitates, with no consideration for *why* the reader may *appear* to be hesitating. And they assume that readers whose "productions" are flawed must be flawed as learners. These unfortunate misconceptions serve only to reinforce the negative self-perceptions of readers who need to revalue.

RMA has the power to release all kinds of readers from the useless negativity associated with an obsession for accuracy, and can foster a climate of real collaboration among all readers in a community of learners. As a proficient reader Bernice was forced to explore reading in a totally new way—to find the reasons for her miscues, to begin to question the reading process itself, and to examine the strategies she incorporated into reading to make it a meaningful experience.

11

Revealing Strategies for a Good Reader

David W. Weatherill

WHY IS IT THAT OFTEN when a reader is asked the question at the end of reading a story, "How well do you think you read the story?" he will reply, "I don't think I read it very good." What has happened during the learning experiences presented to the child, both at school and probably at home, that brought about this feeling of limited success in reading? This chapter explores the reading of an eleven-year-old reader, Lucas, who is considered a good reader by school standards, but not by himself.

LUCAS, THE READER

In school Lucas was classed as an above average reader, but he did not consider himself a very good or avid reader. He did not like to "sit down and read" when he had nothing to do. However, when he decided to read, he would not put the book down until he had completed the "story." When I was working with him, the majority of Lucas's reading was from expository material. He read approximately one narrative story to about five expository pieces, usually written for children much older than Lucas. He was reading the texts of the *Dungeons and Dragons* games in order to plan his strategy to proceed through the different levels to become a Dungeon Master. These texts are written for ages from teenager to adult. But because the interest was there for Lucas, he struggled through the text.

Lucas realized that as he reads he is building background knowledge from which he can later draw. The more he reads and uses this information through planning and playing, the better he understands and interprets the complex set of rules, moves, and creatures required of the game. This is evidence that Lucas is a proficient reader, especially when he is highly interested in the material.

But why did Lucas, who had success in reading in various contexts, consider himself not to be a good and avid reader? In order to try to answer this question, Lucas was evaluated using three interrelated procedures. The first was from the *Reading Miscue Inventory* (RMI). At the conclusion of the RMI, the Reading Interview was administered (see Y. Goodman et al. 1987). The third procedure, retrospective miscue analysis, involved Lucas and me listening to his oral reading and discussing his miscues.

LUCAS AND HIS READING

Lucas read the story "Why The Parrot Repeats Man's Words" (Y. Goodman & Burke 1972b). His oral reading produced a large number of miscues, but his retelling showed that he understood the story. His comments during this retelling, plus the smile on his face when he came to certain aspects of the story, showed that he appreciated the author's humor.

The miscue analysis of Lucas's reading supports his retelling. He was comprehending successfully: 80 percent of his miscues resulted in semantic acceptability, and 91 percent were syntactically acceptable. What he had read not only sounded like language but also maintained the sense or meaning of the story. Lucas did not correct when he produced miscues that were syntactically and semantically acceptable in the story. When his predictions did not result in sensible structures, he self-corrected appropriately. These strategies are revealed by his high acceptability scores. The RMI scores were supported by his comprehensible retelling of the story. The graphophonic scores showed that he had attended to the text rather carefully—84 percent of his substitution miscues showed high graphic similarity, and 62 percent of his miscues had high sound similarity.

At the conclusion of his oral reading, Lucas listened to his reading, following a typescript of the story. I asked him to follow his reading carefully, and when he came to something in his reading that was different from the text or a miscue he thought he had made, he was to stop the tape. That section of the tape was then replayed and we had a discussion to explore why he may have made a particular miscue. Two conclusions emerged from the analysis of these discussions. Lucas revealed both intuitive and conscious knowledge about the nature of language and reading. In addition, he showed that proficient readers are not always aware of their acceptable miscues.

Knowledge of Language and the Reading Process

The following examples supply evidence of what Lucas was able to talk about concerning his reading. Each example provides insight into Lucas's understanding of language:

But just then the farmer's lorikeet spoke up.

The

My Master killed it.

Lucas: Stop! I read *The master* instead of *My master*.
David: Why did you read it that way?
Lucas: It could have been that it followed *the farmer's lorikeet spoke up*.
David: Does what you read make sense in the story?
Lucas: Yes, it does make sense, but not to fit in the story.
David: What do you mean?
Lucas: It makes sense, but not to fit in the story. It could fit in the story, but you would have to change a bit of it.
David: What would you change?
Lucas: Well . . . I don't know.

Lucas was obviously responding to the cohesive difference between *The master* and *My master* but was unable to articulate a reason for this feeling. Further questioning did not assist in finding out why, or what changes he would have to make in order for it to fit the story.

The people were convinced, (and) the judge

was convinced.

Lucas: I left out the *and*.
David: Why do you think you left out the *and*?
Lucas: I said, *the people were convinced, the judge was convinced*.

David: The *and* is missing, why do you think you did it?
Lucas: Because there is a comma there. I never put commas when I am going to put *and* in.

Here Lucas shares a rule he knows about commas and conjunctions in order to explain his miscue.

Man learned of the arrival of the talking

parrot, and the parrot was captured and

in
taken to man's house.
Λ

Lucas: I said *taken into* instead of *taken to.*
David: Why do you suppose you might have said that?
Lucas: *Into man's house* makes as much sense as *to man's house*—it sounds much better, I think.
David: Putting in *into* instead of *to.*
Lucas: Yes.
David: Why?
Lucas: I think you normally say *into a house* instead of *to a house.*

Here Lucas has used his knowledge about language to conclude that *into* is more acceptable in his normal language use.

Lucas did not stop the tape to identify many miscues when what he read was both semantically and syntactically acceptable, and when he produced no change in story meaning. It seems that even in this retrospective process, the reader still reads for meaning rather than for a word-for-word rendition of the text. The following examples support this view:

his
That night he took the bird from its cage

and placed it in a large brass pot.

Lucas substituted *his* for *its* in the text. The miscue is fully acceptable and does not create any change in meaning. He did not stop the tape at this point; therefore, we did not discuss it.

Consideration of Acceptable Miscues

The man began to beat(on)the pot, slowly at

first, then more loudly, until it sounded like

thunder.

Lucas omitted *on* without producing any change to the meaning of the story. He did not refer to this miscue during the retrospective session.

In the final section of this story, Lucas used a strategy mentioned earlier in this chapter. He omitted *and* a second time but did not stop the tape. This may lend credence to the notion that using preselected acceptable miscues selected by the teacher/researcher helps readers revalue themselves. This lends credence to the notion that preselecting miscues may be the only way to assure that readers have an opportunity to analyze high-quality miscues. And an appreciation for the strengths revealed in high-quality miscues is essential in helping readers revalue themselves.

"If you remember," the farmer said, "last night

was calm and clear, and the moon shone with all

its brightness."

Lucas did not stop the tape for miscues which he self-corrected. I was wondering why he did not stop for these corrected miscues when the following discussion occurred:

© *Then*

. . . This is my warning. When man learns

that you can speak his language, he will

capture you and bring you into his house.

Lucas: Stop! Oh, it's all right. I corrected it.
David: What do you mean by this?
Lucas: I have corrected it, so it is right. I do not have to look at it.

This episode suggests that Lucas thinks if he corrects a miscue, it is no longer necessary to analyze it. It is obvious that to Lucas, corrected miscues are not disruptive to meaning, and therefore not worthy of consideration. When we discount the good things we do as readers, we ignore strengths and have a tendency to search for aspects of reading that are problematic.

The discussion at the end of the session with Lucas suggested that not focusing on his strengths allows him to overemphasize the importance of the surface structure of the text.

David: How well do you think you read the story?
Lucas: I don't think I read it very good.
David: What makes you think that?
Lucas: It was just the many mistakes I made. I don't think I should have made as many as that when I am reading. For myself, I try hard not to make mistakes.
David: Were there some areas where you thought you were making a lot of mistakes?
Lucas: Yes.
David: Where do you think they were?

Lucas: Mainly towards the end.
David: How well do you think you understood the story?
Lucas: I thought that I understood it really well. I knew what was happening in the story.
David: If you felt you understood the story, why do you feel you made a lot of mistakes?
Lucas: I knew what the story was about when I finished it, but I think I made too many mistakes. Even the ones I went back to, I think I made too many of them.

Considerations for Lucas and Other Young Proficient Readers

Lucas's reading ability, as identified through miscue analysis and retrospective miscue analysis, shows him to be a proficient reader. His insights into the miscues he generated indicate what he believes about reading and the reading process. His comments about his miscues provide evidence that he has intuitive knowledge about how language works. Lucas's knowledge provides a good starting point to assist him in viewing the reading process as one where all readers produce miscues. Even some good readers like Lucas believe that miscues are the mark of not reading a story "very good." Lucas needs to understand that reading is a risk-taking process in which his own background knowledge and his ability to predict and self-correct selectively as he attempts to construct meaning all come into play during the reading process.

Retrospective miscue analysis allows the teacher to tap the understandings held by the reader before making a final judgment about the reader. Too often decisions regarding a reader are made from an instrument that supplies no data on what the reader knows, or why any "mistakes" were made. Making quick or unrealistic judgments may have an enormous impact on the reader. Lucas has shown that he feels he is not a good reader because he makes too many mistakes. Somewhere, someone has led him to believe that reading must be an exact rendition of the text, yet we know that learners are successful when programs are designed to build upon their language strengths and allow them to appreciate their own abilities. Retrospective miscue analysis can be an integral part of such a program.

Part III

INSTRUCTIONAL STRATEGIES FOR REVALUING

PARTS I AND II ARE THE WORK of teachers/researchers presenting the theory and research that underlie retrospective miscue analysis and that explain how and why RMA works in the way it does. In this section of the book, we turn to teachers' descriptions of RMA used in different instructional settings.

Chapter 12 begins with selections from the unpublished writings of Chris Worsnop, a reading specialist and district consultant who raised a question during a workshop Yetta Goodman was presenting on miscue analysis at a reading conference in the late 1970s in Toronto, Canada.

Chris: Have you ever used miscue analysis with students?

Yetta: No, I'm not sure that they would understand the linguistic and reading process concepts that are necessary to make use of miscue analysis.

Chris: Well, I've been using the RMI (Reading Miscue Inventory) with secondary school students and I am really impressed with the results. The most immediate response is that the students become more confident about themselves as readers. . . . The most amazing thing is that their attendence in their reading classes really improves. They do not want to miss any of the sessions.

Chris told Yetta that he was writing a report about his experiences and that he would send her his work. The RMA researchers in this book have used Chris's unpublished writings for many years for background information on using miscue analysis with readers. Chris helped us consider what happens when students build their own understandings about miscues and the reading process. In his manuscript Chris reports how he had rejected the "reading skills of sequential, bit-by-bit approach" to instruction because the students he was teaching had "for years . . . failed to learn to read despite repeated instruction and practice in what are referred to as the basic skills. The student is given a commercial test, which finds him lacking in these same skills and so the remedy is to give him more of the same, to compound the failure with another dose of it" (Worsnop 1977, 12).

Chris was influenced by the research of Peter Board, who concluded that disabled readers are disabled because they have trusted the instruction they were given. Board found that these readers were in trouble, not because they had failed to learn what the programs had to offer, but precisely because they had succeeded too well in learning what their programs had to offer (1982). Moreover, they had failed to learn the things that were not offered in their programs, but which most proficient readers manage to figure out and learn for themselves. Chris was also influenced by Frank Smith's and Ken Goodman's work on the reading process and became knowledgable about miscue analysis. Because he wanted to help the teachers and students with whom he worked build holistic views of reading through the power of miscue analysis, he decided to develop the RMI as a classroom tool. He began working to make the RMI easy to use, less time-consuming, and applicable in group situations. Over a three-year period, he organized various projects to see how RMI could be adapted to become a teaching tool. The first chapter in this section is based on Chris's projects.

We are grateful to Chris Worsnop for his insights and creative energy in response to the troubled readers with whom he worked. Without his application of what he was learning about miscue analysis and his willingness to share his insights and his unpublished reports with us, retrospective miscue analysis might never have seen the light of day. His work also provides ample evidence that classroom practice informs theory as much as theory informs practice. Each of the chapters in this section reinforces the basic construct of teacher as researcher.

**CHAPTER 12:
THE BEGINNINGS OF
RETROSPECTIVE
MISCUE ANALYSIS**

Chris Worsnop shares his foundational work involving junior and senior high school students in using principles from miscue analysis to analyze their own reading. He describes how classroom teachers and reading specialists were able to conduct sessions to support adolescent readers.

**CHAPTER 13:
READER-SELECTED
MISCUES**

Dorothy Watson and Sharon Hoge describe Reader-Selected Miscues, which is an alternative retrospective experience used to help students become consciously aware of their miscues as they read silently in the classroom.

**CHAPTER 14:
A TEACHER/
RESEARCHER USES
RMA**

The intertwining of teacher and researcher is expressed by Sarah Costello as she describes the instructional applications of retrospective miscue analysis in her middle school classroom.

**CHAPTER 15:
THE READING
DETECTIVE CLUB**

By involving elementary school-age readers in following clues like a detective, Debra Goodman represents another kind of self-study for readers. She talks about its use in her roles as classroom teacher and reading specialist.

**CHAPTER 16:
AT THE CRITICAL
MOMENT: RMA IN
CLASSROOMS**

Using anecdotes and insights from teachers in a range of school contexts, Yetta discusses additional instructional experiences related to retrospective miscue analysis for elementary classroom settings.

**CHAPTER 17:
REVALUING READERS
AND READING**

Yetta and Ann Marek synthesize the research findings and instructional applications described throughout the volume and present their conclusions about the potential of retrospective miscue analysis to transform the ways in which teachers and readers revalue language, readers, and the reading process.

12

The Beginnings of Retrospective Miscue Analysis

Chris Worsnop

WHEN I BEGAN MY WORK with miscue analysis in the 1970s, I was trying to work out a way of sharing the RMI technique with teachers. The reading I had done about the reading process, the sessions in which I observed others using the Reading Miscue Inventory (RMI), and the forms of the RMI that I used as a diagnostic tool, had, in the space of a couple of months, given me more insight and inspiration about the reading process and about teaching reading than had all my years of teaching before. My understandings came from listening to tapes of readers, marking their miscues, and considering how and why the miscues occurred.

As a consultant, I began to discuss my interest in the RMI and what I was beginning to understand with teachers. Teachers curious enough to attend workshops to learn more about the RMI gained understanding about the reading process, and their diagnostic skills improved. Nearly all of these teachers changed their attitudes as a result of their new insights. They became encouragers instead of correctors; they gave more emphasis to a focus on meaning construction in their reading instruction.

Conversations with teachers confirmed for me that the most valuable insights about reading came from listening to the recorded versions of the reading, marking the miscues on a typescript, and speculating on the nature of the miscues. I began to believe that if those students who were having the most difficulty in reading could have experiences similar to the teachers, perhaps they too could undergo positive change.

INVOLVING READERS IN MISCUE ANALYSIS

I started by recording the oral reading and retelling of a seventh-grade girl from a remedial class. Together, we listened to the tape of her reading and marked all the miscues. The student was fascinated; however, the task of analyzing the miscues on the RMI sheets did not engage her—the patterns did not emerge quickly enough and she was not impressed with percentage scores. I was encouraged, though, that a student's enthusiasm could be maintained up to the point of marking miscues on the script. I decided to modify my approach to incorporate a simplified form of miscue analysis with the marking of the script.

Working with other students individually, I followed RMI procedures, including the retelling. After the RMI procedure, we rewound the tape and listened to it immediately together. Whoever heard the miscue first stopped the tape recorder, and we listened again to the miscue until we agreed on what we heard. We would each mark the miscue on our separate scripts.

After each miscue had been marked, we went through a hierarchy of questions:

1. Does what the reader said mean the same as what is in the book?
2. Does what the reader said still make a good sentence?

3.   Does what the reader said look like what is in the book?
4.   Does what the reader said sound like what is in the book?

I used the questions in this strict order to impress students with the fact that semantic consistency is the most important consideration in reading, that syntactic acceptability is next most important, and so on. When analyzing a miscue using these questions, the objective was to get a "yes" answer as soon as possible. If students answered "yes" to the first question, they could skip the other three. If they got a "yes" to the second question, they could skip the last two. If they did not get a "yes" until the third or fourth question, I complimented them for making use of the graphic or sound cues, but then engaged them in discussion, suggesting that if they take risks in response to the graphophonic cues in order to achieve semantic and syntactic consistency, they would get a "yes" earlier in the hierarchy.

The results of this approach were very encouraging. The students showed interest and willingness, and quite easily answered the four questions. Question 2 caused a little trouble at first, but I eventually changed it to "Does what the reader said still sound like language?" and then the students handled it well.

I then wondered if students could work in pairs at this procedure and made arrangements to work with two seventh-grade boys. While one student read, the other took on a teacher's role. The miscue questioning became a three-handed game among the two students and myself, with no apparent decline of benefit to either student. On the contrary, they appeared to gain confidence from each other, and became more willing to take risks. When I checked with their regular classroom teacher, I found that he believed the boys were improving their reading. He also reported that both showed more general interest in school, had improved their attendance record, and were keeping out of trouble. After an initial feeling of elation, I settled down to one of mild optimism, attributing the positive results to the fact that it was now June, close to the end of the school year.

The next year, although I moved to a new job a good distance from my original location, I was eager to carry on my experiments with this modified RMI procedure. I began working with six high-school students who were in a Specific Learning Disability program. The teacher, Ms. Winter, was eager to work with me once I explained the project. I specified that I wanted to work with pairs of students who worked well together. In addition, the students should be having difficulty with reading, yet be motivated to read better. We scheduled sixty-minute periods to meet with each pair of students. I visited the school for half a day a week, and usually met with two or three pairs of students during each visit.

The presence of the teacher in all the sessions did much to overcome the initial misgivings of the students. During the first meeting with each pair I explained the procedure and its purpose, emphasizing that at the same time that they were benefiting from the experience, they would be helping me develop a technique to help other readers. I tried to keep the atmosphere relaxed and non-threatening. The students understood that they could opt out at any time. I asked each student to tell us what he or she believed about reading and to describe any specific difficulties with reading. I also presented some concepts that were going to be stressed, gave the students the four miscue analysis questions, and asked them to read them over and know them for the next session.

Typically, students' responses revealed they believed that reading is saying the words properly. I wanted to show them that reading was much more complex, and that they already had command of some very effective reading strategies for which they were not giving themselves credit. During initial meetings, I led the sessions and asked most of the questions. The students used this initial time to "read" the context of the program. They were "tuning in" to the assumptions and exhortations that they kept hearing from Ms. Winter and me.

READERS WORK TOGETHER USING MISCUE ANALYSIS

We would listen to a miscue and work through the four questions. When a student answered "yes" to the first question (concerned with meaning), I congratulated the reader with statements such as "you're going for meaning" and "you really know what reading is all about." When the first question got a "yes" answer, we usually skipped the other three questions. I would sometimes, however, explore them anyway. I wanted the students to realize that a "yes" to question 1 concerning meaning nearly always resulted in a "yes" to question 2 also. Sometimes we discovered that questions 3 and 4 yielded a "no" answer even with "yes" answers to the first two questions. Through our discussions, the students began to realize that the surface text information is there as a guide, but the meaning and grammar can be maintained without paying undue attention to the graphophonic cues.

Often we found miscues where the answer pattern was "no, no, yes, yes." In these cases, the students readily admitted that they could sound out the word after an attempt or two, but that they still did not understand it. This led the students to insights and realizations that underlined both the importance of meaning and the futility of hesitation. Students commented that they often understood a sentence if they kept reading and missed a word. Yet when they stopped to get the word, they missed the meaning of the sentence. Our role was to support risk-taking. When a student kept reading and omitted a word, we would, when examining that miscue, sometimes find that it made no difference at all to either the meaning or the syntax of the text. At other times, we found that such omissions made only very minimal differences. This was particularly true of function words. But even with content vocabulary items, the students soon learned that, in a long passage, the chances of seeing a troublesome word again in a different context was very high. One of the boys miscued on the word *exciting* five times and got it right the sixth time. The look of satisfaction on his face at that time was worth a great deal.

Our searches through the sentence or paragraph to find why the miscue took a particular form always yielded interesting results. We found that miscues occurred because the reader's eyes were already scanning ahead in anticipation. Frequently, we talked about the effects of the reader's familiarity with the topic of the passage, particularly the effects of previous experience on the different kinds of miscues.

At every opportunity we supported and praised the students. We made sincere, supportive statements such as: "smart miscue"; "high quality miscue"; "go for meaning"; "keep rolling"; "get to the end of the sentence—the end of the paragraph—the end of the chapter—the end of the book"; "take a chance"; "give it a try"; "yes, you can"; "I knew you could." At first these statements came from me or Ms. Winter, who after observing for a while began to take a more active role, similar to mine. Eventually, the students also offered encouragement to each other and occasionally students would volunteer a statement about their own miscues indicating pleasure: "That was smart of me, wasn't it?" When we could not honestly give praise, we discussed what caused the problem and explored intelligent ways to avoid it.

When we finished talking about the miscues, marking them on the typescript, and weighing their quality and importance, we ended up with a script heavily marked with pencil. Ms. Winter and I realized that a marked-up script could be very discouraging to students who are used to associating such marks with negative judgments. We decided to ask the students how well they thought they had read the passage. Nearly always the answer was "badly." We then followed this question by asking how well they had understood the passage. To substantiate the responses, we listened to the retelling and showed the readers how their retellings revealed their knowledge. These discussions allowed readers to reconsider their judgments, and they began to say that their comprehension was much better than they expected it to be.

We modified the procedures in response to the sessions. When a sixty-minute session did not allow enough time to listen to an entire tape, the students volunteered to put in extra time with their Specific Learning Disabilities teacher between my visits, to continue evaluating their miscues.

When it became evident that the four questions did not consider the issue of self-correction, we began asking of each miscue: Was it corrected? Why was it corrected or not corrected? Students immediately gained insights about how the semantic and syntactic cueing systems triggered corrections. Such insights, without exception, became a source of confidence for the students who previously believed that they were not making use of efficient reading techniques. Their corrections showed them that they were being too severe in their self-criticism. Overcorrections began to disappear.

We also made modifications to the retelling. We found that the second student was concentrating so much on listening for miscues as the first student was reading that he or she was not paying attention to meaning. So we gave the second student an opportunity to add to or argue with the reader's retelling. Giving the second student a role in adding to the retelling changed his or her stance in terms of attending to the meaning of the reading.

We acknowledged our respect for the students whom we had been underestimating. We "let them in" on our jargon, using appropriate terms such as *semantic cueing system*, *deep structure*, *miscue*, and *redundancy*.

As time went on, the sessions became more relaxed. The students were able to criticize each other and themselves without the attendant guilt evident earlier. Most of them became more cheerful and confident. During the sessions, they began to verbalize their belief that they might be able to "make it" in reading after all. Ms. Winter began to receive reports of improved work in school, improved class participation, improved relationships with teachers, fewer problems with homework and projects, and improved relationships in the home. One English teacher reported that she could scarcely believe that one girl in the program had volunteered to read aloud in class and then had read well! The students themselves were aware of their progress and attributed it to the program. Test marks and examination results showed improvements in every case. Our biggest problem was erratic attendance patterns.

RESPONSES FROM HIGH SCHOOL

After the school year was over, Ms. Winter and I analyzed the RMI data. The results of the analysis showed that all of the students handled progressively more difficult material while either maintaining or improving their miscue profiles when compared to those with which they had started. We also had a final session with the students, and excerpts from the transcript of these sessions provide interesting insights.

Brian: I just read the novel *Ice Station Zebra*, and I did quite well on the tests and I read it fast.

George: When I read a book now, I just read it, and then I understand it more than I did before. It seems as though at first I was reading and then if I was doing questions, I'd have to go back and read it over again to see what I was doing. Now I can read it and then I will mainly know what it's about and I don't have to really go over the questions again. . . . I thought that you had to know everything that was going on, like in a story every word meant something and that if you put all the words together then you get a story, because every word meant something. Now I feel that some of the words, they're just in there to help out the story and they don't mean anything and it's just that some words really mean something that bring out the story, like before every word meant everything.

Chris: I don't think I was ever trying to tell you that there were certain words that weren't important.

George: What I mean is, the words pull the story together, but there are main points that are more important than those words and I used to go over every word and try to figure out what every single word meant and sometimes it wouldn't even deal with the story, it had no meaning at all.

Graeme: I used to always read the words and I'd get stuck on one word and I'd figure it out for about five or ten minutes.

Chris: How did you figure it out?

Graeme: I just took it by vowels . . . . Now if I read the sentence and I understand the sentence, and a word doesn't mean all that much and I can't really figure it out, I just skip over it and just go on and it's going to make some sense.

Even Louise, who had dropped out of school to go to work, reported benefits from the program:

Louise: Before, I wouldn't even pick up a book.

Chris: What kind of material are you reading?

Louise: Novels. I wouldn't pick up a novel and now I just grab everything I can get my hands on. That's true I do. . . . I find it's not meant to be a chore to read, it's meant to be enjoyable, and instead of having to look at a TV or something like that, you can read a book, and it's much more fun to imagine things in your head than when it's right in front of you like that.

Ms. Winter shared with me other long-term changes in the students. The students that had participated in the program regularly seemed to have benefited greatly as evidenced by increasing grades and developing habits of leisure reading. The students who had erratic attendance had some early successes but later became discouraged about their reading abilities again.

After the project with Ms. Winter ended, I used the procedure with eight ninth-grade students in a special reading class. The whole class of eight was to be involved in every forty-minute session. Only one student read on a given day. All students were invited to add to the retelling and take part in the discussion of miscues. The reading teacher, Ms. Killian, had very limited background in RMI but was an observer and a participant as I conducted the sessions.

Although attendance was again a problem, five of the students had consistently good attendance and attendance at the sessions improved for the other three. No student's attendance became worse. I scheduled my visits more often than for the previous group, and the students knew when to expect my visits. Ms. Killian told me that some of the students showed up only for these reading sessions.

Because of the shorter time period, forty minutes as compared to sixty, we were not able to complete the taping of a reading and an analysis in the time period. We continued unfinished work on the next day. Within a two-week period, Ms. Killian became comfortable with the program and the success she observed in the students. She believed that the program was valuable and that she could operate it on her own. She decided to work with her other class on her own and continue working with me with the eight students. I consulted with her about both classes.

The class she was working with on her own had the same results as the one with which I was working. Our discussions led us to confirm my earlier conclusions about using RMI with students: *the significant difference is the improvement of the students' images about themselves as readers, and that reading improvement and self-confidence are interdependent, subject to setbacks as well as dramatic spurts forward.*

There were pitfalls during all of the projects. There were students who got into trouble in school and at home and fell back into patterns in which they did not value their own learning. For the most part this occurred with students who did not attend sessions regularly and did not participate consistently.

We decided to inform other teachers working with the same students about our objectives, procedures, and progress. In this way, the students received more consistent support throughout their school experiences.

As I concluded these projects, I was left with questions that need to be considered:

- What is the optimum and maximum number of students that can work together in a group using these retrospective miscue analysis procedures?
- What are the ages of students that benefit most from this program, and is there a lower age limit to consider?
- Can students make and analyze their own taped reading without a teacher and maintain the encouragement and support necessary to sustain their self image?

What the teachers I've worked with and I know is that the technique works because it encourages students not to give up on themselves. We discovered that some of the most useful phrases a teacher can use to help students build a positive view of themselves as readers are:

- Give it a try.
- Sure you can.
- I knew you could!

13

Reader-Selected Miscues

Dorothy Watson
Sharon Hoge

WHOLE LANGUAGE EDUCATORS WANT STUDENTS to be in control of their own learning. Such ownership happens naturally outside the classroom, but is sometimes ignored in the classroom. In this chapter, we share a learning strategy, Reader-Selected Miscues (RSM), that not only allows students control over the process of learning to read, but also helps teachers understand pupils' reading behaviors. Teachers can use such information to create appropriate reading strategy lessons that are immediately applicable.

To take control of their reading, students must move to the center of the learning process by becoming *informants*. Informants know that they can empower themselves as learners, inform their teachers, and ultimately inform reading instruction.

Teachers using the RSM strategy encourage students to *reflect* on what they are trying to do as readers, then *share* that information with their teachers and other students. Sharing leads to further reflection, all of which helps learners recognize their own contributions to the reading process and to understand that text and context influence their reading behavior. That process leads naturally to curricular decisions about how learners can improve their reading by building on their strengths while addressing their needs.

READER-SELECTED MISCUE PROCEDURE

One way to implement the RSM strategy is to allow at least thirty minutes for personal silent reading. Students are told that they will be exploring how reading works by examining places in the text that cause them problems. Before the reading period begins, students take several blank bookmarks (approximately two inches by eight inches). They read as they normally would except that when they have difficulty, they place a marker in their books at the trouble spot and continue reading. Ten minutes before the close of reading time, students examine their trouble spots and select three miscues that confused or distracted them and affected their overall understanding or enjoyment of the work. Each student writes a sentence containing a selected miscue on the marker, underlines it, writes his or her name on the marker, and returns all bookmarks to the teacher. Students who have encountered no problems continue reading, while the others can return to reading after handing in the bookmarks. As readers get more comfortable with RSM, they may jot down points in the text they want to discuss, even if they have not made a miscue.

RSM is a procedure that teachers and students can modify for their own comfort. For example, some students put stick-on notes directly on the text at the point of selected miscues. In that case, teachers don't collect the miscues, but discuss them immediately following the reading. Teachers who use bookmarks find that the markers make it easy to collect and classify miscues. Other teachers encourage students to record their miscues in logs; once or twice a week the miscues are classified and discussed. Teachers sometimes ask two or three students to classify the miscues collected by the class prior to discussion. Some teachers ask volunteers to write miscues, within the context of the sentence, on the board. Students who have similar miscues add theirs during discussions. It is also useful, for classification of miscues and future discussion, to write miscues on chart paper that may be referred to quickly.

The first step in the RSM strategy (inserting bookmarks at trouble spots and going on with the text) promotes several important attitudes in students about reading and about themselves as readers. First, the reader, not the teacher or another student, is in control of the process. No one is on hand to call attention to miscues or provide help. The reader and author are allowed their own conversation without interruptions from outsiders.

Second, through class sharing, students realize that everyone, even the most proficient reader, makes miscues. They begin to understand that the goal of reading is not performance perfection, but rather creating meaning.

Third, students have autonomy in selecting and rejecting what they read. For example, no one can tell students, despite real needs and strong motivation, that they must "discard a book if five errors are made on one page." The *readers* decide if the miscues cause loss of meaning or loss of interest, or if the miscues diminish their determination and reduce their staying power.

Fourth, readers become their own monitors; that is, the students become actively involved in the meaning-seeking process. Readers must constantly connect text information with the information in their own heads. They do this by making sure that whatever they read makes sense and that the language is acceptable to them.

Finally, students realize it is okay to keep reading in spite of miscues. The teacher asks students to continue the flow of reading; not to stop to get help from outside the text and outside themselves. They don't have to stop to ask a teacher how to pronounce a word or check a dictionary to find out what a word means. Students sometimes feel they are cheating if they continue reading not knowing every word or concept as they meet it on the page. The act of inserting a bookmark allows them to continue reading with the understanding that if needed they can come back to the trouble spot later.

In the next step of the RSM strategy, students examine their miscues and select three (or a number determined by the teacher and students) that caused the most trouble in terms of losing meaning and disrupting language flow.

At this point, students needn't count their miscues; rather, they learn from them. With the teacher's guidance, students figure out how some miscues may actually help with the construction of meaning, and that some other miscues can be ignored without losing any understanding of the text. That is, they learn that through continued reading, the word, phrase, or concept in question may become clear. This is not to say that all miscues are of high quality—some disrupt meaning. Students must learn to evaluate their reading and in the process become proficient readers.

EXAMPLES AND INFORMATION FROM READER-SELECTED MISCUES

Authors provide information to readers through inference, reference, substitution, ellipsis, example, and definition. Readers take the text and combine it with their own knowledge to create meaning. Readers and authors communicate through a mutual effort.

Seventh- and eighth-grade students provided the following examples in which unfamiliar words or phrases can be understood from information that follows or proceeds in the text. (The trouble spots are underlined once; related explanatory text is underlined twice.)

He's on this <u>café au lait</u> kick where he has to heat the <u>milk separately and then pour it simultaneously with the coffee into a mug</u>.

It's Not What You Expect (Klein 1973)

All that was visible of this alien Wisconsin were slivers of bright sky and fragments of green and gold fields, and just a twinkle, off to the left, of the <u>loch—lake</u>, she corrected herself wearily.

The Secret of Stonehouse

The <u>jodhpurs</u> were her dearest possessions, even though they had been handed down to her from a neighbor's cousin in Doddenkirk. They were a <u>soft black material, with black leather patches inside the knees</u>, and they had been handtailored in London.

The Secret of Stonehouse

"You <u>new</u> here, right? <u>Stranger</u> here? . . . A <u>haole</u>, dat's a <u>stranger</u>. <u>White like you</u>. <u>Not brown like me</u>."

Make No Sound (Corcoran 1977)

Where did they get their food, anyway? "It is <u>pauper's</u> share," his grandmother answered shortly. He wished he had not asked. He hated the picture of his grandmother following after the reapers in the field, <u>scrabbling for the sheaves they dropped</u>, which had by law to be left for <u>paupers</u> to gather.

The Bronze Bow (Speare 1961)

Romey said he knew where there was a big spread of <u>lamb's-quarters</u>, <u>which is a potherb, something like spinach</u>.

Where the Lilies Bloom (V. Cleaver & B. Cleaver 1970)

Readers discovered through discussion that it is not necessary to understand every word in the discourse; some omissions do not change text meaning. Extensive vocabularies may be desirable, but often readers have more to lose than gain by interrupting their reading in order to look up or ask about word meaning. (We might argue that this procedure isn't the way to enhance vocabulary, anyway.) By continuing to read, additional information can be constructed. At the close of the reading, students can decide if a missed word or concept needs attention. A junior high student reasoned that the following omissions were unimportant to the total meaning of his story. He chose to read on.

"I'm glad all animals can't speak," said Lightfinger, "we'd have <u>meningitis</u> within the week. . . ."

. . . and a sheet of <u>corrugated</u> iron covered the main doorway.

The <u>facade</u> of the building was painted over in gray. . . .

It was a typical Borrible hideaway, <u>derelict</u> and decaying. . . .

The Borribles (De Larrabeiti 1978)

Examining miscues qualitatively rather than counting errors informs rather than defeats readers. Through enlightened investigation, readers understand that they often change the author's message, not because they are lazy or careless readers (as they may have been told), but because something in their own personal background is momentarily influencing them. When students are relaxed about their reading, they enjoy sharing miscues that directly reveal their origins in the reader's immediate context (such as signs just read, snatches of recent conversations, or the subject of a movie just seen) or origins that are linked to pervasive or lingering forces in the reader's environment (such as concern with dating, current heroes, familiar expressions, brand names, lines from commercials, poetry and songs, getting a job, or making it through school). For example:

the Pips

King Arthur and his knights . . .

• • •

I scamburger

Jake pulled the rifle out of his scabbard.

● ● ●

A second later he was out again, carrying a roll

Scotch

of sticky tape.

● ● ●

tail

You haven't got the law on your trail, have you?

By studying their miscues, readers recognize that authors may unwittingly cause them problems. Unexpected syntax, conceptual overloading, and lack of text cohesion are set-ups for trouble. After using the RSM strategy on a regular basis, students began to share encounters with texts that cause them to change the author's syntax. Many students self-correct such miscues.

As readers grow confident in their understanding of the reading process they enjoy talking about miscues that, for example,

1) involve syntax:

The driver folds the seat in half ˄ a second.
I'll Get There, It Better Be Worth the Trip (Donovan 1969)

When, with hand reaching tremblingly over hand, he hauled it out, it knocked often against the walls of the well and spilled some of its contents.
"A Mystery of Heroism" (Crane 1963)

2) involve conceptual overload:

Few debutantes have been the recipients of such mass masculine interest upon their presentation. . . . This somewhat unusually large attendance at a rather usual miracle was due to the fact that, like any prima donna, she heralded her arrival and then kept her public waiting almost two weeks.
Karen (Killilea 1952)

3) involve shaky text cohesion:

. . .Or rushes in to pal with an example, when that's what the teacher points me out to be. Hardly anybody wants to hang out with a guy who keeps showing him up all the time.
Henry 3 (Krumgold 1967)

By looking into their miscues, readers begin to appreciate their own contributions to the reading act. They become aware of their correcting strategies including what prompts the correction, when it is necessary to correct, and when it is inefficient to do so. Readers' own strengths become obvious when they can make appropriate substitutions based on text information combined with their own knowledge. Students involved in the RSM strategy over time could easily express why they corrected the following miscues or why they accepted their own substitutions.

hang-up

. . . thought about names and the gaining of them, a major preoccupation

with him.

The Borribles (De Larrabeiti 1978)

Chance

But Donald was in a good mood now, and she didn't want to jeopardize

it.

The Secret of Stonehouse

A girl in the back laughed just a little too long. Mr. Rawling merely flicked

stopped

his eyes at her, and she subsided.

The Boy Who Could Make Himself Disappear (Platt 1968)

With practice, students can determine the difference between miscues that are so detrimental that meaning is distorted or slips away as opposed to miscues that do not cause any disruption to their conversation with the author.

From the wealth of available data directly provided by the students, the teacher classifies the miscues, finds persistent problems, and constructs strategy lessons that address problems while capitalizing on readers' strengths. Usually, teachers find that students first report difficulties with unknown names, foreign and unknown words, and dialect variations.

Unfamiliar names:

In the distance Kiser Please, high on his tractor, was creating clouds of furious, black dust.
Where the Lilies Bloom (V. Cleaver & B. Cleaver 1970)

. . .Frederick Douglass said that spring, in Rochester's Corinthian Hall . . .
Sojourner Truth, a Self-made Woman (Ortiz 1974)

And off in the distance were the volcanoes. Farthest off, with snow on top of it, was Mauna Kea. . . . Nearer were Mauna Loa and Kilauea. . . .
Make No Sound (Corcoran 1977)

At the end of the display, someone started to sing the Marsellaise, then someone else joined in. . . .
When Hitler Stole Pink Rabbit (Kerr 1972)

Foreign and unknown words:

> "The Mayor of Paris has decided to award prizes for the twenty best French compositions written by children taking the <u>certificat d'etudes</u>," she explained. "It seems that you have been awarded one of them."
>
> *When Hitler Stole Pink Rabbit* (Kerr 1972)

> She laughed and ran down into the yard and hid herself behind a flowering <u>rhododendron</u> and peered out at us through its white, lacy veil.
>
> *Where the Lilies Bloom* (V. Cleaver & B. Cleaver 1970)

> Oliver was making smoked oyster sandwiches on <u>Kommisbrot</u> with Boston lettuce.
>
> *It's Not What You Expect* (Klein 1973)

Unfamiliar dialect and eye dialect:

> Thieves they are, just like us, only they call it finding. <u>A copper</u> would call it stealing by finding.
>
> *The Borribles* (De Larrabeiti 1978)

> "Lord have mercy, look at him. He's <u>sicker'n</u> a dog. He don't even know we're here, he's that sick."
>
> *Where the Lilies Bloom* (V. Cleaver & B. Cleaver 1970)

> "<u>Chillun</u>, I talks to God, and God talks to me."
>
> *Sojourner Truth, a Self-made Woman* (Ortiz 1969)

> "<u>Aye, go it, lass</u>," Heather sang.
>
> *The Secret of Stonehouse*

> "I <u>spik</u> you later. Now I <u>spik dis lil malihini</u>. . . . What your name? . . . <u>Bruddahs</u>? Two <u>mo' Baxters</u>, yeah? . . . We be back <u>bumbye</u>."
>
> *Make No Sound* (Corcoran 1977)

> Like as not we'd be <u>pizened</u> from all that reddenin' on her fingernails.
>
> *Me and Jim Luke* (Branscum 1971)

Unfamiliar use of familiar words:

> Aunt Imie was fat with really tiny legs, like a bird, and she <u>dipped</u> snuff and gossiped a lot.
>
> *Me and Jim Luke* (Branscum 1971)

> Johnny regarded a tea brewed of fennel leaves as a <u>specific</u> against what the settlers called "fever and ague."
>
> "Johnny Appleseed and Aunt Mattie"

READER-SELECTED MISCUES BEYOND THE WORD LEVEL

After extended use of the RSM strategy, students often talk about monitoring their own comprehension beyond the word level; they share miscues involving larger linguistic units like phrases and clauses. The following trouble spots involve an analogy and an idiom.

> Collins jerked out his arm and canteen with the same motion that a man would use in <u>withdrawing his head from a furnace</u>.
>
> "A Mystery of Heroism" (Crane 1963)
>
> Then there was a man <u>who left town under a cloud</u>.
>
> "My Secret World"

As readers become more sophisticated in their use of the RSM strategy, they share miscues that involve "interrupters" within sentences:

> Earth is too big, and <u>too many uncontrollable (and often invisible or unnoticed)</u> forces are at work to make such study possible.
>
> "Can Earth Survive?" (*Newsweek* 1981)

Readers who have continued experience with RSM often report problems with the relationship between a sentence or phrase and the surrounding text:

> He glanced to the side, at his father. As if they were schoolboys in the principal's office. <u>Alex thought darkness might be made light on a secret smile</u>. His father sat looking ahead. Alex knew his father had seen him on the periphery of his vision and for the moment he felt lost.
>
> "The Car Thief"
>
> Once a year, or maybe twice if there's a wedding among his kinfolks, he may spruce up; but generally fancy clothes do nothing but <u>adorn the wall of the big room and feed the moths</u>.
>
> (Source unknown)

The RSM activity involves discussion among students who have similar reading problems. When the readers who made the miscues above discussed their selections, they were first of all surprised to discover that their problems were common ones shared by other readers. During early use of the strategy, students talked about spending a great deal of time trying to determine the pronunciation of words and names. After the teacher helped them with naming strategy lessons (Y. Goodman et al., in press), the students decided that it was better to substitute a nickname, a nonword, a letter, or a synonym for the unknown name or word and to continue their reading. If the word were foreign, they felt it important to know this, but it was not necessary to be able to pronounce it. The following examples helped the readers understand the naming strategy:

STRATEGY LESSONS

Val

It is called the Valkyrie.

B-70 Monarch of the Skies

But to continue my story, you see I've not finished yet, when we arrived

Pren

at the Prenungracht.

The Diary of Anne Frank (Frank 1956)

Man   *Rich*   *Sil*

Manfred von Richtoven was born in Silesia.

Flying Aces of World War I (Gurney 1965)

L

Lavenia, get on with your spinning.

The American Book of Horse Stories

The students concluded that if they continued their reading, they could make their own decisions about whether or not they needed or wanted to learn to pronounce a particular name or word. For example, Tim, whose hobby was marine life, felt it important to be able to pronounce *Cyanea Capillata* in the sentence, "The largest of the jellyfish is Cyanea Capillata." Other students agreed that because of his interests Tim would enjoy researching the Cyanea Capillata—including learning how to pronounce the name, but for them it held no appeal and their time would be better spent in other ways.

Dialect mismatches caused readers problems until they saw that they could translate from the author's to their own preferred expressions, all without loss of meaning. Readers shared the following dialect preference substitutions.

there

"I forget my sack. I left it back yonder."

Where the Lilies Bloom (V. Cleaver & B. Cleaver 1970)

among

. . . there are good technicians amongst them. . . .

The Deserters

Way

"Clear up in the foothills? That's a fair way, all right."

Tuck Everlasting (Babbitt 1975)

started

. . . I took a basket and some knives and lit out for the Trail Creek.

Where the Lilies Bloom (V. Cleaver & B. Cleaver 1970)

IMPLICATIONS

The RSM strategy gives students the chance to gain control of their reading in a supportive instructional environment. Readers can choose materials that appeal to them and can then evaluate their own process. Conventional reading programs require students to master the smallest units of language before progressing to the next unit. Many materials, in conventional programs designed for less proficient readers, are based on the idea that vocabulary should be controlled. The RSM strategy dispels these and other nonproductive notions about reading, learning, and teaching. Through RSM, readers are invited to select materials they have interest in and are helped with units of language (words, sentences, total text, ideas) as the reader selects them for study. Vocabulary and related concepts are learned within authentic context that is of interest to the reader.

The RSM procedure provides learners with a continuous accounting of their reading process and strategy use while giving the teacher information about each reader's strengths and needs as well as information about particular texts. The use of RSM can help ensure that the reader is at the heart of the program, that the instruction is personalized and authentic, and that individual readers have the opportunity of sharing and learning within a supportive community.

14

A Teacher/Researcher Uses RMA

Sarah Costello

Reading is like a puzzle. The more you read the more pieces of a puzzle you have. If a miscue makes it easier for a reader to read a book, then it is a good miscue.

—Kirb, a seventh-grader

KIRB'S COMMENT documents a shift in his understanding about the reading process after participation in many collaborative retrospective miscue analysis (CRMA) sessions. His is a powerful statement that answers many questions I initially had before I became involved in researching RMA as an instructional strategy in my seventh-grade classroom. In this chapter I describe how retrospective miscue analysis (RMA) sessions evolved as an instructional strategy in my classroom. It encapsulates seven years of action research, involving experimentation, evaluation, and reflection, culminating in my development of collaborative retrospective miscue analysis.

Previous to my middle school experience, I taught in an elementary school, implementing a progressive whole language program in kindergarten through third grade. I had a strong theoretical background in the reading process and was familiar with the procedures of miscue analysis. I was comfortable working with emergent readers. The students felt good about themselves as readers. Reading was fun!

Then I was transferred to a junior high school, where teaching was a totally different experience. Students struggled with reading. They believed they were poor readers. When I took the students to the library I found their book selection strategies limited to counting the number of pages in the book before checking it out. I was frustrated and concerned. How could I help these students realize their full potential as readers?

I began to discover some interesting things. I was under the impression that I was teaching a typical reading class and that students were grouped heterogeneously. It was not until later, through casual conversation with another teacher, that I learned some of my classes were the remedial reading classes. I assumed that the "R" next to the course number signified the course title, Reading. In fact, "R" stood for remedial. The school system placed all the low proficiency readers into the same class. The students viewed themselves as poor readers and the school reinforced this view by their scheduling procedures.

Miscue analysis provides valuable diagnostic information, but with five classes of 35 students it was impractical to do a miscue analysis on every student. How could I put my theoretical understandings of the reading process to practical use? I wondered if understanding the reading process would help the students become more proficient readers. And if so, how could I share this information in a meaningful way?

About that same time retrospective miscue analysis as an instructional strategy

(RMA) emerged as a topic of discussion in one of my university classes. We discussed the work of Ann Marek (1987) and Chris Worsnop (1977). RMA was significant because it suggested that understanding one's own reading strategies helped students revalue themselves as readers.

I was intrigued. Having readers discuss their miscues retrospectively seemed like a fascinating way to incorporate information about the reading process, and to highlight successful reading strategies. Students would have an opportunity to observe themselves and others while engaged in the reading process.

I had many questions about the use of RMA in my classroom. I wondered what impact talking about miscues would have on my students' attitudes toward reading. I wondered if talking about reading miscues in a collaborative group of their peers would help students evaluate their own reading strategies in a positive way. Would understanding the reading process help the students become more efficient, effective readers? Could seventh graders understand the concepts involved in the reading process, the cueing systems, and the strategies? I decided to implement RMA groups in my classes and see what benefits the students gained from participation in these groups.

EARLY CLASSROOM RESEARCH

The purpose of the RMA groups was to help students develop an understanding of the reading process and to give them an opportunity to see their strengths in reading. Initially I had to determine what structure would work within the rotating schedule. Then I had to decide what the students had to know to function effectively in the RMA groups. Finally I had to figure out how to convey that information to the students in a meaningful way

During the first week, classroom instruction concentrated on fifteen-minute discussions about concepts related to miscues and reading. I explored three concepts before we started the RMA groups. First I introduced the concept of miscues. I explained that we did not call unexpected responses "mistakes" because often the word "mistake" has a negative connotation. I wanted to dispel the notion that miscues were simply random occurrences. We talked about the fact that when people read they do not produce an exact reproduction of the text. Miscues provide valuable information about what the reader is doing when reading. Second, I wanted my students to understand that all readers miscue. The students were non-believers, as most people are when they first learn about the concept of miscues. Believing is in the hearing! Third, I introduced the concepts of predicting and confirming strategies related to the syntactic, semantic, and graphophonic cueing systems. I decided to use the same vocabulary that is used in miscue analysis. My students had experienced low level classes and lacked self-confidence in themselves as readers. I wanted to interact with them as intelligent, thinking young adults. I decided, therefore, to introduce the concepts using those words and define them in the context of our miscue discussions. I found that students had no problems understanding and using the vocabulary in class discussion or in the RMA groups.

I formed five heterogeneous groups, each containing six students. The RMA sessions were conducted at the beginning of each class while the rest of the students were engaged in Sustained Silent Reading. I participated in the RMA session, listening to the dialogue and asking questions related to the miscues. In that way I could facilitate the discussion of the miscues and help with any procedural problems.

The groups operated on a rotating basis. Usually it took two or three days for a group to complete an RMA session. On the first day a student would read a complete text, followed by a retelling, into a tape recorder. When the reader finished, a volunteer would rewind the tape. The reader would then get a typescript copy of the reading on which to mark miscues (I prepared these in advance).

Protocol For Miscue Discussion

Text/Misc.	Semantic	Syntactic	Graphophonic	Self-Correct Need?
She /Judy	yes	yes	No	No / No
foot / front	yes	yes	yes	No / No

1. Did the miscue make sense? (Semantic)

2. Did the miscue sound like language? (Syntactic)

3. Did the miscue look like what was in the text? (Graphophonic)

4. Did the reader self-correct? (Self-correct)

5. Did the reader need to self-correct? (Need?)

What is the reader's strength? _____

Figure 14-1

Everyone would listen to the taped reading and follow along on the typescript. When anyone in the group heard a miscue they would tell the student in charge to stop the tape. The student would rewind the tape and all would listen again for the miscue. After discussion and reaching consensus, the students marked the miscue on the typescript in the same way I marked miscues and filled in a protocol sheet I developed for this purpose (Figure 14-1). They would write the language from the original text and the miscue in the "text/miscue" column, and then answer questions related to the miscues. The students marked *yes* or *no* as they discussed each question. At the end they listed the reader's strengths based on the miscue.

It was my role to help the students focus on their strengths. By having students write down readers' strengths, the readers left the session knowing they had strengths in reading. Often, for the less proficient readers, their strengths were related to knowledge about the graphophonic cueing system.

The questions related to self-correcting strategies stimulated rich discussions. Asking whether the reader self-corrected and considering whether the reader should have self-corrected kept the focus of the discussion on the meaning of the miscue. They would explore whether the miscue changed the meaning of the text. Often the proficient readers would make substitution miscues that revealed their predicting strategies. This focused the group's discussion on how readers construct meaning. The discussions following the miscue examples demonstrate this point.

my class
"I do not allow crying in the classroom,"

said Mrs. Gorf.

Terry: Yes it does. It makes sense because *class* and *classroom* are the same thing.
Carolyn: Do you think you should have changed it?

Terry: No. It helped because it's the same thing.
Kirb: 'Cause you are predictable.
Terry: 'Cause I saw *class* and I didn't see *room* and I just read fast.

After the session, the protocol sheets were turned into me, and I noted additional information about the miscues the reader made. This gave me an indication about what strategies the reader was relying on when reading. I kept the protocol sheets in a permanent folder with other information I kept about the students' reading strategies. For example, I had notations of miscues on an index card collected during informal miscue analysis on the students as they read orally to me during reading conferences. By collecting these miscues, I could share a successful reading strategy with the reader or comment on an interesting miscue that I observed.

Reading material was selected from Scholastic *Scope* magazines and short stories from old basal readers. Materials that were most effective were short, interesting, relevant, and complete pieces that students could read in ten to fifteen minutes. Initially selection of material took some time, but once I had a range of reading materials, I just kept adding to my resources, always looking for new and appropriate materials that students could read independently.

The RMA sessions laid the foundation for all the work we did in reading that year. The concept of miscues and our understanding of the reading process permeated the classroom. We became comfortable when we heard miscues that the students or I made when reading from the board or overhead projector, and we could laugh about them. Classroom etiquette developed that would not allow students to interrupt each other when reading. Students had to be given the chance to use their own self-correcting strategies. We compared these responses to telling someone the answer to a riddle before they had the chance to figure it out for themselves.

Other reading experiences occurred during the year that were supported by what we were learning in the RMA groups. We read books and discussed them in ways that demonstrated our understanding of those books. We had Book Society on Fridays, during which we sat in groups, drank tea, and talked about the books we were reading.

The RMA groups worked very well that year. Readers were selected on a volunteer basis: no student was forced to read. For the most part, students weren't shy or embarrassed about reading. However, one student did negotiate a time to complete his RMA session with me individually because he did not want to read in the group. He still participated in the other RMA sessions and had the opportunity to observe others reading. The students were very businesslike when they got their materials and assembled their groups, and they seemed to love working in small groups.

At the end of the year, I asked the students to evaluate the RMA groups and state what they had learned. Three significant points emerged from their responses. Students said that they had learned it was "okay" to miscue. Many students commented that they found out "everybody miscues." Finally, they discovered that certain peers, peers they defined as "good readers," made miscues. Their written responses included comments such as, "I was surprised that Lisa miscues" or, "I didn't know that Gabriel miscued when he read."

The myth that good readers produce an exact rendition of the text was dispelled by actual observation. Students began to revalue themselves as readers. Through observation of themselves and their peers they began to recognize reading as something more complex than sounding out letters on the page. Observing other students reading helped them to develop a more realistic view of the reading process. Would understanding the reading process help them become more efficient, effective readers? I was convinced that the use of RMA sessions in the classroom as an instructional strategy was worth further investigation.

The following year positive changes occurred at the school. The middle school philosophy was adopted by the district. This meant that tracking procedures were eliminated and students were organized into teams. Teams provided a support base for the students, and they had fewer teachers to interact with on a daily basis. Teachers were expected to collaborate with other teachers on the team, planning themes and creating consistent discipline policies. More attention was given to preparing the students for the transition from elementary to middle school and from middle to high school. I was given a two-hour block of time for teaching reading and language arts, and I continued my RMA work with the new principal's support.

I strengthened and improved the organizational structure of the RMA groups. At the end of each session a student would volunteer to read during the next session. In this way, I was able to prepare appropriate readings ahead of time. Each group had a basket with all the necessary materials. There was a chairperson in charge of each group who knew when each group was supposed to participate in the RMA sessions. It was the chairperson's responsibility to 1) set up the tape; 2) assemble the students; 3) hand out the readings; and 4) get the group started on the RMA procedures in the workroom located in the back of the classroom. Each group had a blank tape with the students' names listed on it in the basket.

I expanded my whole class lessons about the reading process to include various examples of miscues, especially those used by efficient readers and their different, effective reading strategies. I collected the protocol sheets which listed the miscues for each reader to determine his or her specific strengths. That year the students did not mark the typescript because I decided it detracted from the focus of the sessions. I wanted the focus to be on the reading and the dialogue about miscues and strategies, and not on marking the typescript correctly. I originally intended to sit in on the whole RMA session, but classroom dynamics were such that I often had to leave the group, so that for the most part they worked on their own.

During that year my principal videotaped each teacher for evaluation purposes, and later provided the tape for us to view on our own. She chose to videotape a segment of the RMA group discussion in the workroom and the tape reveals students engaged in a fascinating discussion about reading—on their own. The students were involved in discussing a substitution miscue, *the* for *a*, as follows:

Anna: Doesn't *the* mean one thing? *A* means anything, not a particular thing.
Tony: It's not that big a deal.
Carlos: But it still means the same thing.

In this discussion about the reader's substitution miscue, the focus of discussion is on constructing a meaningful text. The discussion opened up a range of possibilities for miscue discussion: for interpreting the text; for understanding the reading process; and for considering linguistic questions. This event signaled a pivotal point in my understanding of the RMA sessions. I began to recognize the importance of the discussion about miscues that was going on among students. Initially I wanted readers to understand the reading process and observe each other while they were actually reading. My purpose for the RMA groups slowly changed as I realized the power of the conversation. The questioning, the debating, and the support were all valuable parts of the RMA sessions.

At this point a new question emerged as I began to wonder about the impact of RMA sessions on successful readers. I knew the less proficient readers were making many important discoveries about their own reading strategies and the strategies of proficient readers. They had a chance to listen to proficient readers and observe their successful reading strategies. RMA sessions improved their self-esteem, as evidenced by their increased self-confidence. For example, students who never before volunteered to read aloud in class now raised their hands to read. These students began to question an author's choice of words and recognized their ability to manipulate the text because their miscues "made it sound better." But what benefits were the proficient readers gaining from the RMA sessions? Or would discussing miscues disrupt the reading process for them?

DEVELOPING CLASSROOM RESEARCH

I had the opportunity to be involved in an RMA research project led by Yetta Goodman and Ann Marek (see Chapter 7) in which proficient and non-proficient seventh-grade readers participated. Yetta and Ann selected students from my classes because they knew I was discussing miscue analysis and the reading process with my students. I decided this would be a excellent opportunity to explore the influence of RMA on proficient readers. First I will discuss my classroom instruction, which was informed by my action research. Then I will discuss my findings concerning proficient readers (see indepth discussion of Bernice, Chapter 10). This information comes from observation, notes, and videos the research team collected about the lessons I conducted in class.

Classroom Instruction

Before we began the RMA miscue sessions, I organized lessons for the whole class similar to those I developed for previous classes, including:

- Lesson 1: Process of learning
- Lesson 2: Reading the world
- Lesson 3: Interpreting the world; perceptions about reading
- Lesson 4: Miscues; strategies readers use
- Lesson 5: Cueing systems readers use to construct meaning
- Lesson 6: Qualities of miscues
- Lesson 7: Volunteer student produces a taped reading in class.

During the first lesson we brainstormed and discussed three prerequisites for learning to occur:

1. Students must want to learn.
2. Students must be in an environment where they can safely take risks and make mistakes.
3. Students must be in an environment where they have many opportunities to practice.

The students realized these prerequisites were related to anything they want to learn: riding a bike, riding a skateboard, or learning a new dance.

The second lesson involved the students logging all the reading they did in one day, including after school, at home, and in school. (See Figure 14-2.) They brought their charts to class the next day and we discussed the amount of reading they did in any given day and the function reading served for them. This often led to new questions and interesting discussions. Is math reading? Do words on commercials count as reading? This activity helped students see how much they read and to expand their definition of reading.

The next lesson focused on the students' interpretations of the world. We discussed how people with different experiences perceive the same thing in different ways by examining some perception activities on an overhead projection. For example, I used a popular picture which can be seen as an old woman or a young woman, depending upon which figure a person perceives first. Another picture I use is one which may be perceived as a vase, or as profiles of two faces. These activities always get the discussion off to a great start. One person's perception is not better than another's, they are just different.

Material	Informational	Environmental	Recreational
Science book	X		
Stop sign		X	
Seventeen Mag.	X		X
Commercial TV	X	X	X

Figure 14-2

Riddles are effective tools for discussing multiple interpretations because the author expects a reader will think one way and then provides a twist for the purpose of surprise. Following are two examples of the riddles I use.

1. Some months have thirty days; some have thirty-one. How many have twenty-eight? (All of them.)
2. You are lost in the woods. You are freezing and you find a cabin. You have only one match and you enter the cabin and see a kerosene lamp, an oil heater, and a wood burning stove. Which would you light first? (The match.)

Authors have agendas too. This is a wonderful way to discuss the role of the author in creating miscues. Nancie Atwell, in her book *In the Middle* (1987, 217), includes an excellent discussion and list of riddles she uses in her class which help students begin to look at the reading process from a different perspective.

Toward the end of the discussion I present another perception activity to facilitate discussion about what effective and efficient readers do when reading (Figure 14-3). Students read the phrases. The proficient readers usually don't re-member reading the second *the* or *a*. This leads into a wonderful discussion about predicting and confirming strategies. "What is reading all about?" the students ask. Together we discover that reading is about creating a meaningful text, not reading every word exactly as it is in the text. If reading is simply sounding out words on a page, as the students so often suggest, why don't readers see the inserted word? Finally, we talk about how efficient, effective readers sample, predict, and confirm when creating a meaningful text.

In the fourth lesson, we discuss strategies used by readers. This discussion centers around the concept that miscues are influenced by what readers expect to see, relating this to the previous lesson on perception. In addition, I present exam-

```
PARIS
IN THE
THE SPRING
```

```
ONCE
IN A
A LIFETIME
```

Figure 14-3

ples to demonstrate how we all use predicting, sampling, confirming, and self-correcting strategies. For example, we predict what a book will be about when we look at the cover. We predict words that we expect to see in a story.

After that discussion we brainstorm the strategies students use when they come to a word they don't know. The following is a sample of the items students generally list:

1. Sounding out the word
2. Skipping the word
3. Asking someone
4. Looking it up in the dictionary
5. Stop reading.

The fifth lesson focuses on the following cueing systems that readers use to construct a meaningful text:

* Semantic: Making meaning
* Syntactic: How language works
* Graphophonic: Sound/graphic relationships
* Pragmatic: Information about the world

I define the cueing systems and explain that students intuitively know and use this information because they are proficient users of language. We discuss the fact that they would never say: "Jack ran up the have," or "Give me the put." By generating many examples like these, we discuss how much the students already know about language.

The next lesson focuses on the quality of miscues readers create. We discuss the miscues and analyze them in relation to the cueing system while each student responds to their protocol sheet. An example includes:

                                 Judy
"I'm really bored," said Julie, "Why don't

we go out and play?"

Students consider:

1. Did what the reader said mean the same thing as what was in the text?
2. Did what the reader said sound like language?
3. Did what the reader said look or sound like what was in the text?

During the final lesson, the whole class discussed the procedures of the RMA sessions so that they would know what was expected in the RMA groups. A volunteer student read a story into the tape recorder with the whole class following along on the typescript. We then discussed the miscues. This became a tedious process because it was difficult for all the students to hear the tape recorder. The reader became defensive trying to justify his miscues to the whole class. The more work I did with RMA the more convinced I became that small group settings were the most effective way to conduct RMA in the classroom.

**Individualized RMA
Sessions**

As part of the NCTE seventh-grade study, I conducted individualized RMA sessions with four proficient readers to determine what impact RMA had on successful readers, wondering whether discussing miscues with proficient readers would disrupt the reading process for them. Using session organizers (see Appendix B), miscues were organized to focus on specific strategies that the reader was using. As we looked at miscues and discussed possible reasons why the reader made them, we were able to identify strategies the reader was using.

The readers I worked with were identified by their teacher, their school test records, and their peers as good readers (see Chapter 7). In the context of our RMA sessions I discovered these students had as unrealistic a view of the reading process as did the less proficient readers. Frequently there were contradictions between what they said about their reading and what they actually did when reading. When confronted with these discrepancies they blamed themselves. All the proficient readers gained insights from the RMA sessions. Kelly is an example of a reader who revalued herself over time.

Kelly exhibited good strategies when reading, and her miscues provide evidence of her reading proficiency. Following are two miscues she produced while reading "Western Gladiators":

⊘calf [laughs]
The cave never had . . .

• • •

certain
. . . by special cells . . .

Kelly laughed when she substituted *calf* for *cave*, revealing her self-monitoring strategy as she reads and strives to make sense out of the text. As Kelly explained, "I laughed because it sounded funny . . . then I corrected it because it didn't make sense." Kelly's substitution of *certain* for *special* reflects her proficient use of predicting strategies. This is an excellent example of a miscue that shows her appropriate use of the syntactic and semantic cueing systems. When Kelly was asked about that miscue the following discussion occurred:

Sarah: What was your miscue?
Kelly: *Certain* for *special*.
Sarah: Do they look alike?
Kelly: No.
Sarah: Why do you think you made that miscue?
Kelly: Maybe it sounds better.
Sarah: Did you self-correct?
Kelly: No.
Sarah: Why not?
Kelly: Because that makes sense.

After involvement in the RMA sessions Kelly showed more confidence in herself as a reader, saying, "Maybe it sounds better." Kelly discovered interesting things about herself as a reader. As she listened to herself on tape she was fascinated with the things she heard. After four RMA sessions during which Kelly listened to the tapes and discovered she inserted and omitted words, she commented "I know it's okay to do that, but I just never knew that I did that when I was reading." As their RMA sessions continued, the proficient readers I worked with challenged the author, the text, and even me in defending their answers. They were empowered by their understandings.

I decided my next step was to document what happened in the collaborative sessions, and my doctoral dissertation topic emerged.

COLLABORATIVE RETROSPECTIVE MISCUE ANALYSIS (CRMA)

The purpose of my dissertation research was to document what happens when students with a range of proficiencies work together in a small collaborative group and talk about reading miscues. I wondered whether shifts in understanding and perceptions about reading occur without a teacher continuously present to facilitate the discussion. As a classroom teacher I found it difficult to sit in on collaborative retrospective miscue analysis (CRMA) sessions for more than fifteen minutes because other classroom responsibilities interrupted my participation. I wanted to know if CRMA sessions could still be productive if the teacher joined the group only during the last ten minutes of the discussion.

I decided that four students was an optimum group size to allow opportunities for all students to contribute. From past experience, I knew that in groups of five or six, the voices of the less outgoing students are often lost.

Students were interviewed to assess their perceptions about reading. I presented strategy lessons about miscues and reading strategies following the lesson plans I discussed above, and students then worked in CRMA groups. Each student read a text and participated in a CRMA session on the text they read. Groups met twice a week during class for a fifty-minute period. One day the students would do a reading and then begin the CRMA, which they completed the following day.

I analyzed the students' responses during the semester for shifts in perceptions in the following areas: the reading process, reading miscues, and reading strategies. There were significant shifts in understanding and perceptions about reading as well as changes in the use of reading strategies for all the students involved.

CRMA groups created a successful environment in which the students could discuss reading and the reading process. The students were comfortable in the groups because, as they reported, they "weren't so nervous," and they were "with their equals." In an environment where students practice, take risks, and make miscues, learning occurs on many different levels. A transformation in students' thinking and reading proficiency occurs as students transact with the text, gain new understandings about themselves as readers, incorporate new information about the world, and learn to function successfully in a collaborative group.

It is significant that major shifts in the understanding of miscues and the reading process emerged for each student as they were discussing their own reading and their own miscues. All students discovered aspects of their own reading strategies, some that were effective and some that weren't so effective. José recognized that "trying to read perfect" made him miscue more. Terry recognized that she miscued because she "was expecting to hear that (the miscue)" in the text. Carolyn commented that she miscued because she wanted to find out what was going to happen in the story. Kirb stated that he knows that "all readers miscue, but it doesn't matter as long as the story makes sense." The students changed as readers, and their understanding of the reading process changed as well.

Text selection for CRMA needs careful consideration. The text influenced the discussions as students offered their thoughts and reactions, and powerful discussions emerged from the students' interpretations. When Terry finished reading about "Mrs. Gorf," (Sachar date unknown), José responded, "Aww, he ate the apple." When discussing José's reading of "Pedro and Diablo," (Hayes date unknown), Kirb said, "Wouldn't it be neat if that happened?" They often critiqued the literature, saying whether they liked a particular story or not. José and Kirb both rejected the author's choice of ending in "Western Gladiators." Reading, responding to, and rejecting literature while transacting with the text is a powerful mediator for learning.

Group dynamics is an important consideration. The context of the collaborative group provided opportunities for students to learn effective ways of negotiating, influencing, and supporting others in the group. When José was vulnerable about his miscues the group reassured him that all readers miscue. They learned to support each other, listen to each other, and debate differences of opinion. The students went to great lengths to have other students understand their interpretations of a miscue. Terry went so far as to get a piece of tape to demonstrate what she meant about taping a note *to* a box and taping a note *into* a box.

"Look," said Peter, pointing to a note

into

taped to the bottom of the box.

José:	*Into* the box.
Terry:	*Into* the box.
Terry:	Did the miscue make sense?
Carolyn:	No.
José:	Yes.
Terry:	Yes. Yes it does. *Into* the box.
Kirb:	You tape something *into* something? It doesn't sound right.
Terry:	Yes. You can tape something *into* something. Look. I'm putting, taping this *into* my right hand.
Kirb:	*Into*???
Carolyn:	*To the bottom of the box.* Shouldn't it be *to the bottom of the box*? You can't tape something *into* . . .
Terry:	Okay, you can't tape something *into* something.

The group discussed the miscue and decided that *to* and *into* do indeed have different meanings in the context of this text.

The teacher plays a valuable role in the CRMA sessions. When the teacher joins the discussion, his or her professional judgment supports each reader in maximizing their full potential. Teachers mediate by asking questions and directing attention to proficient uses of strategies. The teacher draws attention to contradictions, helping students come to terms with inconsistencies between what they say they are doing and what they actually do as they read. The discussions with the teacher cannot be planned; they emerge from the group discussions.

My inquiry into what happens when students sit together and talk about reading miscues without the constant direction of a teacher led me to an appreciation of the depth of discussion of which readers are capable. Students discussed dialect differences, the role of the author and the text in influencing miscues, and how reading speed is influenced by many different variables. They discussed a wide range of miscues, including substitutions, insertions, and omissions. They discussed high-quality miscues and low-quality miscues, focusing on meaning construction. They acknowledged that some miscues didn't matter as long as the text made sense to the reader.

As the CRMA sessions progressed, the tone of the sessions changed. In the beginning of the study the students expected the reader to produce an exact reproduction of the text: If a reader miscues, the miscue should be corrected. By the fourth session student comments shifted to a qualitative stance. Students began asking questions such as, "Did it make sense?" "Did you know what the word meant?" and making comments such as, "You didn't need to correct it because it would have been a waste of time." They soon determined that only miscues that disrupt meaning need to be corrected. As they conferred about miscues it was surprising how quickly the students' attention shifted from the influences of the text to the reader's role in constructing a meaningful text.

All the students benefited from participation in the CRMA sessions. The depth of the discussions and interpretations that went on in these groups over eight weeks make it clear that when CRMA sessions are embedded into a classroom structure where discussion of the reading process is part of the ongoing language arts curriculum, the proficiency of readers increases dramatically.

15

The Reading Detective Club

Debra Goodman

I FIRST DEVELOPED THE READING Detective Club (D. Goodman in press) for Jacob and Michele. It was summer, and we spent five weeks together in daily tutoring sessions as part of my "Diagnosis and Corrections" courses on my way to a master's degree in Reading.

It's funny how those distasteful medical words stick in my head so that I can't remember the rest of the course title. A Chapter 1 reading teacher at the time, I called my tiny closet classroom the "reading center" rather than the medical term "laboratory." Just semantics, of course, but semantics are crucial in the effort to help readers revalue the reading process and, ultimately, themselves as readers.

Michele, who was entering third grade, was willing to try anything, but having difficulty with reading in her classes in school. Jacob was also entering third grade, but had repeated the second grade. He was a confirmed believer that he was a failure as a reader, and argued against any evidence to the contrary. He was also an extremely bright child whose parents read to him a great deal. Michele and Jacob were a good team. Michele was willing to plow through any text. Jacob refused to read, but would sit beside Michele and supply the concept terms with which she struggled.

He refused to believe that his ability to listen and predict text meaning had anything to do with reading. Like many adults he could not accept that reading involved "guessing." It was Jacob who helped me realize that children as well as adults are often more comfortable with the term "predicting" than with the more common word guessing. With his reluctance to guess, imagine how he felt about miscues.

Jacob put up such a resistance to reading on his own that I needed to place him in a situation where he was forced to read without my help. Like many kids his age, he liked the *Nate the Great* stories, and so I wrote the first reading detective cases for Jacob and Michele to solve without me. In order to solve the cases, they had to figure out the meaning of missing words. This pushed both children to focus on seeking meaning rather than trying to sound out letters.

I placed Michele between Jacob and myself and refused to help them. If they got stuck, I told them to just treat that part of the text like another mystery word and continue reading. Jacob and Michele were, of course, thrilled to see their names in print. Being detectives made the process of predicting text and coping with miscues more acceptable to Jacob.

This was the chronological birth of the Reading Detective Club, but the idea has grown from several other practical and theoretical roots, such as reading strategy lessons, cloze procedures, concepts of the Literacy Club, and revaluing, without which the Reading Detective Club would not have been born.

READING STRATEGY LESSONS

Miscue analysis helps us to see that reading strategies can be described in several broad categories. We see readers using processes in order to construct meaningful text: perceiving, predicting, confirming, and integrating. We see readers transacting with the language cueing systems: the graphic system of letters, logos, and pictures used in written text; the lexico-grammatical system of how ideas are represented by words and grammatical structures; and the semantic system or meaning system. Other systems involving literary qualities, cultural beliefs, personal experiences, and the setting in which the reading occurs also influence the reader's construction of meaning.

All readers use these strategies when they are reading, but most of us aren't aware of the reading strategies that we're using. Yetta Goodman and Carolyn Burke (1980) developed the idea of strategy lessons to help readers become more aware and conscious of strategies that help them construct a meaningful text (see Y. Goodman et al. 1996). Unlike typical skill instruction, strategy lessons involve readers in reading whole texts selected or written to explore some aspect of the reading process.

As I experienced and wrote a variety of strategy lessons with my students, I saw that these learning experiences went beyond helping students to use reading strategies. Students learn a great deal about language. When students became aware that they were using a variety of reading strategies, they understood that they were in control of the reading process and could select the reading strategies. This gave them confidence in themselves as readers.

The Reading Detective Club is really a series of strategy lessons through which students can explore the reading process as young linguists. Jacob felt that he required adult assistance and could not read independently. I wanted to develop strategy lessons that could be done independently of adult assistance. Even the instructions would be embedded in the text.

COMBINING THE CLOZE PROCEDURE WITH MISCUE ANALYSIS

Teachers who explore applications of miscue analysis in the classroom are daunted by the factor of time. It may be practical to use the RMI in a lab or with a few students, but it is difficult to use with an entire class.

Adapting cloze procedures with insights from miscue analysis provides another technique for understanding students' reading. In a traditional cloze test, the reader reads a text with every seventh word missing. The tests are scored based on how many exact responses the reader predicts. The traditional cloze procedure does not include evaluating the quality of responses in terms of maintaining the meaning of the text.

I helped Margaret Lindberg, a researcher at Wayne State University, field test a miscue cloze procedure with a written retelling (Lindberg 1977). In Lindberg's procedure, cloze responses are treated as miscues and coded for syntactic acceptability, semantic acceptability, and meaning change. Students read an entire story. After the first page or so, there is a passage in the story where every tenth word is replaced by a blank space. The students are asked to fill in every space.

After they finish reading and responding to the story, the readers retell the story in writing on a form asking open-ended reading miscue inventory (RMI) questions such as: *Write down what you remember from the story. Is there anything else you remember? Tell a little about each of the characters in the story.* When they finish, the teacher reads the retelling and may ask a few more questions to extend what the student has written. Additional responses are recorded on the retelling form.

This adaptation of the cloze procedure actually has some advantages over an oral RMI. It works extremely well for a large group of students. Because it is a silent reading procedure, it actually provides a more authentic reading context for older students. It also provides qualitative information about each reader. It suggests future individual or group strategy lessons.

I used the procedure to determine which students I should work with in the reading center. The best feature of the cloze procedure is the lack of graphic cues in the missing words. This frees up the readers to search for meaning rather than "sounding it out." This procedure also forces readers like Jacob to recognize that they *must* use other cueing systems besides graphophonics when they read.

After using this procedure for evaluation, I began to explore its use for retrospective miscue analysis by having students discuss their responses. Working with third and fourth graders, I used predictable stories or familiar folk tales and encouraged them to work in pairs.

After the students had an opportunity to complete their cloze stories, I would put the sentences on a chalkboard or chart paper and list all of the answers that students came up with. Some basic questions such as "Do these responses make sense?" or "Why did you come up with your responses?" got some great discussions rolling.

Some of the blank spaces highlight specific strategies such as predicting, confirming, re-reading, or reading ahead. At other times we would get into linguistic analysis. In some blank spaces, such as *Once upon a* _____, all of the readers would choose the same response. Other blanks, such as *The little pig built* _____ *house out of straw*, elicited only a few responses. What is it about the text that limits our choices as readers? Do writers always have unlimited choices, or are their choices limited too?

In still other cases, such as *The wolf walked* _____ *the road*, there were many possible responses. This is often the case when the word is an adjective or preposition. In these cases, we might see how many more words could fit in a blank space. The students really enjoyed playing with language and coming up with funny or bizarre responses.

The cloze activity and subsequent discussions allowed my students not only to view themselves as readers, but also to see how adept they really were at constructing meaning from written language. I praised them highly for their cleverness in making discoveries about our linguistic system. They began to see themselves as active members in the Literacy Club.

JOINING THE LITERACY CLUB

Frank Smith (1988) talks of children joining the Literacy Club, when they see themselves as members of our literate society. He says that we join clubs because we identify with the members of that club. We don't have to be expert, or even proficient, in order to join a club. We join a sailing club because we want to learn to sail, and other members of that club help us to become sailors. We don't have to know how to read to join the Literacy Club. We do have to see ourselves as readers or potential readers.

Jacob saw himself as a nonreader, and so he refused to read. Being retained for a year sent a strong message to Jacob about his ability and about himself as a person. This retention of a child who had such strong oral language ability, as well as a strong interest in the written texts read by his parents, shows how testing and minimal competency standards have overtaken our common sense as educators. Jacob's experiences in school only helped to convince him that he couldn't read.

By the time I met Jacob, at the age of eight, his conviction that he couldn't read was an almost insurmountable barrier to his learning to be a reader. He and his parents viewed his non-reading as a handicap that they had to accept but not overcome. Before Jacob would be able to learn to read, he had to change his beliefs about himself.

In my reading center, I saw many fourth and fifth graders who were turned off to reading. I met second graders who were already strongly convinced that they were failures at reading. These children struggled valiantly to "read" according to their teacher's instructional definition of reading. Dana, a first grader, was in a classroom where word recognition was the instructional base. She was a "Swiss Cheese Reader." She would read one word at a time, leaving out any words she didn't recognize. Dana's oral reading sounded exactly like a word list, and had about as much meaning to her.

William came from a classroom with a phonics approach. He was a "Perseverator," struggling, usually unsuccessfully, over and over again to sound out each word. He would often end up with nonsense words that meant nothing at all.

Parents are drawn into the cycle of hopelessness. On parent-teacher conference night, Alicia's parents came into the room very upset. Alicia's teacher wanted her to repeat first grade because she wasn't reading. I showed Alicia's parents her dictated stories and expressed my confidence that she would blossom into a reader.

Danny's mom sat down and burst into tears. She had heard nothing good about Danny at any of his conferences. The worst problem seemed to be his spelling and his handwriting. As a fourth grader he did very poorly in these areas. Should she get him a tutor for these areas? I assured Danny's mother that Danny had a fine mind. I showed her his amusing stories, and his scientific observations of our classroom plants. When he gets to sixth grade, I told her, he wouldn't receive separate handwriting and spelling grades. Instead, he will receive one grade for language arts. My hunch is that these areas, which are given so much emphasis in elementary school, would become non-issues for him in middle school.

Parents of children in Chapter 1 and other remedial reading programs often hear nothing but bad news and discouragement from their child's classroom teachers. I told them a different story about their child. I showed them the writing and reading their child had done with me. We laughed together, and strategized how to be teacher and advocate for the child. As I write these words, my stomach churns and tears come to my eyes. I think this is because I have also been a parent in similar circumstances.

In my reading center and in my classroom teaching, I tried to recreate the rich literate environment that leads most of our students to become readers without the struggles that some students endure. I read to the children and encouraged them to listen to tapes and read to each other. We organized a collection of favorite and familiar texts, starting with nursery rhymes and predictable books.

Contrast the stories about Dana, William, Alicia, and Danny with the children learning to read now in the Dewey Center in inner city Detroit. The Dewey Center is a K-8 public school with a whole language philosophy. When I wrote this chapter, I was teaching there as the school librarian. In the first-grade room, large signs tell the students: "I can read, I can write, I am a scientist, I am an author," and so on.

Three prominent signs in the middle of the room read: "We plan. We do. We share." These three positive statements form the basis for a student-centered, inquiry-based curriculum, and also reflect the rhythm of the day. In addition to immersing the students in a variety of language experiences, the students take responsibility for their learning as well. When the first graders enter the room, they get down on the floor to sign up for their reading workshop choice. The early birds help the teacher decide what choices they should have. Then they write on the morning message sheet in invented spellings.

With this expectation and trust in their ability to negotiate the written text in their classroom, most of the students, no matter where they are in emergent literacy, think of themselves as readers and writers. Mindy LePere, a combination first/second-grade teacher, asked me to take a look at some second-grade students. It was late in the year and she was very concerned about their reading ability and whether they would survive third grade. I conducted an RMI session with several of these readers, and was amazed at how they differed from the "Swiss Cheese

Readers" and "Perseverators" I had known before. These children all described themselves as readers. They said they liked to read. When I asked them to read a story to me, they confidently constructed a meaningful text. If they had to choose between graphic cues and making sense of a story, they always chose making sense.

John had not completely grasped the alphabetic principle of the English writing system, but he still "read" me a meaningful story from the book that I gave to him. Following each RMI, I talked with the children about how smart they were. I pointed out the reading strategies that they were using with great success. It surprised me to learn from Mindy that these interviews also brought changes in the children. They went back to the classroom viewing themselves in a new light. John returned to the classroom and began to write stories, something he had never done before.

Brian Cambourne (1988), in his conditions for learning, says that learning doesn't happen without "engagement," where the student makes an active decision to be a learner. Cambourne says there are three crucial elements that must be present in order for a child to become engaged in learning. Learners must see themselves as potential doers; they must see the relevance of what they are learning to their lives; and they must feel safe to take risks and make mistakes.

Michele was a risk-taker. She enjoyed reading with Jacob and me, especially when I helped her to find materials that were interesting to her. She knew it was okay to make mistakes and was willing to keep reading. Jacob, with his quick mind and strong background in listening to written texts, was actually a more able reader than Michele, yet he did not feel he was a good reader, and he resisted reading. Unless Jacob could be convinced that he was a reader, Michele would soon pass him by because he was unwilling to read. He was so convinced that he had a reading problem that he set up elaborate systems to avoid becoming literate. I worried that he was in danger of becoming a self-described adult "nonreader."

REVALUING: DEMYSTIFYING THE READING PROCESS FOR CHILDREN

The student's attitude about learning has always seemed critical to me. My concerns about learning stages and ability levels became non-issues after watching students make great leaps following a pivotal change in how they perceived learning and themselves as learners. Sometimes this change is the result of making an important discovery about literacy. When young children discover that those two yellow arches with the red letters stand for McDonald's, there's no turning back. Later, they learn that print carries a message in a story, that there is a relationship between the sounds of our language and the written language, and (in an alphabetic writing system) that the relationship is alphabetic.

In upper elementary school, students discover how novels with extended plots differ from short stories or books from the *Ramona* or *Encyclopedia Brown* series, in which every chapter is a story. At this point they become novel readers. We can explore these issues with students in strategy lessons or literature discussions, but each student must discover how to be a novel reader for themselves.

The first step in helping children to revalue reading and readers is to revalue the reading process for ourselves as teachers. Instead of diagnosing students' deficiencies we need to examine what students know and help teachers, parents, and the students themselves to marvel in their ability to learn language. Instead of worrying about the students' performances, we need to search for ways of connecting students with authors, poets, books, magazines, and other printed material that will help them to see that reading has a role in their lives.

Instead of worrying about the students' "reading level" we need to help ourselves, the students, and others in their lives to see how they are already proficient readers and writers when they want or need to read and write. (Can they read a TV guide? Is that easy reading?)

Instead of quizzing kids to see if they are really reading, we need to help them find materials that they get excited about so that they have that "couldn't put it down" experience.

Instead of threatening a child with poor grades or detention, we need to be the child's greatest advocate. We need to exude confidence that this child is a reader, will be a reader, and can read.

This means that we have to be learners, readers, and risk-takers ourselves. It isn't an easy task. My own son, Reuben, has a lot in common with Jacob. He is also a bright child whose interests surpassed his ability and patience with written text. His early experiences also left scars that made him refuse to read. I have told everyone—his teachers, his father, and Reuben himself—that he doesn't have a reading problem. I insisted that he can read anything he wants to, such as menus in restaurants and trading card reference books. Though I may have felt my confidence shaken inside, I persisted with my stance for Reuben's sake. I knew that if I expressed the slightest doubts, he would begin to see himself as a nonreader.

Reuben, even as a seventh grader, resisted reading. He was a victim of a large homework burden, which left little time for reading. But he knew that he could read and he had no difficulty reading anything he wanted or needed to read.

There is no mystery to being a good reader, I tell Reuben and all of my students. Good readers are kids who like to read. They read a lot and they become good readers. It's that simple. If you want to be able to read better, find something that you really want to read and read every day.

When we get together in our Reading Detective Club, I ask the students how they learned to ride a bicycle. I picked riding a bicycle because it's something that they didn't learn to do in school. If kids don't like riding a bicycle, they can consider learning to swim or skate or whatever they enjoy most (see Demetrius' and Deandrea's stories, Figures 15-1 and 15-2).

When we get together to share our stories, we always find three main components of learning to ride a bicycle: You have to want to. You have to practice. You have to fall down. Children can see how hard they worked to learn to ride a bike, even though they didn't think of it as practicing. They all laugh about the accidents they had while learning to ride. The best riders, I remind them, still fall down when they try something new. The best baseball players hit the ball only three out of ten times at bat.

Exploring the learning process for bicycle riders many times has made me realize two other conditions for learning. First, you have to have help. But this help is different from the kinds of instruction that children experience in school. Bicycle riders' help takes the form of experienced riders who gear their assistance to the learner. The learner usually is in charge of the assistance.

Finally, you have to have access to a bike. This has important social and political implications for teachers. Who has access to books? Where are books kept? Who has time for reading?

It's easy to make the connections to reading. Readers are people who want to read and have some reason for reading. Reading requires practice, but the practice should be enjoyable and should involve reading and not other exercises. And all readers make miscues.

Some students will argue about the miscues. Some will even argue that they have learned to ride a bicycle without ever falling. These students, like Jacob, may have to struggle to become literate. My son Reuben also was uncomfortable with making mistakes. Much of his reluctance to read was the result of his desire for the smooth, perfect reading that he perceived in adults. "Your Grandpa Ken has a theory about that," I told him finally. Discussing theories of how reading worked helped Reuben to see things in a new light. He, as a student, could understand how the reading process worked. This made him feel intelligent and wise. He doesn't think much of any language arts teacher who has not heard of Kenneth Goodman's theories.

How I learned to ride a bike

On Monday, February 18th 1989 –
my 5th birthday I got a lot of presents
and a lot of money but then my brother
came in with a big box and he told
me to open it I did it was a bike
then I went outside to ride it, It
still had training wheels thow then
the next day my brother took off the
training wheels then I didn't want
to ride it. Then I went down the
street to my friends house and
jumed on his bike and ran into
a bus. and then I went and got
my bike and teased him and that
is how I learned how to ride my
bike

By Demetrius

Figure 15-1 Demetrius Learns to Ride a Bike.

There are many parallels between reading and detective work. Readers make guesses, explore these guesses, look for clues (or cues), and manage to make sense of a complex symbol system. The analogies and metaphors come very easily.

Upper elementary students love being part of a club, and they love to pretend. I play it up big. They are famous detectives. At the end of the semester, they will get their detective badge. Because I want the experience to be successful, our first case, "The Case of the Missing Word" (D. Goodman in press), is extremely easy:

THE CASE OF THE MISSING WORD

Jacob is a famous detective. He has solved many important cases.
One day, Michele came to see Jacob. She said, "I have a case for you."
Jacob said, "What is it?"
Michele showed Jacob a book. She said, "I wanted to read my book, but my dumb brother crossed out some words. Now I can't read it. Can you help me?"
Jacob said, "Did your brother say anything about the words?"
"Yes," Michele said, "He said it is the same word. He said it is a word he doesn't like."

THE READING DETECTIVE CLUB

Jacob said, "I think I can solve this case."
Here is page one of Michele's book:

Hi. My name is Jim.
I have one brother and one xxxxxx.
My brother is Sam. My xxxxxx is Lisa.
I am ten years old, and my brother is twelve.
My xxxxxx is a baby. She is two.
I like my brother, but my xxxxxx can be a real pest.

What is the missing word? _____

Deandrea

How I learn to Ride my Bike
and I was 5
years old
my mother bout me a bike
and the same day I got my
bike I tuak my bike out
side and Rold it I got
on it and start Rideing it. but
the frist time I feal off
of it but I got back on and
tride agind the second time I
feal but I got right back on
it and rirde agina and I fealed
agina, but I said this time I am
Not going to fall I got on it one
more time but this time I did
Not fall so I kape rideing my
bike so the my mother got
me bigger bike it was call
a 5 speed the I New how to
Ride a bike but the 5 speed
was just a little hard
because it dident have
No brakes you could Pattle
backward That was fun +
that is the End thank You !

Figure 15-2   Deandrea Learns to Ride a Bike.

"Guess what?" I tell the kids before handing out the case, "Today we have our first case." They gasp. They are super excited. They solve the case in a jiffy. "That was easy!" they say.

"You are great detectives," I say.

In my small reading center groups, the students worked in pairs and then we discussed the story as a class. When I have a Reading Detective Club in a large group or whole class setting, I divide the students into teams of four or five. These teams stay together throughout the reading process study. After students find the missing word, they go through the story and underline or highlight the clues that they used to find the missing word. With their teammates, they talk and write about what clues helped them solve the case. Then we come together and discuss the case and the process we used to solve it.

In one fourth-grade club, many of the students said, "As soon as I saw *brother*, I knew it was *sister*." Some of the students reported using other clues. Earline said, "The clue that made me know [the missing word] was when she said 'My XXXXXX is a baby.' And when she said, 'She is two.'"

Students also reported their thinking process. Damali said, "The clues where *sister* was the only thing . . . Everything else didn't make sense. So I put *sister* because it fit the space."

I asked who made a prediction other than "sister" for the first missing word. Students were reluctant to share their early miscues, but I encouraged them to go ahead. Finally Eamon raised his hand.

Eamon, who has two brothers and no sisters, had predicted the word would be *friend*. But, he said, "I know it was *sister* because it couldn't be *friend* because it said it can be a pest."

Shira, who has many older brothers and sisters, predicted *nephew*. After reading the second sentence, she changed her guess to *niece*. Her hypothesis was so strong that her entire group decided the missing word was *niece*. We all read it carefully and concluded that *niece* made as much sense as *sister*.

After discussing what clues we used, I told the students that they were describing clues that help us figure out meanings. We called these clues *meaning clues*. We talked about whether every word in the story was equally important in solving the mystery. I asked the students to write their opinions on the back of their papers.

Eamon wrote, "NO!" in large letters, adding, "Because some give more dafanishen and are more inportint."

Carlton, thinking of the detective process, wrote, "No. Brother is not impoted as Lisa or sister."

Demetrius wrote, "I think no because if you say a word like polution or nopoluttion is more important and it makes more sense."

Shira wrote, "Some words are more important than other words. Because some are whorser than others. like Bad words."

Demetrius and Shira's comments show that they have already integrated the "Case of the Missing Word" into other experiences and ideas about words. Alicia does the same, coming up with a different opinion, "Yes [all words are equally important] because if I find a word in a story I ask, but if the same word is in another story I will know it." Alicia seems to feel that reading is a process of knowing words, even though we have just been talking about how readers make guesses and find clues in order to make meaning. By fourth grade students have developed strong conceptions about the reading process.

The next time I met with that group of detectives, we revisited "The Case of the Missing Word" by starting a list of things that detectives do to make meaning. I wanted to help them see how they could use these strategies in other reading experiences, so I asked them, "Now what would you do if you were reading and you came to something you didn't know?"

"Sound it out!" shouted Stacy.

When we interview students, most of them say they "sound it out" even though they are not in a phonics-based program. Our students do reflect the whole language philosophy in other interview questions, such as "How would you help someone learn to read?" Most of our students say, "I would read to them." When asked "How did you learn to read?" most of our students report they learned to read at home, reflecting how authentic and unobtrusive the school reading program appears to them.

But the notion that reading is sounding out words is so strong in our culture that Stacy felt this was the strategy she used in the cloze procedure in which students *can't* sound out the words. They are forced to consider that they are using other strategies when they read. Still, Stacy was not convinced.

I didn't argue with her. The Reading Detective Club provides opportunities for students to explore the reading process like psycholinguists or educators do. As the teacher, I try not to prescribe what that process is or should be. Instead, I set up situations where students confront some aspect of the reading process. Later, I help the students to describe what they have learned.

In order to use more common language to identify the cueing systems, we call semantic cues *meaning clues*, lexico-grammatical or syntactic cues are called *language clues*, and graphophonic clues are *graphic clues*. Graphic cues also include pictures or logos. Other cueing systems we have identified are *pattern clues*, such as rhymes or repetitions, and *memory clues*, involving the child's previous experiences with a text or type of text.

After the "Case of the Missing Word," the cases become more difficult. We continue to work in small groups and share our responses and reasoning after the case is over. We add to our list of reading detective strategies as we go along.

The students find they must put their heads together. They have to read ahead and reread in order to think of responses that make sense. In "The Case of the Messy Hands," Michele's little brother put dirty hands on his book. This left smudges all over the page where words belong. The detectives see how language clues interact with meaning clues.

In the sentence *One day the* [smudge] *pigs decided to go out into the world to make their* [smudge], most of the students predicted *three* or *little* for the first smudge. Some students shared how they predicted *pigs* until they saw that the word pigs followed the smudge. The language of the story ("The Three Little Pigs") and their own knowledge of the story grammar helped to prompt their guesses.

A few students had different responses for the [smudge] pigs, and we had fun thinking of possible responses such as: fat, porky, greasy, stupid, brave, and so on. Once we had a long list of possibilities, we could discuss adjectives and how they are used in stories.

For the second smudge, most students predicted *house, houses,* or *homes.* Some students were frustrated as they worked on that smudge. They noticed that the next sentence said, *Each little pig built a* [smudge]. They were uncomfortable with the repetitiveness of the two sentences, showing their awareness that authors try not to be too redundant. Most of them decided to use the same word twice, although one group wracked their memories and came up with the phrase *make their fortune.* I might have changed this process if I had chosen the word *seek* instead of *make.* Still, this ambiguity led us into a discussion of clues that go beyond simple meaning, involving our knowledge of stories and of the craft of authors.

The "Case of the Torn Page" uses a rhyming poem as the text. In addition, I included some of the first letters of words. This brings the graphic cueing system back into the picture. These additional clues make the detective process easier on the one hand since they provide additional information. However, they also restrict the detective's selections. Students try hard to find rhyming words, but learn to recognize that meaning is the first priority.

Eamon's mother dropped in while we were working. She saw how the first word of a couplet was often missing, and suggested to his group that they work backward to solve the case. Eamon's group was the most successful at coming up with a rhyming poem.

In addition to the cloze activities, I use a variety of other strategies to explore reading. Most of these strategies have come from activities used to help teachers explore the reading process. "The Case of the Goldfish" explores the common problem of reading unfamiliar proper names. "Is Your Mom at Home?" is filled with deliberate mistakes to help students see that no one reads with total accuracy. "The Norful Snig" is a nonsense story that helps students to see how we use language clues (lexico-grammatical cueing system) when we read, and how we can answer test questions without even understanding the story.

In addition to these learning experiences, I involve students in literacy research as well. They list everything that they read from the time they get up until the time they go to bed. They interview a variety of adults about what they read on and off the job. They observe younger students who are learning to read during a reading partner experience. We explore retrospective miscue analysis (RMA) procedures involving students in analyzing their own miscues. Retrospective miscue analysis takes more time than the Reading Detective strategies, but it produces amazing results. When we look at the first few miscues, the children answer the question "Why did you do that?" with pat responses like: "I was just careless." "I wasn't thinking." "I was being lazy." But after pushing students to discuss their responses, they begin to realize that there is a thought process involved in every miscue. They are able to supply explanations for miscues that I would never have guessed if I had been doing the analysis by myself.

The students involved in this experience see themselves in a new light. They see themselves as thinking readers who are actively involved in constructing meaning. They even face standardized testing with confidence as we remind them to be detectives and find the clues they need to pass the test.

We want our students to be problem posers and problem solvers in every area of schooling. The Reading Detective Club helps kids view themselves as problem solvers. Students who are involved in problem solving in other areas of the curriculum often make connections for themselves. When I tell them that reading detectives make predictions, they say, "That's like when we estimate in math."

As detectives, students learn that being a good reader is not a mystery; it just takes practice and common sense. As Curtis said, "We read more and more and we got the answer."

16

At the Critical Moment: RMA in Classrooms

Yetta M. Goodman

AS A TEACHER EDUCATOR, I know that the only way to confront teachers about their views of the reading process is to involve them in doing miscue analysis on their students' reading and then help them understand why the students make miscues. Often, teachers in my classes tell me that after doing even one miscue analysis on one of their students, they can never "listen to kids read in the same old way again." Although I knew that I wanted to help readers understand the reading process in a similar way, I did not consider involving readers in their own reflective miscue analysis until Chris Worsnop suggested the idea.

Through the reading strategy lessons that Dorothy Watson, Carolyn Burke, and I are always developing and updating (Y. Goodman et al. in press), we recommend experiences to help students become consciously aware of the reading strategies they use, the intuitive knowledge they have about the language cueing systems, and the degree to which their strategies and language knowledge help them in constructing meaning. Dorothy Watson and Sharon Hoge's "Reader-Selected Miscues" (Chapter 13); Debra Goodman's "The Reading Detective Club" (Chapter 15); and Sarah Costello's "Collaborative Retrospective Miscue Analysis" (Chapter 14) are also ways of involving students in becoming conscious of the reading process in classroom settings. We help students become aware that many of their miscues and the strategies they use in response to those miscues are of high quality and positively influence their reading development. We hope that we also help them dispel the notion that all miscues interfere with their construction of meaning as they read.

However, we haven't been very systematic about involving students in asking the kinds of questions that we have found helpful over the years in understanding miscue analysis and constructing a transactional sociopsycholinguistic view of the reading process.

Classroom teachers knowledgeable about the reading process began to experiment with ways of engaging students in thinking about their own reading and in talking about the kinds of things that happen as people read. As teachers such as Sarah Costello, Chris Worsnop, Debra Goodman, David Weatherill, and the others who are authors or have been featured in this book became knowledgeable about the reading process through miscue analysis, they began to consider that their students might benefit from exploring miscue analysis procedures. These teachers adapted miscue analysis concepts in their own classrooms or clinical settings. Some of them, like Ann Marek and Sarah Costello, did formal studies with readers to explore the potential of retrospective miscue analysis, but many teachers use miscue analysis procedures daily in their classrooms to engage students in discussions

---

Each classroom documentary was written in collaboration with the teacher—Alan Flurkey, Wendy Hood, Don Howard, and Debra Jacobson, respectively.

about the reading process and to explore together how people read in general and how individual students read in particular. Through these discussions and explorations, students reflect on their knowledge about the reading process.

Fortunately, I am in contact with a number of these teachers/researchers and they often share with me the kinds of experiences they design for their students. These teachers are well informed. They have conducted formal miscue analyses with their students, and they use formal miscue analysis with at least some students on a regular basis. They also keep up-to-date about miscue analysis by attending conferences and reading new information. Many of them write for professional publications and make presentations at conferences and workshops to help inform their teaching colleagues. I owe the teachers I talk about in this article and the authors of the chapters in this book a great deal because they continuously influence my own professional development and theoretical understandings of the reading process. I count them among my most valued colleagues and provide vignettes from some of them who use miscue analysis in various ways in clinical and classroom settings.

DON HOWARD'S PRIMARY CLASSROOMS

Don Howard has been adapting retrospective miscue analysis in response to his students and their needs for the sixteen years that he has been teaching primary through fifth grades. For most of those years he has been a second and third grade teacher. He considers himself a whole language teacher and has won wide acclaim and awards for his teaching. His students respond to his gentle support and the rich learning environment he establishes in his classroom by exhibiting a great joy for the learning that occurs in the classroom community that Don helps to establish.

RMA came to Don when he was reading a big book to his second graders. He spontaneously made a few miscues during his reading and two girls corrected him. He was surprised at their response since he believed that neither of these girls was reading as proficiently as others in his class. He not only accepted the children's corrections with grace, but also chose to discuss with them the strategies and language cueing systems that he was using that were responsible for his miscues. He then decided to make miscues intentionally in such a way that students would notice so he could use the critical teaching moments to legitimize miscueing and focus children on their own knowledge about language and reading. But once the kids became aware that he made miscues and didn't mind talking about them, he did not have to fake making miscues. His students noticed most of the miscues he made spontaneously as he read. And Don began to exploit his miscues whenever they occurred. He talked about how they helped him be a good reader and that they were his way of always trying to understand what he is reading.

Don believes that kids feel very comfortable when they see adults making mistakes. In an environment where the authority figure in the class makes mistakes, it becomes legitimate for students to make mistakes as well. In such an environment students are willing to take risks because they become aware that mistake-making is simply a natural part of learning. Don makes this last statement explicit during appropriate moments in the classroom and encourages his students through open-ended discussions to believe and talk this way themselves.

Don discusses with the students that there is nothing wrong with making miscues. He uses the term *miscues* with his students. Rather than condemning a miscue as something that is wrong, Don and the kids explore the reasons learners make miscues. They decide together that some miscues are good ones and some are not, depending on the degree to which they make sense. The good ones are to be celebrated and accepted as helpful to their learning. The bad ones need to be fixed if possible. They discuss which miscues need to be corrected and which do not need to be worried about because they don't interrupt the story.

While working with third graders, Don has monthly reading conferences in order to hear each of his students read and help them focus on their effective and efficient reading strategies. He spends about ten to fifteen minutes individually with each student. Once he realizes some students need greater support than others, he schedules more time for them. In order to have the students read something they have not read before, they either bring a book to the conference that they are reading and start reading orally where they left off their silent reading, or they choose from a range of books that Don has set aside for reading conference purposes that are not usually accessible to the students. As students read aloud to Don, he makes notes about their miscues and their reading strategies. When they finish their reading and complete a retelling, he asks them if they noticed anything about their reading that they would like to talk about. Usually they say that they had a hard time with a particular word. Don discusses why they thought it was hard and the strategies that the child used in trying to build meaning throughout the story. They decide together which strategies were helpful and which weren't. They discover that some strategies work better than others. Then Don uses his notes to focus the student on high-quality miscues, appropriate self-correction, and keep-going strategies. Don believes that this procedure strengthens their confidence in themselves as readers. Many students overuse or fixate on a single strategy such as sounding out. By focusing them on the range of strategies that are possible and they are capable of, he helps them become more flexible readers. They come to know that it is acceptable to change strategies; if one thing doesn't work then they are encouraged to try others. At the end of each session, they decide which alternative strategies were useful and then the student selects one strategy that he or she will focus on during the next few weeks.

Don's class is always engaged in a great deal of silent reading, so they have many opportunities to try out the alternative strategies. Immersion in lots of silent reading and time for reading in class are important components of this kind of instruction. Don says that he and the students talk about reading strategies and the role of making miscues daily. It just becomes a natural part of their daily teaching and learning conversations.

Don has extended his concept of miscues and RMA to science and math. The students in his class keep individual learning logs in which they write about the strategies and problem-solving that seems to work to help them learn and why they believe a particular strategy worked. Since it is too cumbersome for the students to keep a learning log in each subject matter area, Don has them keep one log with a different chapter for each area: Math Learning Strategies, Science Learning Strategies, and Reading Learning Strategies. When the class comes to a strategy that has worked for them, the kids take about three minutes to jot down in their learning log what they have learned, how they learned it, and why it worked. This helps them to think and express in language their own learning and reading processes.

The discussions Don and his class have about strategies and making mistakes have led to a list of reading strategies that is posted in the classroom and that the children can readily talk about. From a video on strategies developed by the University of Wisconsin, the kids became aware of a strategy they call "Plant the seed before you read." The students discuss the importance of bringing to their minds everything they know about a topic before they read about it. Other strategies that they have discovered and listed include: "Go Back and Read Again," "Read Forward," and "Keep Reading." The language is the language of the students; the concepts are ones that we all recognize as legitimate reading strategies. The kids realize that they can understand a good deal of a story or article without knowing every word. They explore how to select available clues such as pictures and other aspects of the surrounding text to understand what they are reading.

Don extends his discussions of miscues to writing and spelling as well. His class became aware of spelling strategies through a demonstration that Sandra Wilde (1993), who has done extensive research on spelling, did in their class. The kids became aware that the word *sno* written on the board was not conventionally spelled. So they started playing around with how many ways the *o* sound is represented in English. They did an *o* sound search around the room. They found the sound in many words on bulletin boards, in libraries, and on books and papers on display, and they began to categorize different spellings of the *o* sound. They extended their search to their homes and did an *o* sound search with their parents. They added their new knowledge to the categories they had brainstormed which they were keeping on an *o* sound chart which is displayed for students to use whenever they write.

Don values his students, their language, and their learning. And in the environment he organizes, the students value themselves and each other.

DEBRA JACOBSON— READING RESOURCE TEACHER

The philosophy in Debra Jacobson's school is that special support staff should work directly in the classroom with teachers and children and not simply pull children out of the classroom for special attention. Although she has had many years of experience in all the elementary school grade levels, at the present time, she is working collaboratively with third grade teachers. They plan much of the curriculum together, since a reading program is not relegated to a single time of the day but is integral to the learning experiences that take place in all areas of the curriculum.

One of the experiences she plans is to present a reading strategy lesson to the whole class that she believes will benefit all the students. A recent lesson included discussing with the students their ability to predict as they read and guess an appropriate word or phrase for a context when they are not sure what the word is. She started this lesson by reading aloud an interesting and relevant story to the class and stopping at selected places, asking the students to predict and make a good guess about what they think will come next. She wrote the students' guesses on the board in two columns: Good Guesses and Bad Guesses. Eventually the students participated in writing on the board. They decided under which heading their guesses should be listed after a class discussion. They wondered what cues they used to make their guess and how prediction and confirmation helped them decide whether their guess was good or not. They continued this procedure throughout the story. It didn't take long for the kids to discover that their guesses are almost all good because they made sense with the language that came before and after in the text. Debra supported this discovery by explaining to the students, using their rationale for the guesses that they made, that much of what they read is behind the eye, the knowledge they already have in their heads, and not between the eye and the page. She used their predictions to show that their guesses are educated ones based on their knowledge of the world, their knowledge of language, and their knowledge of what has come before in the story.

Then she had the students take a book they had been reading or find a book and work in pairs. The students read to each other and when they came to something they didn't know, they helped each other by having their partner make a good guess and then discussed the choices. Once the students were reading with each other, Debra and the other classroom teacher walked around the room and listened to the conversations. If help was needed, they responded accordingly, but most of the time this opportunity provided them with insights into the way the students handled the task. They received a great deal of information about students' knowledge about the reading process and the language cueing systems when they heard the students support each other's good guesses and then help each other explain what it is behind the eye that helps them make appropriate predictions.

Debra also works individually and in pairs with some fourth and fifth grade students. She pairs the students thoughtfully so that they complement each other's strategies and in that way the students can support each other. Recently, she was working with Barry and Jorge. Barry took lots of risks, produced many nonwords, and kept reading even though his miscues didn't always make sense. Some of his miscues were acceptable within the story and he did self-correct others. As a result, he produced a story that had a semblance of meaning. Jorge, on the other hand, was not willing to take risks. He stopped when he came to something he did not know and looked to Debra or Barry for help. If he did not get help fairly quickly, he was either likely to skip a word or just give up and stop reading.

In this setting, Debra asks students to select a book they would like to read and to decide who will read aloud first. Debra stops the students at the end of a passage that she carefully selects as a stopping place. Her selection depends on the high-quality miscues the students make or on the insights the students show as they talk to each other.

Because of Jorge's anxiety in reading print and his unwillingness to take necessary risks, Debra occasionally provided him with words or phrases, although she watched the text carefully and whenever the language was highly predictable she was able to get Jorge to predict. Barry followed Debra's lead and sometimes provided Jorge with a word, but more often tried to help Jorge focus on the cues in the text that preceded the word that had stopped Jorge's reading.

On the other hand, whenever Barry read, Jorge often said to him, "you messed up" or "you goofed"—providing evidence that he considers miscues, regressions, and self-corrections not to be the mark of good reading. As the boys read, Debra jotted down notes about the comments the boys made and their miscues, especially high-quality miscues, syntactically and semantically acceptable predictions, and self-correction strategies. At an appropriately-selected moment, Debra engaged the boys in discussion about their reading. She pointed out to the students the high-quality miscues that they were making and the strategies that they used when they were not making sense and discussed with them how this helped them. She focused on their strengths as much as possible but at the same time helped them see what strategies they used that disrupted their meaning making.

Barry's reading provided more miscue strengths than Jorge's. Debra reminded the boys that Barry would say a word that did not make sense, keep on reading another phrase or to the end of the sentence, and then self-correct. She explained that this kind of reading is not "messing up" or "a goof" but a good way to use problem solving when they read. She helped the boys understand that this strategy "keeps the fabric of the reading intact."

When Jorge paused a long time, looking at a word or searching Debra's face for a response, Debra (after at least ten seconds of wait time) asked him to think of the language that came before and after to see if it could help him decide on the word he needed. Barry worked with Jorge in this way, and Debra discussed what she was doing with Jorge's mother, who used a similar strategy with him at home, since she read with Jorge fairly regularly. As the boys developed ways to make sense from their reading, they began to value their additional strategies.

Debra believes that when students watch each other make different kinds of miscues and respond with alternative strategies, they begin to incorporate new strategies into their repertoire. Debra works with other teachers in her capacity as a resource teacher. Sometimes she works individually with a student and at other times she works in the classroom with the whole class or with small groups. Debra shares her understandings not only with students, but also with teachers, developing a community consciously concerned with the revaluing process.

**WENDY HOOD—
KINDERGARTEN
THROUGH THIRD
GRADE**

Wendy Hood is teaching a bilingual kindergarten class again, after a number of years of teaching second and third grades. She believes that retrospective miscue analysis concepts have a place even with her kindergartners. She often has two or three students during the year who begin to construct meaning, transacting with the print in a book. When she sees this happening, she works individually with these children while her other students are involved in other learning experiences. Robin was such a reader. Wendy could tell that he was establishing an intuitive awareness of the relationship between print and oral language, although he did not believe Wendy when she told him that he was a reader already.

For example, during a whole-class shared reading using a big book called *Freight Train* by Donald Crews (1978), most of the children predicted *going* in response to the page which said: *moving through daylight*. Above the sounds of the other children, Wendy heard Robin's lone voice saying *moving*. Wendy turned to him in surprise and asked: "Why do you think that's *moving*?" He replied with an air of confidence: ". . . 'cause the *m*."

Wendy decided to help him become consciously aware that he was a reader by involving him in talking about his reading. In order to plan for such an experience, Wendy is always conscious of the importance of the written text she selects for such purposes. She selected a predictable book that had a high correlation between text and illustration but that shifted in a different way than the more common predictable books with which Robin was most familiar.

Wendy chose *Eek, A Monster*, a book in which boys and girls are chased by a monster. The language of the text would build and repeat common phrases such as: *Boys. Boys run. Boys run up. Boys run down.* Toward the end there is a page where the pattern changes, eliminating the noun: *Jump up*. While reading, Robin demonstrated a number of things that he knew about reading. He knew how to handle a book in terms of directionality and moving continuously through the text page by page. He made good use of the illustrations. But he also knew that the printed language he read as *Boys run* was different than what he said when he looked at the picture: *the boys were running*. In other words, he knew that what he saw in the illustration and the written language were not exactly correlated.

Retrospective miscue analysis helped Robin discover his power over print. When Robin got to the page that says: *Jump up*, he read: *Boys jump up*. He looked closer at the print and read: *Boys*. With his index finger, he touched the word *jump*, and again read *boys*; he touched the word *up* and read: *jump*. He picked up his finger, moved his head closer to the print, sat up triumphantly, and read: *jumped up*.

Wendy used this critical moment to get this five-year-old to reflect on his reading. "Tell me about what you just did."

Robin replied, "It was supposed to say *Boys* but there weren't enough words and that word is *jump* (pointing again to *jump* in the text). It has the *j*."

And Wendy said, probing a bit, "How did you know that wasn't *boys*?"

And he said, "It's *jump* like on the other page," and he turned back to a previous point in the text where the word *jump* was first introduced.

Wendy said, "That's a good thing to do when you read. You thought about what it would be and when it didn't match what you saw, you thought about it again."

And Robin responded, "I could read," and proceeded to finish reading the story.

Wendy plans similar opportunities for her second- and third-grade students to explore the reading process. She adapts experiences from the New Zealand model of teaching reading and writing (Ministry of Education 1985, 1990). In addition to rich language and literacy experiences integrating the use of science, math, and social studies experiences, Wendy uses guided reading strategy lessons with small groups or individuals on a regular basis.

She also regularly listens to the children read orally. She uses miscue analysis in an informal way, without taping the students, noting the degree to which each child is making sense and the strategies they use on 5 × 7 cards which she keeps handy in a file box. She notes high-quality miscues, predicting strategies, omissions which suggest a lack of risk-taking, multiple attempts at individual words, appropriate use of correction strategies, and so on. She asks for a retelling and notes any things that come up in the retelling that can help her understand the student's reading. When she notices, based on the kinds of miscues they make, the strategies they use, and their retellings, that a group of children might benefit from a discussion about a specific strategy use, she brings them together in a small group.

She takes special care in the selection of the texts she uses in these small group lessons. She uses texts that she becomes familiar with so that she notices if the children are making miscues common to most readers. For example, when she uses a familiar text, she can tell whether the students overuse the surface graphic features of the text or if the students have a strong need to produce sensible sentences that have very little in common with the printed text. She chooses texts that have familiar language and concepts and that support the strategies she will discuss with the students.

She asks the students to read the first page and stop. When all the students have finished, she discusses first what they understood from the story, always focusing on meaning prior to a discussion about any other aspect of the reading. Next she asks them if anything in the passage gave them trouble. She also asks the other students if they had a similar or different experience in that part of the text. The group then participates in a discussion about reading strategies and the opportunity is taken to predict subsequent text and the reading continues. Discussions and the interruptions are kept to a minimum to avoid disrupting the flow of the story.

In one group, she remembers that none of the students knew the word *mirror* when they came to it in the sentence *He looked into the mirror* . . . on the bottom of a page toward the end of the story. The story *Nick's Glasses* (Cachemaille 1982) is about a boy who cannot remember where his glasses are and they end up being on his forehead. It is a take-off on a folk tale of an old man looking for his glasses and finding them through logical elimination of possibilities. Wendy noticed that when Eli came to the bottom of the page, he hesitated for a few minutes and then turned to the next page, which showed the main character's face centered within a frame. Eli looked back at the word on the previous page and said: "That says *mirror*."

"How did you figure that out? What makes you think that's *mirror*?" Wendy asked. Wendy queries kids' responses regardless of whether the responses are the expected ones or not. That way students don't become convinced that she only questions them when their responses are wrong, as many teachers do, and the students consider all of their answers thoughtfully.

Typical of kids' responses early in her work with them, Eli said, "I sounded it out. See . . . mmmiiiirrrooooaaarrr."

Wendy responded by saying, "You don't call that mirroar, do you? Take another minute and think about what you did."

Then Eli was able to report: "I knew he was going to find them . . . I wondered where he could be looking that started with an *m*. I then looked at the next page and saw him looking in the mirror and then looked back at the word and I knew it was *mirror*."

After the other kids discussed whether they agreed or disagreed with Eli's explanation and why, Wendy summarized the literacy lesson they had all shared with Eli. She said, "You did a lot of good things as you were reading. You knew that you wanted the story to make sense and knew he had to find his glasses. You knew that it would be in a place so you were looking for a place word—we call that a noun. You also used what you know about the sounds of the language because you looked at the first letter of the word. You used the illustration to help you and decided the word was *mirror* and then you checked yourself by looking back at the word to see if all your thinking about it was right. You did a lot of hard work on that. You used a lot of good strategies and it worked for you."

Because of Wendy's knowledge of miscue analysis, a number of her teacher colleagues and the principal have asked her to do miscue analysis on other students in her school when there is uncertainty about how to help a particular child. Wendy believes that miscue analysis provides teachers with very rich and helpful information about readers. But she says this knowledge is independent of the reader. RMA, she believes, adds an expanded dimension to her insights into a child's reading because she has additional understandings provided by the reader. She can use that knowledge to help the reader build the confidence necessary to support the student's reading development.

ALAN FLURKEY—FROM SPECIAL EDUCATION TO GRADE ONE

After several years of teaching self-contained special education classes and learning disabilities resource, Alan Flurkey took a leave of absence to pursue studies in language and literacy. During that time he was a member of the research team that conducted the RMA project with adolescents reported in Chapter 7. Near the end of his leave, he chose not to return to his special education position and decided instead to teach first grade. In this setting, he hoped to gain a closer look at the processes of emerging literacy from the theoretical framework about literacy learning that he was developing. He wanted to see "learning to read" happening first-hand. But while Alan felt comfortable arranging a classroom to support literacy development, he wasn't prepared for his first day and remembers thinking how small the children were.

Alan knows that to support literacy development, kids need a breadth of literacy experiences surrounded by good literature. He collected a variety of book shelves, easels, and carousels which hold the nearly 1,000 books in his classroom: author sets, predictable books, big books, book tapes, nonfiction books, magazines, newspapers, and poetry. Classroom walls literally drip with poetry charts and photocopies of the cover of every "read-aloud," author study, or inquiry topic book read to the class. Read-aloud is used extensively: to provide frames for opening and closing the day, to study authors, science, or social studies, and to expose children to the beauty of poetry and to the power of novels.

Alan provides extensive blocks of silent reading time for the children, supplying them with a choice of reading materials and activities. When Alan works with children in small groups or individually, other children may choose from a number of activities: read from the classroom library, read with a friend, listen to a book tape, author their own books, plays, or poetry, write in correspondence journals, write in reader response logs, write using the computer—participating in the literacy activity of their choice.

Alan believes that once a teacher understands miscue analysis, that teacher cannot avoid seeing readers construct meaning as they transact with print. Alan says that he is rarely consciously aware of using miscue analysis in the classroom because it has become second nature to him. In addition to discussions with his students in small groups or individual conferences, he surreptitiously eavesdrops on students as he passes by their desks or encounters them reading in pairs. He uses these opportunities to make notes of their uses of predicting and confirming strategies or whether the readers appear to be overly concerned with surface features of text. He notes the types of words, structures, or concepts that seem to cause difficulties and uses that information to target mini-lessons or big book experiences.

Just as Alan was not fully prepared for his initial encounter with first graders, he also was not prepared for the language students used to talk about reading. He knew that his special education students could discuss miscues with sophistication, but had not expected similar sophistication from first graders. On one occasion early in his first year, he noted that Maureen, one of his more confident readers, produced a miscue, regressed to the beginning of the sentence, self-corrected, and read on:

ⓒ

As he turned the corner he ~~saw~~ *was* the lion.

Even though Alan works to focus readers' attention away from individual words toward a focus on meaning at the text level, he interrupted Maureen when she finished reading the page.

Alan: I noticed that near the top of the page you stopped, backed up, and then continued to read, and I'm just wondering what you were thinking about. Why you did that?
Maureen: You mean up here? (pointing)
Alan: Yes.
Maureen: Well, when I got to the middle of the sentence, it didn't make sense so I just started over.
Alan: What didn't make sense?
Maureen: Well, I thought it was going to say, like: " . . . he was scared. . ."—was scared of what was there. . .
Alan: So then what did you do?
Maureen: It didn't say that so I just started over.
Alan: Uh, huh. So why did you, uh, so what was it in the sentence that made you turn back?
Maureen: Well, it wouldn't make sense to say, like: ". . .he was the lion" so I just went back.

Alan reports that he was surprised that this very young reader was so confidently employing predicting, confirming, and self-correction strategies. She also was clearly aware of how and when she was using these strategies and was able to discuss her reading strategies with confidence. Most surprising to Alan was the realization that this first grader was using the same language to describe her sense-making process that his special education students had used and that he had heard seventh-grade readers in the RMA research study use. Maureen used the term "make sense" several times in her analysis of her own thinking.

Alan used this experience as a platform for further opportunities for exploring the reading process with first graders. Big book experiences work especially well for this purpose. On one occasion while reading the predictable book *Greedy Cat* by Joy Cowley (1983), Alan covered the words and phrases at the end of selected sentences. The purpose was to focus on using context to make sensible predictions.

Text: Mum went to the store and got some [sticky buns (covered)].
Alan: What do you think the story should say here?
Student: Bread.
Alan: Why?
Student   Because it's in the picture—it's in the grocery bag.
responses: It's gotta be food, 'cause it's in the pattern of the book, like it was sausages and bananas before, and like that.
            I think it's gonna say "loaves of bread" because the paper is longer. It's covering up more than one word.
Alan: Do we need to look under the paper to know what's going on?
Student   No, 'cause we know it's food and from the picture.
responses: And we know Greedy Cat is going to eat it.

Later, the class read the story again and compared the text with their predictions. At this time Alan and the kids discussed the use of graphophonic cues to aid in confirming predictions.

Alan describes using older "buddy readers" as one of his most successful activities. He observed that young children seem to display a different quality of respect and intensity when they are with children two or three years older than themselves than they do with adults. To capitalize on this, Alan invited several buddy readers into his classroom from the third and fourth grade. Although this is a rather common practice, Alan taught the basics of miscue analysis to the older "buddy readers," using principles like:

- When a reader pauses at an unknown word, just wait it out and watch what they do.

- When a kid "asks for a word," instead of reading the word for them, ask them what they think should go there. If they guess sensibly, fine. If they can't manage a guess, then encourage them to keep reading. If their guess doesn't make sense, encourage them to go on anyway and watch what they do later in the sentence, paragraph, or when they next encounter the same word.

Discussion of these principles gave the older readers alternative ways to respond to their first-grade buddies other than "sound it out." In this way, Alan taught the older readers helpful reading strategies to use in support of the first-grade readers and at the same time, the older readers received validation for their own reading strategies and became more consciously aware of their use.

Like Don Howard, Alan employs the same spirit of exploration of language to spelling and writing. For a variety of reasons, some children come to school believing that words always need to be spelled conventionally. Alan broached the topic of spelling by asking: "So why is spelling important, anyway?" Again, he was taken by the sophistication of kids' reasoning: So people can read what you write; So it can make sense; So it can look nicer. Alan then helps his first graders come to understand that they know a lot about the sounds of language which they can use when they spell and that it is okay to suspend the conventional rules of spelling in order to get on with the business of writing.

Knowledge of miscue analysis helps Alan make a conscious effort to draw children away from a word-centered view of reading, as the following exchange demonstrates. When approached by a student who was critical of his own reading because, in the student's words, "I couldn't get some words," Alan responded by saying: "But did it affect your understanding of the story?" "No," replied the student. Alan said, "Well, then I guess it didn't matter. You know, it's okay to 'not get' words."

In Alan's classroom, children quickly learn that "asking for a word" when reading or spelling when writing is not a fruitful line of pursuit. Alan keeps his role as a teacher—always supporting young readers' efforts to control the reading process—at the center of his interactions with them. Alan extols the virtue of patience and faith in the learning process and the abilities of young readers. He emphasizes that there are no periods of non-growth; rather, he likens times when children appear to be marking time as quiet periods of gathering momentum before explosive periods of growth. One of his favorite examples is red-haired Elizabeth, who ostensibly learned to read in the space of one weekend in April. The word "ostensibly" is important here because it carries with it the realization that months of read-aloud, shared reading experiences, big book experiences, authoring stories and poems, playing, and thinking had preceded and supported the "overnight breakthrough."

Alan's observations with "miscue eyes and ears" suggest to him that for some children, gaining control over the reading process appears to be a gradual, zigzag path. For others, it seems like the flipping on of a light switch. Alan has learned to honor his kids' unique ways in becoming readers. He believes that if you invite kids into an enriched learning community and give them the time and the support they need to grow, they will become readers and writers.

GENERAL CONSIDERATIONS

Based on discussions with the knowledgeable professionals whose classroom teaching has been presented, there are a number of issues I want to address regarding using RMA in classroom settings: the knowledgeable professional, critical-moment teaching, and the difference between students' inquiry into the reading process and direct instruction.

Knowledgeable Professional

It is obvious from the accounts I have documented that these teachers are knowledgeable about miscue analysis and the reading process. It is not possible for teachers to examine students' miscues thoughtfully if they are unaware of the theory, the research, and the understandings about the reading process that emanate from doing miscue analysis. There is no question that participation in miscue analysis and retrospective miscue analysis is in itself a learning experience. It is impossible not to be affected by examining miscues and asking "what knowledge do these readers have about language and the reading process that caused them to make the miscues they did?" I am still amazed at the new things I keep learning whenever I do miscue analysis on yet another reader.

However, miscue analysis is based on understanding concepts about language and learning processes and anyone beginning to explore the possibilities that RMI and RMA provide for classroom use should be open to reading, attending conferences, registering for classes, or engaging in discussions with others about miscue analysis theory, research, and practice. A number of references that are good starting points include *The Whole Language Catalog* (1991) and the *Assessment Supplement* to the catalog (1992) by Ken Goodman, Lois Bird, and Yetta Goodman. They have an extensive number of articles listed in the index under miscues, miscue analysis, and reading process (pp. 440–441 in the *Catalog* and pp. 187–188 in the *Supplement*).

Another area of knowledge that facilitates success in using RMA is an ability to analyze and select texts that reveals what students know and challenge their reading proficiency. As Wendy Hood describes in her interactions with her students, reaching for appropriate material not only is supportive to the reader but allows the teacher greater insights into what the reader knows and what the reader is doing. Although we sometimes ask students to choose their own reading material or provide them with two or three options and encourage them to select what is most interesting to them, there are times that text selection is in the hands of the teacher/researcher. Text selection cannot be taken lightly. Teachers' knowledge about how texts work, the influence that text has on the nature of readers' miscues, and the perceptions that students have about written texts are all considered in text selection. Other features of text selection include literary quality, conceptual load, grammatical complexity, interest and relevance to the reader, truthfulness, varying text style, and genre, among others. When I was in New Zealand, I participated in a teacher study group as they examined appropriate material to use with students during guided reading. This was a wonderful discussion and revealed to me the knowledge teachers have about what makes a good reading book for students. Margaret Mooney (1988) discusses criteria to take into consideration in text selection in *The Whole Language Catalog* (119–121) and Margaret Meek (1988) explores the role of the text in what readers learn.

Critical Moment Teaching

The teachers represented in this chapter and in this book who use retrospective miscue analysis in their classrooms are masters at making the most out of the critical moments that emerge daily as students ask serious questions about their reading. I am often intrigued, though I hope not in a condescending way, by the seriousness with which students begin to talk about the process of reading when their responses are treated with respect and when they begin to believe that the people they are talking to think that they have important things to say. I always remember a Australian fifth grader discussing his reading with me at length and finally saying, "if you don't know what it is you just do your best . . . you have a go."

The supportive repartee that regularly occurs between the teacher and individual students is common practice in the classrooms of great teachers. Often in a matter of a few minutes, the teacher moves the student toward a significant understanding and the learner experiences an intuitive leap (Bruner 1960)—the insightful *aha* moment. The classroom interactions of the teachers in this book are filled with such moments. Possible critical learning/teaching moments happen whenever teachers or students read aloud in the class—whenever the students ask questions about what they are reading as they are struggling with new concepts or challenging language.

But such teaching moments can also occur when students are reading aloud to each other and they notice each others' miscues. In such settings, Debra Jacobson helps students establish critical teaching moments with each other. Students, with the help of a knowledgeable teacher, learn to explore the nature of miscues, when it is helpful to call others' attention to miscues, and when it is best to allow the reader to continue. Teachers can encourage kids to listen for the miscues announcers make on television or family members produce at home. During cross-age tutoring programs or in multi-age classrooms, it is especially important to help the students explore responses to each others' miscues based on developing knowledge about miscue analysis and the reading process.

Many teachers produce tape recordings for listening centers to accompany books they want kids to read or that are the students' favorites. I know teachers who spend hours rereading to make the tapes completely accurate. I suggest that high-quality miscues be left on the tape and if a student notices, the teacher has another critical moment when the student asks a question about the miscue and reflects on its meaning.

One of the early steps in using retrospective miscue analysis in classrooms, then, is to capitalize on the number of times during the school day when it is appropriate to talk about reading and the reading process. These critical moments occur incidentally and informally and usually take no more than a few minutes. It is easy in the many situations described in the vignettes above to get the students to consider that; their miscues reflect an overuse of surface information: persevering; sounding out; sitting for a long time trying to get the next word. These short circuit strategies result in miscues that most often disrupt an understanding of the reading. On the other hand, they soon discover that miscues which make sense, sound like language, and fit the text are supportive to their construction of meaning.

Direct Instruction versus Inquiry or Treating Readers as Linguists

How is what Don Howard did when he engaged his students in an *o* sound search different than direct instruction of sounds in workbooks and basals? In Don's classroom the differences between inquiry into linguistic information and direct instruction on the *o* sound become quite apparent. Don is not teaching rules listed in spelling and reading texts that prescribe the rules for spelling the *o* sound. Rather, he is supporting or establishing opportunities for his students to study the possibilities available in the language. The students are inquiring into language use in the same way a linguist interested in the same questions might do. Responses that the students bring to the discussion are not considered right or wrong, but respected and treated as tentative hypotheses. There are many opportunities to talk and think about language; to debate and disagree. Textbooks might be consulted at this point in the study, but not for the purposes of finding a single correct answer. Rather, textbooks and any other reference materials are used as resources that can be critically examined and sometimes even rejected, based on what the students are discovering. The exploration is ongoing and doesn't end with an absolute rule. Children are not graded on their ability to know the *o* sound. Evaluation is based on the strategies students use to discover, to inquire, to ask appropriate questions, to wonder, and always to keep searching.

Retrospective miscue analysis must always be presented to students in settings that encourage them to ask their own questions about their reading; in other words, to self-reflect and to find a variety of ways to develop a range of alternative strategies to use to solve the problems they face as they read. In such settings, students explore reading in the same way that linguists do, wondering about language and how it works. Any attempt to turn RMA into formulaic procedures to be followed slavishly can turn an essentially problem-solving and inquiry-oriented experience into direct instruction. Then the quality of RMA ceases to exist. On the other hand, as students and teachers explore language together to understand the reading process, everyone in the classroom learning community continues to learn about language, about reading, and about the world.

17

Revaluing Readers and Reading

Ann M. Marek
Yetta M. Goodman

DURING THE YEARS WE HAVE worked with students and colleagues in exploring the use of retrospective miscue analysis, we have come to understand readers and reading in new ways. We have also learned much about teachers/researchers, and about reading instruction and evaluation. But as much as we have learned, we acknowledge that much remains for discovery. The intent of this chapter is to share some final thoughts and to pose a number of questions which continue to intrigue us as teachers and researchers.

Retrospective miscue analysis provides readers with a window on the reading process. In the hands of knowledgeable teachers, it is a powerful tool in helping readers discover for themselves the sociopsycholinguistic transactional model of the reading process. Through RMA sessions, readers begin to see the process more holistically, they begin to revalue their own abilities, and they in turn become more proficient readers. We know that even proficient readers like Bernice often don't value themselves as good readers, and retrospective miscue analysis can benefit them as well.

Retrospective miscue analysis forces us to examine questions about self-evaluation and self-reflection in reading. We wonder why talking and thinking about reading improves reading proficiency. We are intrigued with the fact that as a person begins to define himself or herself as a reader or a writer, there is an impact on reading proficiency. As we examine these questions, we continue to explore others. We hope those who find this volume useful will help us in that process.

As we look at readers who benefit most from RMA and other revaluing strategies, we often discover people who have defined themselves as nonreaders or poor readers. They are insecure about themselves as learners. Participating with someone whom they conceive to be knowledgeable provides them with the opportunity to organize a zone of proximal development (Vygotsky 1978). Working with an adult tells them that they are worthy of attention, and respect from another shows them they have value. As they talk about reading in this setting, or with their peers, they come to see that they know a lot about language. They may not have academic terminology, but they are capable of talking, wondering, and learning more about language itself. We must not underestimate the power of such a shift in attitude. It transforms people into learners who take charge of their own learning—who define themselves as readers: literate human beings capable of learning what they want to learn.

It is through RMA discussions that the student comes to demystify and demythify reading, concepts Barbara Flores has helped us understand as she describes

DEMYSTIFY AND DEMYTHIFY

myths about bilingual readers (Flores 1982; Flores et al. 1991). There are many myths that even proficient readers believe: that reading is an accurate word-by-word response to print; that readers have to read slowly and carefully; that if they had appropriate doses of phonics at the right time and in the right way it would help them solve all their reading problems. They believe that good readers always read fluently, know most of the words, remember everything that they read, and rarely make mistakes. They aren't aware that their own knowledge and experiences are important in understanding what they read. Reading is a mystery to people who think that good readers have somehow found magic solutions to becoming proficient readers. These mythical beliefs are documented again and again by readers in responding to the Reading Interview.

During retrospective miscue analysis discussions, it is easy to respond to the myths as the participants explore the range of strategies that are available in order for readers to construct meaning. Talking about these myths in a class or small group settings helps readers who lack confidence become aware that all readers—even the best readers—do things in reading that they always thought marked them as poor readers. It is important, therefore, to include in such discussions a wide range of readers so that less confident readers come to understand the reading strategies and language cueing systems that all readers use, including those they consider to be good readers.

The more teachers know about the reading process, the more they can point out to students as Don Howard does (see Chapter 16) that even teachers make miscues and use predicting and confirming strategies as they read. Knowledgeable teachers can help students become aware of their own strengths by substituting appropriate semantic and syntactic features of the text or by making a miscue that is a result of some complex linguistic structure or conceptual knowledge.

Even in discussions with proficient readers in graduate classes, exploring the reading process leads to demystifying and demythifying the reading process. First we ask students whether they believe they are poor or good readers. We ask those who consider themselves to be poor readers what they do that they consider problematic and list those items on the board. Then, the students who believe that they are good readers respond to the items listed. It isn't long before the students realize that all readers basically use the same reading strategies. The use of context, the nature and complexity of the content and the material, reading rate, levels of interest, appropriate and inappropriate reading strategies, and intuitive and conscious knowledge about language cueing systems are all issues we explore.

Having students collect data on the reading experiences in their homes and communities also explodes various myths about what counts as reading and who counts as a reader. In this way, students discover that they and the people they know do lots of reading—and not just books, magazines, or newspapers. They discover the pervasiveness of literacy events in their communities and begin to consider themselves literate members of literate communities. They come to understand that reading and writing are not simply school subjects. They begin to break down myths about illiteracy and about what constitutes a literate society.

Serious talk about the reading process with students helps to turn something that seems a mystery to them into something that students can discuss intelligently and come to believe that they control. Debra Goodman's (Chapter 15) sharing with her students that reading is a detective game in which the reader as detective is always looking for meaningful and linguistic cues gives them a great deal of power over their reading. More than a century of reading instruction has reduced reading to a set of skills to be mastered and fostered a common sense notion that reading can be achieved by simply sounding out words. As a result, most readers are aware of the graphophonic cues. However, their understanding about the relationship between the sound system and written systems of language is influenced by many myths. Many such students use their "sounding out" skills as an initial cue, rather than using syntax and semantics as cues for prediction, and graphophonic cues as part of their confirming strategies. Such students look for simple letter-to-sound correspondences rather than making use of the complex relationships between graphic patterns and phonological patterns influenced by the syntactic and semantic context of the written material.

Self-reflection about their reading is an important step to demystifying and demythifying the common sense beliefs about reading that many readers hold. Through these processes (demystifying and demythifying), readers and teachers come to appreciate their own strengths, they recognize the knowledge they must have about language and their world, and they revalue themselves as readers.

RISK-TAKING

Risk-taking is a concept that does not have a strong research base and it would be helpful if more teachers/researchers found ways to document the role of risk-taking in learning. In order to use language with confidence, students need to feel comfortable making mistakes, asking "silly" questions, and experimenting in ways that are not always considered conventional. It is obvious to those of us who work closely with readers of all proficiencies that the students who have a "keep going" strategy in reading are those who become avid readers. They are willing, for the most part, to take the necessary risks to sustain struggling with the text at times because they are confident that eventually they will construct meaning.

Students who lack risk-taking often become, as Peter Board (1982) would say, instruction-dependent personalities. They are not eager to assume responsibility for their own understanding of a written text. They become dependent on the teacher and the instructional program. Like Debra Jacobson's student Jorge (Chapter 16), they disengage from the text, looking with soulful eyes at the teacher's face or the ceiling for help. They are depending on resources outside of themselves.

When readers are in environments that encourage risk-taking with teachers who respect them as knowledgeable about their own reading, they begin to depend on themselves as the most important resource to answer their questions as they read. Other supplemental resources are necessary for all readers, but not without conscious awareness that the initial step in problem solving is to rely on their own independent resources and to believe that they are smart enough to do so. In environments where students are encouraged to become active in solving their own problems as the central focus of learning, risk-taking is an integral part of exploring the world. Students are immersed in rich environments which include a range of resources and opportunities to explore the power and limits of language use. They ask their own questions as they are involved in their reading and writing, not only about problems in the world, but also about their personal problems and dreams.

REVALUING

Throughout the retrospective miscue analysis sessions, we witnessed transformations in readers' beliefs about the reading process and about their strengths as readers. The RMA sessions document a shift for readers of all levels of proficiency from a "text reproduction" model of the reading process to a "meaning construction" model. Early in the sessions, several of the readers stated that all their miscues needed to be corrected—that their miscues were the result of careless reading. Other readers, like Rolando, were able to verbally articulate a more meaning-centered model of reading, even at the outset, but despite those stated beliefs, Rolando read as though exact reproduction of the text were the goal for reading. He, like Bernice, was effective, but not efficient.

Over time, however, our readers began to assert justifiably that many of their miscues did not require correction, that meaning was constructed despite the miscues, and that the interaction between the text and the reader had prompted most of their miscues. They became sensitive to miscues which so distorted the text that a need for reprocessing was signaled, and they also were sensitive to nuances in text which should be preserved even when miscues did not disrupt meaning in a major way.

Finally, they showed evidence of gaining control over the reading process as they found the confidence to assert that in many instances the miscues they made were "better" than the words used by the authors. Readers had grown more confident and had decided that "making sense" was the essential component of reading for meaning.

They became confident in exploring the meanings of what they read. They controlled the text, the making of meaning, and built their own personal meanings in transactions with texts, yet these meanings were often modified through shared conversations. It is only when people talk about what they've read that they come to know the social meanings of texts.

A positive relationship had been established between perception and process—one in which the strengthening of readers' perceptions about their reading abilities led to more risk-taking and more reading, which in turn reinforced positive self-perceptions. This cycle of revaluing can be visualized in the following model:

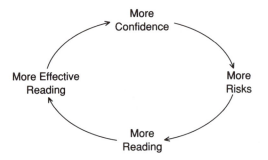

The model recognizes that, ultimately, the most natural way to improve reading is by reading; but readers in trouble are often so lacking in confidence that they are unable to proceed on their own. When low levels of confidence are influenced by instruction that stresses errorless reading, readers can become immobilized. As Sarah Costello informed us about her adolescent readers: "The readers viewed themselves as poor readers and the school reinforced this view" (Chapter 14). What retrospective miscue analysis offers is a way for readers to come to new understandings about reading and to use that information to become the kind of confident, proficient readers they want to be. Listen, again, to the words of Gina, Marlene, Rolando, and Kari as they reflected upon their experiences at the end of our work with them.

Gina showed that while discovering the reading process, she had discovered some things about the world as well: "I find that it is quite interesting to read, I must admit. I am surprised that people write such a lot of rubbish, though. And I never knew that before." Gina had learned more than a little about the power that literacy has—to help individuals examine and evaluate their worlds. To discover, to accept, to reject.

Ann asked Marlene, "How do you feel about your ability to continue to improve your reading?" She replied, "I can do it. It will take a lot of practice and reading a lot on my own." In defining herself as a reader, Marlene has gone a long way in releasing herself from the confining labels of the past: moving away from her view of herself as a dyslexic, learning-disabled child toward her view of herself as a capable, motivated young woman who is a reader.

Ever the realist, Rolando reminded us that "everybody has to probably make a mistake. Nobody's perfect." And although he was talking about making miscues in reading, we think his statement has implications for teachers/researchers as well. We must continue to be risk-takers ourselves, as we attempt to refine and extend the potential of retrospective miscue analysis.

We are encouraged by the words of Kari, who told Joel, "Everyone loves to read, they just don't know it yet." We revel in her optimism, and hope that as we continue to explore retrospective miscue analysis and similar strategies, more children and adults will discover that they love to read. If Marlene believes she can do it, we know she and others will.

Appendix A

Reading Interview

Name _____ Age _____ Date _____

Occupation _____ Educational Level _____

Sex _____ Interview Setting _____

1. When you are reading and come to something you don't know, what do you do?

   Do you ever do anything else?

2. Who is a good reader you know?

3. What makes _____ a good reader?

4. Do you think _____ ever comes to something she/he doesn't know?

Goodman, Yetta M., Watson, Dorothy J., and Burke, Carolyn L. 1987. *Reading Miscue Inventory: Alternative Procedures.* Katonah, NY: Richard C. Owen Publishers, Inc. Reprinted by permission.

5. "Yes" When _____ does come to something she/he doesn't know, what do you think she/he does?

   "No" Suppose _____ comes to something she/he doesn't know. What do you think she/he would do?

6. If you know someone was having trouble reading how would you help that person?

7. What would a/your teacher do to help that person?

8. How did you learn to read?

9. What would you like to do better as a reader?

10. Do you think you are a good reader? Why?

Appendix B

RMA Session Organizer

Reader _____

Date _____

Text _____

Tape-Recorder Counter Number	Miscue	+/−
_____	_____	_____
_____	_____	_____
_____	_____	_____
_____	_____	_____
_____	_____	_____
_____	_____	_____
_____	_____	_____
_____	_____	_____
_____	_____	_____

Notes:

This form is a prototype. Various versions are referred to in this book.

Appendix C

RMA Response Form

SESSION _____

Session focus, if any _____

READER _____

RMA QUESTIONS:

READER FOCUSES ON:

*Reproducing Text   **Constructing Meaning

1. Does miscue
   make sense?

(each miscue is listed)   (reader comments are quoted)

_____   _____

_____   _____

2. Did/should
   correct miscue?
   (as above)

3. Why did reader
   miscue?
   (as above)

4. Miscue affect
   understanding?
   (as above)

NOTES _____

_____

_____

_____

This form is a prototype. Various versions are referred to in this book.

Appendix D

Burke Interview Modified for Older Readers (BIMOR)

1. When you are reading and you come to something that gives you trouble, what do you do? Do you ever do anything else?

2. Who is a good reader that you know?

3. What makes _____ a good reader?

4. Do you think that _____ ever comes to something that gives him/her trouble when he/she is reading?

5. When _____ does come to something that gives him/her trouble, what do you think he/she does about it?

6. If you knew that someone was having difficulty reading, how would you help that person?

Original by Carolyn Burke, adaptations by Watson, Dorothy and Chippendale, Ene-Kaja. 1979. Describing and Improving the Reading Strategies of Elderly Readers. Monograph, Joint Center for Aging Studies, University of Missouri, Columbia, MO. Reprinted by permission.

7. What would a teacher do to help that person?

8. How did you learn to read?

9. Is there anything you would like to change about your reading?

10. Describe yourself as a reader. What kind of reader are you?

11. What do you read routinely, like every day or every week?

12. What do you like most of all to read?

13. Can you remember any special book or the most memorable thing you have ever read?

14. What is the most difficult thing you have to read?

Appendix E

Closing Interview

1. How do you feel about yourself as a reader?

2. Do you have any different attitudes toward reading than you had at the beginning?

3. Have there been any changes in your reading as a result of our sessions? Describe.

4. How do you feel about your ability to continue improving your reading?

5. Generally speaking, what do you think about the sessions we spent together?

Note: Questions from the Burke Interview Modified for Older Readers will be asked again during the Closing Interview, where appropriate.

Marek, Ann M. Retrospective Miscue Analysis as an Instructional Strategy with Adult Readers. Unpublished doctoral dissertation, University of Arizona, Tucson, AZ. Reprinted by permission.

Appendix F

Miscue Analysis Procedure I Coding Form

Goodman, Yetta M., Watson, Dorothy J., and Burke, Carolyn L. 1987. *Reading Miscue Inventory: Alternative Procedures.* Katonah, NY: Richard C. Owen Publishers, Inc. Reprinted by permission.

MISCUE ANALYSIS PROCEDURE I CODING FORM

© 1987 Richard C. Owen Publishers, Inc.

READER _____ DATE _____

TEACHER _____ AGE/GRADE _____

SELECTION _____ SCHOOL _____

LINE No./MISCUE No.	READER	TEXT	1 SYNTACTIC ACCEPTABILITY	2 SEMANTIC ACCEPTABILITY	3 MEANING CHANGE	4 CORRECTION	MEANING CONSTRUCTION (See 2, 3, 4)			GRAMMATICAL RELATIONSHIPS (See 1, 2, 4)				5 GRAPHIC SIMILARITY			6 SOUND SIMILARITY		
							No Loss	Partial Loss	Loss	Strength	Partial Strength	Overcorrection	Weakness	H	S	N	H	S	N

COLUMN TOTAL

PATTERN TOTAL

PERCENTAGE

a. TOTAL MISCUES _____
b. TOTAL WORDS _____
a ÷ b × 100 = MPHW _____

(Goodman, Watson, Burke)

References

Allington, Richard. 1983. "The Reading Instruction Provided Readers of Differing Reading Abilities." *Elementary School Journal,* Volume 83, issue 5, pp 548–559.

Atwell, Nancie. 1987. *In the Middle: Writing, Reading, and Learning with Adolescents.* Portsmouth, NH: Boynton/Cook.

Barnitz, John G. 1980. "Linguistic and Cultural Perspectives on Spelling Irregularity." *Journal of Reading,* January, pp 320–326.

Board, Peter. 1982. "Toward a Theory of Instructional Influence: Aspects of the Instructional Environment and Their Influence on Children's Acquisition of Reading." Ph.D. diss., University of Toronto, Toronto, Ontario, Canada.

Bridges, Allayne. 1985. " 'Ask a Silly Question . . .': Some of What Goes on in Language Comprehension Tests." *Child Language Teaching and Therapy,* Volume 1, issue 2, pp 135–148.

Brown, A. L., Campione, J. C., and Day, J. D. 1980. "Learning to Learn: On Training Students to Learn from Texts" (Technical Report No. 189). Urbana-Champaign, IL: University of Illinois, Center for the Study of Reading.

Brown, Joel, Marek, Ann, and Goodman, Kenneth S. 1994. "Annotated Chronological Miscue Analysis Bibliography" (Occasional Paper No. 16). Tucson, AZ: University of Arizona, College of Education, Program in Language and Literacy.

Bruner, Jerome S. 1960. *The Process of Education.* Cambridge, MA: Harvard University Press.

Cambourne, Brian. 1988. *The Whole Story: Natural Learning and the Acquisition of Literacy in the Classroom.* New York, NY: Scholastic.

Coles, Richard E. 1981. "The Reading Strategies of Selected Junior High Students in the Content Areas." Ph.D. diss., University of Arizona, Tucson, AZ.

Costello, Sarah. 1992. "Collaborative Retrospective Miscue Analysis with Middle School Students." Ph.D. diss., University of Arizona, Tucson, AZ.

Flores, Barbara. 1982. "Language Interference or Influence: Toward a Theory for Hispanic Bilingualism." Ph.D. diss., University of Arizona, Tucson, AZ.

Flores, Barbara, Cousin, Patricia, and Diaz, E. 1991. "Transforming Deficit Myths about Learning, Language and Culture." *Language Arts,* Volume 68, pp 369–379.

Goodman, Debra. In press. *The Reading Detective Club.* Bothell, WA: Wright Group Publishing, Inc.

Goodman, Kenneth S. 1964. "The Linguistics of Reading." *Elementary School Journal,* Volume 64, issue 8, pp 355–361.

———. 1969. "Linguistics in a Relevant Curriculum." *Education,* Volume 89, issue 4, pp 303–306.

———. 1973. "Miscues: Windows on the Reading Process." In K. S. Goodman (ed.), *Miscues Analysis: Applications to Reading Education.* Urbana, IL: ERIC and National Council of Teachers of English.

———. 1976. "What We Know about Reading." In P. D. Allen and D. Watson (eds.), *Findings of Research in Miscue Analysis: Classroom Implications.* Urbana, IL: ERIC and National Council of Teachers of English.

———. 1982. "Revaluing Readers and Reading." *Topics in Learning and Learning Disabilities,* Volume 1, issue 4, pp 87–95.

———. 1984. "Unity and Reading." In A. C. Purves and O. Niles (eds.), *Becoming Readers in a Complex Society. 83rd Yearbook of the National Society for the Study of Education: Part I.* Chicago, IL: University of Chicago Press.

———. 1986. "Revaluing Readers and Reading." In G. Williams, D. Jack, and K. S. Goodman, "Revaluing Troubled Readers: Two Papers" (Occasional Paper No. 15). Tucson, AZ: University of Arizona, College of Education, Program in Language and Literacy.

———. 1993. *Phonics Phacts.* Portsmouth, NH: Heinemann.

———. 1994. "Reading, Writing, and Written Texts: A Transactional Sociopsycholinguistic View." In R. B. Ruddell, M. R. Ruddell, and H. Singer (eds.), *Theoretical Models and Processes of Reading* (pp 1093–1130). Newark, DE: International Reading Association.

Goodman, Kenneth, Bird, Lois, and Goodman, Yetta M. 1991. *The Whole Language Catalog.* Santa Rosa, CA: American School Publishers.

———. 1992. *The Whole Language Catalog Supplement on Authentic Assessment.* Santa Rosa, CA: American School Publishers.

Goodman, Kenneth, and Burke, Carolyn. 1973. "Theoretically Based Studies of Patterns of Miscues in Oral Reading Performance" (Final Report Project No. 9–0375, Grant No. OEG-09-320375-4269). Washington, DC: U. S. Department of Health, Education and Welfare, Office of Education.

Goodman, Kenneth, and Goodman, Yetta M. 1977. "Learning about Psycholinguistic Processes by Analyzing Oral Reading." *Harvard Educational Review,* Volume 47, issue 3, pp 317–333.

Goodman, Kenneth, Smith, E. Brooks, Meredith, Robert, and Goodman, Yetta M. 1987. *Language and Thinking in School, 3d ed.* Katonah, NY: Richard C. Owen Publishers, Inc.

Goodman, Yetta M. 1980. "The Roots of Literacy." In M. P. Douglass (ed.), *44th Claremont Reading Conference* (pp 1–32). Claremont, CA: Claremont Reading Conference.

Goodman, Yetta M., and Burke, Carolyn. 1972a. *Reading Miscue Inventory, Manual for Diagnosis and Evaluation.* New York, NY: Macmillan Publishing Co.

———. 1972b. *Readings for Taping*. New York, NY: Macmillan Publishing Co.

———. 1980. *Reading Strategies: Focus on Comprehension, 1st ed.* Katonah, NY: Richard C. Owen Publishers, Inc.

Goodman, Yetta M., and Marek, Ann M. 1989. "Retrospective Miscue Analysis: Two Papers" (Occasional Paper No. 19). Tucson, AZ: University of Arizona, College of Education, Program in Language and Literacy.

Goodman, Yetta M., Watson, Dorothy, and Burke, Carolyn. 1987. *Reading Miscue Inventory: Alternative Procedures.* Katonah, NY: Richard C. Owen Publishers, Inc.

———. In press. *Reading Strategies: Focus on Comprehension, 2d ed.* Katonah, NY: Richard C. Owen Publishers, Inc.

Hanson, Geane R. 1992. "My Thinking Chair: Daydreaming in the Lives of Children." Ph.D. diss., University of Arizona, Tucson, AZ.

Harste, Jerome, and Burke, Carolyn. 1977. "A New Hypothesis for Reading Teacher Research: Both the Teaching and Learning of Reading Are Theoretically Based." In P. D. Pearson (ed.), *Reading: Research, Theory and Practice; Twenty-sixth Yearbook, National Reading Conference.* Minneapolis, MN: Mason Publishing.

Haynes, M., and Jenkins, J. 1986. "Reading Instruction in Special Education Resource Rooms." *American Educational Research Journal*, Volume 23, issue 2, pp 161–190.

Hill, Clifford, and Larsen, Eric. 1983. "What Reading Tests Call For and What Children Do" (Final Report for Grant #G-78-0095). New York, NY: Columbia University, Teachers College, Institute for Urban and Minority Education and Program in Applied Linguistics.

Hoffman, James, and Clements, R. 1981. "A Descriptive Study of the Characteristics of Miscue Focused Verbal Interactions between Teacher and Student during Guided Oral Reading" (Final Report). Washington, DC: National Institute of Education. ERIC Document ED 200946.

Irwin, Pi, and Mitchell, Judith. 1983. "A Procedure for Assessing the Richness of Retellings." *Journal of Reading*, Volume 26, issue 5, pp 391–396.

Lindberg, Margaret. 1977. "A Descriptive Analysis of the Relationship between Selected 'Pre-Linguistic,' Linguistic, and Psycholinguistic Measures of Readability." Ph.D. diss., Wayne State University, Detroit, MI.

Lingren, Ernest. 1970. *The Art of the Film*. New York, NY: Collier Books.

Long, Catherine P. 1984. "The Effectiveness of the Reading Miscue Inventory and the Reading Appraisal Guide in Graduate Reading Programs." Ph.D. diss., University of Arizona, Tucson, AZ.

Marek, Ann M. 1987. "Retrospective Miscue Analysis as an Instructional Strategy with Adult Readers." Ph.D. diss., University of Arizona, Tucson, AZ.

Meek, Margaret. 1988. *How Texts Teach What Readers Learn.* England: Thimble Press.

Menosky, Dorothy. 1971. "A Psycholinguistic Description of Patterns of Miscues Generated during the Reading of Varying Positions of Text by Selected Readers from Grades Two, Four, Six and Eight." Ph.D. diss., Wayne State University, Detroit, MI.

Ministry of Education. 1985. *Reading in Junior Classes.* Wellington, New Zealand: Learning Media.

———. 1990. *Dancing with the Pen.* Wellington, New Zealand: Learning Media.

Mooney, Margaret. 1988. *Developing Life-long Readers.* Wellington, New Zealand: Ministry of Education.

Page, William D. 1973. "Clinic Uses of Miscue Research." In K. S. Goodman (ed.), *Miscue Analysis: Applications to Reading Instruction* (pp 65–76). Urbana, IL: ERIC and National Council of Teachers of English.

Piaget, Jean. 1971. *Psychology and Epistemology* (A. Rosin, trans.). New York, NY: Grossman.

Smith, Frank. 1988. *Joining the Literacy Club: Further Essays into Education.* Portsmouth, NH: Heinemann.

Stephenson, Marisu. 1980. "Using Principles of Miscue Analysis as Remediation for High School Students." Unpublished manuscript, University of Arizona, Tucson, AZ.

Taylor, Denny. 1991. *Learning Denied.* Portsmouth, NH: Heinemann.

———. 1993. *From the Child's Point of View.* Portsmouth, NH: Heinemann.

Vygotsky, Lev S. 1978. *Mind in Society.* Cambridge, MA: Harvard University Press.

Wilde, Sandra. 1993. *You Kan Red This!* Portsmouth, NH: Heinemann.

Wong, Bernice. 1987. "How Do the Results of Metacognitive Research Impact on the Learning Disabled Individual?" *Learning Disability Quarterly*, Volume 10, issue 2, pp 189–195.

Worsnop, Chris M. 1977. "A Procedure for Remedial Reading Instruction Based upon Miscue Analysis Research and Techniques." Unpublished manuscript, Canadian Education Department.

———. 1980. *A Procedure for Using the Technique of the Reading Miscue Inventory as a Remedial Teaching Tool with Adolescents.* ERIC Document ED 324644.

References for Stories Used by Readers

Babbitt, Natalie. 1975. *Tuck Everlasting*. New York, NY: Farrar, Straus, and Giroux.

"Bill Evers and the Tigers." 1972. In *My City*, ed. Bank Street College of Education. Toronto, Canada: Macmillan.

Branscum, Robbie. 1971. *Me and Jim Luke*. New York, NY: Doubleday.

Cachemaille, Christine. 1982. *Nick's Glasses*. Wellington, New Zealand: Learning Media.

"Can Earth Survive?" *Newsweek*, Fall 1981.

Cleaver, Vera, and Cleaver, Bill. 1970. *Where the Lilies Bloom*. Philadelphia, PA: J. B. Lippincott Co.

Coles, Joanna. 1986. *The Magic School Bus at the Waterworks*. New York, NY: Scholastic.

Corcoran, Barbara. 1977. *Make No Sound*. New York, NY: Atheneum.

Cowley, Joy. 1983. *Greedy Cat*. Wellington, New Zealand: Learning Media for Ministry of Education.

Crane, Stephen. 1963. "A Mystery of Heroism." In Thomas Gullason (ed.), *Complete Short Stories and Sketches of Stephen Crane*. New York, NY: Doubleday.

Crews, Donald. 1978. *Freight Train*. New York, NY: Greenwillow.

De Larrabeiti, Michael. 1978. *The Borribles*. New York, NY: Macmillan.

Donovan, John. 1969. *I'll Get There, It Better Be Worth the Trip: A Novel*. New York, NY: Harper & Row.

Goodman, Y. and Burke, Carolyn. 1972. "Why the Parrot Repeats Man's Words." In *Readings for Tapings*. New York, NY: Macmillan.

Goodrich, Frances. 1956. *The Diary of Anne Frank*. New York, NY: Random House.

Gurney, Gene. 1965. *Flying Aces of World War I*. New York, NY: Random House.

Hall, N. C. date unknown. *The Platt & Munk Treasury of Stories for Children*. New York, NY: Platt & Munk. Stories include: "The Country Mouse and the City Mouse," "The Boy and the North Wind," and "The Goosegirl."

Hayes, date unknown. "Pedro and Diablo." In *The Day It Snowed Tortillas*.

Kerr, Judith. 1972. *When Hitler Stole Pink Rabbit*. New York, NY: Coward, McCann & Geohegan.

Killilea, Marie. 1952. *Karen*. New York, NY: Prentice Hall.

Klein, Norma. 1973. *It's Not What You Expect*. New York, NY: Pantheon Books.

Krumgold, Joseph. 1967. *Henry 3*. New York, NY: Atheneum.

MacLean, Alistair. 1963. *Ice Station Zebra*. New York, NY: Fawcett Crest.

Morgan, Carol McAfee. 1955. "Anita's Gift." In *A New Home for Pablo*. New York, NY: Abelard-Schuman, Ltd.

Ortiz, Victoria. 1974. *Sojourner Truth, a Self-made Woman*. Philadelphia, PA: Lippincott.

Platt, Kin. 1968. *The Boy Who Could Make Himself Disappear*. Philadelphia, PA: Chilton.

Sharmate, Marjorie. 1972. *Nate the Great*. New York, NY: Coward McCann Geohegan.

Sobol, Donald. 1966. *Encyclopedia Brown*. New York, NY: Bantam Skylark.

Speare, Elizabeth George. 1961. *The Bronze Bow*. Boston, MA: Houghton Mifflin.

"The Man Who Kept House." date unknown. In *Treats and Treasures*. Toronto, Ontario: Nelson.

Van Allsburg, Chris. 1982. *Jumanji*. Boston, MA: Houghton Mifflin Company.

———1983. *The Wreck of the Zephyr*. Boston, MA: Houghton Mifflin Company.

Every effort has been made to include complete bibliographic information on the texts used in the retrospective miscue analysis sessions. Please excuse any omissions, and please send any additional reference information to the publisher.

Index

Abandoning a correct form 32
Accuracy 61, 64, 73, 74, 75, 82, 84–85, 98, 100, 120, 123, 124, 132–134, 138, 141, 174, 187, 204
Adolescent readers 96–97
Adult readers 3, 47, 51, 53, 71
Age 22, 42, 47
"Aha" moments 200
    See also Critical moment teaching
    See also Teachable moments
Allington, R. 103
Anxiety
    effects of 68
At-risk 108, 109, 113
Attendance patterns 108, 114, 154, 155
Attitudes 1, 6, 54, 65, 69–70, 87, 88, 97
    influence of grades on 124–126
    influence of RMA on 97–100
    and schooling 124–127
Atwell, N. 171
Authentic texts 15, 38, 164, 178
Authority of text 123–127
    See also Text reproduction model
Avoidance behavior 71

Background knowledge and experience 65, 98, 100, 114, 116, 135–136, 137, 139, 143, 147, 153, 194
Beliefs about reading 88–89, 92–95, 102, 111–112, 179
    conflicting with reader actions 96–97
    relation to strategies 87–88
    use of 95–96
    See also Perceptions about reading
    See also Self-perceptions
Bilingual readers 14
Bird, L. 199
Board, P. 9, 104, 149, 205
Bridges, A. 129
Brown, A.L. 102
Brown, J. 22
Bruner, J. 200
Buddy readers 198
Burke, C. 9, 18, 21, 24, 26, 34, 40, 41, 42, 52, 89, 90, 109, 110, 120, 143, 163, 178, 189

Cambourne, B. 181
Campione, J.C. 102
Case study 49
Clements, R. 103
Closing Interview 69–70, 215

Cloze stories 178, 186
Coding
    Procedure I
        miscue types for 26
        selecting miscues for 26, 28
        syntactic acceptability 28
    Procedure III 35–36
        graphic similarity 35
        meaning change 35
        semantic acceptability 35
        syntactic acceptability 35
    in RMA 42
Coding Form 27, 29–33
    Procedure I blank form 216–217
    Procedure III 35–36
Coherence 15
Cohesion 7, 15, 144, 160
Coles, R. 100
Collaborative Retrospective Miscue Analysis (CRMA) 3, 44, 165
    Early versions
        impact of 168, 169, 170
        protocol sheets 168, 169, 172
        questions 167
        sample lessons 170–172
        session organizers 173
        setting up for 166–167, 169, 170
        typescripts 166–167
    Later version 174–175
        lessons 174
        optimum group size 174
        role of the teacher 175
        text selection 174
Complex miscues
    substitutions 25
Comprehending 143
Comprehension 29, 51, 52, 53, 61, 109, 110
    Gina's 68
    Marlene's 75, 78, 79, 80, 81
Conceptual load 160
Confidence 15, 18–19, 38, 42, 52, 56, 63, 70, 82, 95, 98, 104, 155, 173, 206
    and selection of miscues for RMA 43
Confirming 23, 63, 93, 99, 121, 166, 171–172, 192
Constructing meaning/constructing meaning model 7, 10, 15, 17, 18, 23, 24, 69, 82, 96, 98, 100, 103, 109, 110, 111, 113, 116, 123, 139, 145, 147, 151, 158, 167, 175, 178, 186, 194, 200, 205–206
Context 15, 16, 67, 82, 117, 153
Control 69, 78, 100, 103, 104, 157, 158, 164, 206

Corrections 5, 23, 36, 45, 53, 57–58, 59, 61, 63, 64, 73, 74, 76,
    77, 85, 90, 93, 97–98, 103, 109, 121, 123, 124, 133, 134,
    138, 144, 146, 154, 173, 191, 195
    coding 26, 31–32
    as defined by Kari 122
    marking 26
    partial 32
    unsuccessful 32
    and patterns for grammatical relationships 34
    See also Abandoning a correct form
    See also Overcorrection
    See also Self-corrections
Costello, S. 44, 189
Cousin, P. 107
Critical teaching moments 190, 200
    See also "Aha" moments
    See also Teachable moments
CRMA
    See Collaborative Retrospective Miscue Analysis
Cultural difference 6, 14
Curriculum 22
Cycle of failure 16–17

Day, J.D. 102
Demystification of the reading process 38, 181, 203–205
Demythification of reading 203–205
Dependency
    See Instructional dependency
Development 34, 46–47, 53, 67–69, 111, 140
    of model of reading through RMA 56
Diagnosis 8, 13
Dialect 6, 9, 22, 24, 26, 29, 35, 64, 90, 127, 161–162, 164
    and coding sound similarity 33
Diaz, E. 107
Dictionary use for reading 7, 9, 46, 54, 55, 69, 72, 82, 95, 112,
    120, 132, 158, 172
Direct instruction 200–201
Disconfirming 23, 28, 32
Disequilibrium 18
Dyslexia/dyslexic 4, 8, 13, 14, 53, 71, 72

Eavesdropping on readers 39, 96
Eclecticism 56
Effective reading 8, 10, 25, 73, 74, 82, 86, 92, 95, 100, 103, 104,
    139, 171, 205
    documenting 52
Efficient reading 8, 10, 23, 25, 66, 74, 92, 95, 100, 103, 104, 110,
    113, 139, 171, 205
    and selection of miscues for RMA 43
English 28, 29, 90, 118, 135, 139
Environmental print 16
Expectancies of teacher/researcher in miscue analysis
    See Miscue analysts' expectancies
Expected response 21, 24, 32
Expression, reading with 56, 71

Flores, B. 107, 203–204
Flurkey, Alan 196–199
Fry Readability Formula 65, 79, 80

Genre 4, 34, 40, 41
    editorials 59
    fictional narratives 65
    informational 7
    nonfiction 65, 68, 123

and miscue patterns 65
and readability 65
Gist of the text 57, 60, 140
Good and poor readers 3, 5, 6, 7, 8, 75, 87–105, 119, 173, 204
    beliefs about reading 92–95
    initial models of reading 95
    knowledge of confirming process 93
    knowledge of cueing systems 93
    knowledge of predicting process 93, 94
    mythologies about 103
    time for revaluing 90
    unit of text focused on 95
Goodman, D. 177, 189
Goodman, K. 11, 21, 22, 29, 39, 40, 51, 110, 111, 112–113, 116,
    117, 129, 199
Goodman, Y. 9, 16, 18, 21, 24, 26, 34, 40, 41, 42, 51, 52, 89, 90,
    109, 110, 117, 120, 143, 163, 178, 189, 199
Goodman model of reading
    See Transactional sociopsycholinguistic model
Goodman Taxonomy 21
Grading
    and attitudes 124–126
Grammatical function 21, 28
Grammatical relationships 67, 79, 80, 81, 82
Grammatical transformations 21
Graphic similarity 21, 100, 103, 110, 134, 137, 144
    coding 32–33, 35
    Gina's 66, 67, 68
    Marlene's 79–82
Graphophonic cues 167, 179, 186, 204
    Bernice 132–3
    Gina 66, 68
    Kari 123
    Lucas 144
    and text difficulty 68, 152, 153, 198
Graphophonic system 22, 23
Grouping 165
    and teacher attitudes 125–126
Guessing 60, 120, 121, 177, 183, 192
    See also Prediction

Harste, J. 89
Haynes, M. 103
High-quality miscues 7, 24, 43, 45, 76, 110, 146, 153, 158, 191,
    193, 195
    increase in 69
Hill, C. 129
Hoffman, J. 103
Holistic approach/model 7, 11, 13, 89, 96, 99, 111, 141, 149
Hood, Wendy 194–196
Howard, Don 190–192

Ideating 112–113
Inference/inferencing 15, 16, 18, 23, 32, 121
    as defined by Kari 122
Initiation of reading 22
Insertions 7, 100, 103, 108, 127, 173
    coding 26
    marking 26
Instructional dependency 9, 16, 18, 72–73, 78, 98, 104, 149, 205
Instructional experiences 100
Instructional models 9, 14, 55–56
Instructional strategy 40
Interests 114–115

Intonation shifts 109
 coding 26
Irwin, P. 25

Jacobson, Debra 192–193
Jenkins, J. 103

Kindergarten and RMA 194
Kinesthetic approach 71, 132
Knowledge of the world 6
Knowledgeable professionals 199

Language 16, 22, 40, 92–93, 94, 102, 116
Language cueing systems 116, 166, 172, 178
 in RMA 45
 and reader talk 93
Language sense/knowledge 28
Larsen, E. 129
Learning disabled 4, 8, 13, 14, 152
Lindberg, M. 178
Lingren, E. 120
Linguistic knowledge
 descriptive 128–129
 prescriptive 128–129
Literacy Club 179
Literate environment 69, 180, 196
Long, C. 22

Making meaning 5
Making sense 45, 53, 59, 61–65, 76, 77, 78, 84–85, 120, 134, 135,
  136, 137, 140, 144, 145, 179, 193, 197, 206
Marek, A. 22, 131, 166, 189
Marking procedures 25–26, 34
 during RMA sessions 43
Meaning centered 5
Meaning change 178
 coding 30–31, 35
 compared across texts 67
 relation to semantic and syntactic acceptability 30
 and patterns for constructing meaning 33–34
Meek, M. 199
Memorization 9, 55, 56, 72–73, 138
Menosky, D. 25, 117
Metacognitive processing/talk 102, 116
Metalinguistic knowledge 49, 87, 92–93, 102–103
Metalinguistic talk 87
Metaphors 50, 93, 128–129
Mexican American 5, 107, 114
Ministry of Education of New Zealand 194
Misarticulations
 marking and coding 26
Misconceptions 7–8, 51, 58–59, 65, 96, 102
Miscue 21, 24, 166, 190–191
 concept of 96, 97
Miscue analysis 21
 relation to RMA 40
 unit of analysis 34
Miscue analysts' expectancies 24, 30, 33, 73, 84–85, 129
Miscue types 25–26
Miscues affected by analogies/idioms 162–163
Miscues affected by foreign language/language variation 159,
  161–162, 163–164
Miscues affected by text chunks 162–163
Miscues affected by unfamiliar names and words 159, 161–162
Miscues per hundred words 36
 Gina's 66, 67, 68

Kari's 123
 Marlene's 72, 79–82
Mitchell, J. 25
Models of reading
 See Constructing meaning/constructing meaning model
 See Holistic approach/model
 See Phonics model
 See Skills approach/model
 See Spell-it-out model
 See Subskills approach/model
 See Text reproduction model
 See Transactional sociopsycholinguistic model
 See Word oriented model
Mooney, M. 199
Motivation to read 4, 7, 65, 69, 73, 170, 182

Next word syndrome 16
Nonreader 14, 54, 71, 86, 179, 181, 182, 200
Nonwords 16, 36, 38, 83, 124, 125, 163, 193
 marking 26
 and miscue selection in CRMA 43

Observed response 21, 24, 26
Omissions 5, 46, 75, 92, 101, 103, 108, 120, 140, 146, 153, 159,
  173, 195
 marking 26
 coding 26
Overcorrection 66, 154
 and selection of miscues for RMA 43
Ownership 69, 73, 77, 84

Page, W. 129
Partials
 coding uncorrected partials 26
Pathologizing reading difficulty 14, 15
Patterns for constructing meaning 33–34
Patterns for grammatical relationships 34
Pauses
 marking and coding 26
Perceiving 112–113
Perceptions of reading 7, 10, 18, 38, 46–51, 52, 54–55, 56, 60,
  64–65, 69, 70, 79, 89, 93, 99, 102, 104, 112, 113,
  132–133, 147, 168, 174
 contradictions in 134, 173
 influence on strategies 100–101
 meaning construction views 98, 99
 relation to reading process 206
 text bound view 98, 99
 See also Constructing meaning/constructing meaning model
 See also Holistic approach/model
 See also Phonics model
 See also Skills approach/model
 See also Spell-it-out model
 See also Subskills approach/model
 See also Text reproduction model
 See also Transactional sociopsycholinguistic model
 See also Word oriented model
Perceptions of RMA 83
Perceptions of teaching 140
Perceptual information 15, 171–172
Perseverator 180–181
Phonics 102, 127
 See also Sound similarity
 See also Graphic similarity
Phonics model 56, 94

Phonological similarity
    See Sound similarity
Piaget, J. 18
Plain vanilla remedial readers 14
Practice 11, 14, 73, 83, 111, 170, 174, 182
Pragmatic knowledge 94
Predictability 65, 179, 193, 194
Prediction 15, 21, 23, 25, 32, 74, 75, 93, 94, 99, 101, 112, 116,
        117, 120, 137, 138, 139, 147, 166, 171–172, 177, 185,
        192, 195, 197–198
    awareness of strategy 53, 61
    as defined by Kari 122
    and partial acceptability (syntax) 28
    See also Guessing
Preselection of miscues 146
    See also Selection of miscues
Presenting 112–113
Proficient readers 14, 22, 51, 66, 75, 95, 103–104, 109, 110, 113,
        147, 167
Proficient reading 10, 23, 101, 123, 141, 171, 174
    influences on 100
Pronunciation 7, 9, 94, 95, 119, 137, 138, 158, 163
Punctuation 7, 128, 132, 145
Purpose 65

Questioning techniques 40

Readability 65
Reader characteristics
    and selection of miscues in RMA 42–43
Reader interests 18–19, 41, 65
Reader profile 36, 42, 52
Reader-selected miscues 42, 45, 157–164
    classifying 158, 161
    discussion of 163–164
    number of miscues selected 157
    procedure for 157
    qualitative examination of 159
Readers in trouble 15
Reading
    as decoding 6
    purposes for 7
Reading conferences 191
Reading Detective Club 183–187, 204
    kinds of clues 186
    origins 177
    relation to strategy lessons 178
    sample text 183–184
Reading Interview 9, 41, 51–52, 54, 56, 69–70, 72, 89, 93, 99,
        109–110, 111, 112, 132, 138, 209–210
    Burke Interview Modified for Older Readers 213–214
    Closing Interview 215
Reading Miscue Inventory (RMI) 21–22, 66, 143, 151, 178
    effects on attitudes 97–100
    familiarity with for research 88–89
    instructions to readers 25
    materials for 90
    Procedure I 22, 24–34, 66–67, 73, 79–81
        coding form 216–217
    Procedure II 22
    Procedure III 22, 34–38, 131
    Procedure IV 22
Reading models 53
    See also Models of reading
Reading process 21, 23, 24

Reading strategies
    See Strategies
Reading strategy lessons
    See Strategy lessons
Reading the world 170
Regressions 101, 103, 193, 197
    See also Repetitions
Remediation 4, 6, 10, 13, 16, 17
Repeated attempts 195
Repeated readings 92, 110
Repetitions
    marking 26
    See also Regressions
Retelling 98, 103, 109, 153, 154, 195
    Gina's 66
    Kari's 123
    Lucas's 143
    written form 178
Retelling guide 25
Retelling procedures 25, 34, 36
    alternate formats 41
    holistic scoring scale 25
    in RMA sessions 41, 46
Retrospective Miscue Analysis (RMA) 22, 38, 147, 165–166
    adaptation of 51
    case studies 49–50
    conduct of RMA session 43–47, 92
        arrangement of setting 44
        explaining to students 44
        guide for 44
        suggested discussion questions 45–46
    familiarity with for research 89
    impact of 69, 154–155
    initial session of 41, 90
    influences on readers 92, 118
    as instructional strategy 49, 118
    materials 90
    nature of reader participation 41
    non-formulaic use 201
    origins of 39, 149, 151–156
    outline of 47
    preparation for sessions 41–43, 90
    purposes of 40–47
    questions 45–46, 53, 92, 151–152, 167, 172
    reader/student reactions 73
    response form 90, 212
    selection of miscues 42
        for group work 43
        maximum number of preselected miscues 42, 52
        by student/reader 42, 45
        by teacher/researcher 42–43, 52–53
        use with younger children 42
    session organizer 90, 91, 211
    stance of teacher/researcher 39
    use of conferences 44
    use of jargon in 154
    use of logs 44
    use with groups 44
    used as instructional tool 40
    used as research tool 40
    and knowledge of RMI 39
    See also Revaluing
Revaluing 1, 3, 11, 15, 17–18, 39, 75, 86, 88, 90, 96, 101, 104,
        105, 111, 113, 128, 141, 146, 168, 181, 203, 205–207

Reversals 58
Risk taking 15, 18, 99, 138, 147, 153, 170, 174, 181, 182, 190, 193, 195, 205, 206
RMA
    See Retrospective Miscue Analysis
RMI
    See Reading Miscue Inventory

Sampling 23, 63, 99, 117, 121, 171–172
    as defined by Kari 122
Schema/schemata 23, 98
Second language influences 90
Selecting miscues 42–43, 90, 146
    See also Preselection of miscues
    See also Reader-selected miscues
    See also Retrospective miscue analysis
Selection of cues 15, 18, 23
    awareness of strategy in RMA 53
Selection of material 24–25, 92, 169, 195, 199
    in CRMA 174
    involvement of reader in RMA 41, 46
    and motivation 65
Self-blame 8, 17, 173
Self-correction 11, 21, 25, 88, 92, 94, 99, 101, 103, 132–133, 135, 136, 137, 146, 147, 154, 167, 172, 191, 193, 197
    example 32
    and miscue selection in RMA 42
    and partial acceptability 28
Self-evaluation of miscues 53, 79, 104, 172, 203
Self-monitoring 15, 18, 78, 79, 158, 162, 173
Self-perceptions 4–5, 10, 15, 17, 19, 23, 40, 41, 46, 49–50, 52, 53–69, 82, 83, 88, 104, 140–141, 143, 153, 155, 165, 168, 179, 187, 203
    blame 8, 17, 173
    carelessness 115–116, 117, 187
    cheater 4, 54, 59
    contradictions 8, 61, 173
    lack of trust 11
    laziness 8, 92, 96, 187
    not paying attention 123
    and selection of miscues in RMA 45
    See also Attitudes
Semantic acceptability 21, 25, 31, 36–37, 79, 88, 92, 100–101, 103, 110, 136, 143–144, 145, 175, 193
    coding 29, 35
    partial acceptability 29
    relation to corrections 77
    relation to meaning change 30
    relation to syntactic acceptability 29, 152
    and patterns for constructing meaning 33–34
    and patterns for grammatical relationships 34
    and selecting miscues for RMA 43
    See also Selecting miscues
Semantic system 15, 22, 23, 58, 173
Skills approach/model 7, 9, 14, 16, 89, 94
Skipping words/text 58, 69, 70, 72, 75, 93, 110, 120, 153, 155, 172
    See also Strategies, types of: skipping
Smith, F. 179
Social context 6
Sociopsycholinguistic transactional model
    See Transactional sociopsycholinguistic model
Sound similarity 21, 94, 100, 103, 144
    coding 33
    Gina's 66–68, 78–82

Sounding like language 45
Sounding out 7, 9, 14, 16, 18, 93, 95, 98, 100, 110, 127, 132, 137, 140, 172, 179, 180, 186, 195, 204
Spanish 5, 6, 90, 94, 107, 118, 138
Special education 4–5, 71
    See also Dyslexia/Dyslexic
    See also Learning disabled
Speed of reading 7, 8, 23, 42, 46, 54–55, 60, 75, 83, 92, 97, 108
Spell-it-out model 55–56, 57, 61, 73
Spelling 192, 198
Standardized tests
    See Tests
Statistical analysis 34, 35–36
Stoppers 74, 79
Strategies
    across the curriculum 191
    for coping 19
    knowledge of 102
    productive/non-productive 9, 18, 46, 52, 57
    relation to attitudes and beliefs 89
    types of
        ask someone 72, 98, 109, 110, 111–112, 132, 172, 198
        concentration 56, 60
        confirming 93, 99, 121, 179
        inferencing 121–122
        looking ahead 69, 137, 138, 191
        looking back 95
        memorization 56
        naming 90
        persevering 100
        predicting 93, 94, 120, 122, 179
        read-on 11, 54, 55, 61, 69, 93, 112, 120, 137, 138, 153, 158, 179, 186
        reread 69, 70, 93, 112, 179, 186, 191
        sampling 121, 122
        sense making 38, 57, 64, 80, 83, 93, 96, 97–98, 99, 102, 123, 127, 134, 137, 138, 169, 191
        skipping 11, 72, 93, 110, 111, 112, 117, 172
            See also Skipping
        substitution 82, 93, 103, 120
        terminating 23, 122, 172
        use of illustrations 195–196
    uncovering in RMA 45
    universality of 204
    and cueing systems 21, 23
    See also Confirming
    See also Dictionary use for reading
    See also Memorization
    See also Prediction
    See also Pronunciation
    See also Sampling
    See also Skipping words/text
    See also Sounding out
    See also Speed of reading
Strategy lessons 163, 178, 189
    across the curriculum 191
    naming 163
    similarity to RMA preselected miscue sessions 42
    whole class focus 170–172, 192
Stephenson, M. 131
Strengths 11, 15, 17, 38, 43, 52, 66, 146, 160, 167, 193
Subskills approach/model 7, 9, 89, 97–98
Substitutions 46, 57, 92, 100, 103, 108, 109, 115–116, 120, 123, 124, 125, 127, 134, 140, 141, 144, 160, 163, 164, 167, 169, 173

coding 26
  bound morphemes 26
  reversals 26
examples 28, 29, 30–31, 32–33, 35, 36–38
marking 25
  complex miscues 25
  involving bound morphemes 26
  nonword 26
  reversals 26
  and graphic similarity 36
  and semantic acceptability 37
  and syntactic acceptability 37
Surface text features 7–8
  and selecting miscues for RMA 43
See also Selecting miscues
Suspended judgement 120
Swiss cheese reader 180–181
Syntactic acceptability 21, 25, 31, 36–37, 79, 88, 92, 100–101,
    102, 103, 109, 110, 127, 144, 145, 175, 193
  coding 28, 35
  Gina's 67–78
  Kari's 123
  Marlene's 79–80
  partial acceptability 28
  relation to meaning change 30
  relation to semantic acceptability 29, 152
  and selection of miscues for RMA 43
Syntactic system 15, 22, 23, 58, 173

Talk about reading 87
  See also Metalinguistic talk
Taping 25, 34
  in RMA 41, 45
Task recognition 22
Taylor, D. 17, 118
Teachable moments 64
  See also "Aha" moments
  See also Critical teaching moments
Teacher judgment 88
Teacher-made miscues 190
Teacher ratings 22
Teacher/researcher 39–40, 42
Teacher response 98–99, 100, 124
Teacher role
  in CRMA 175, 181–182
  in RMA 18–19
Tentativeness 15, 74
Terminating 23, 122, 172
  as defined by Kari 122
Tests 6, 13, 14, 15, 17, 18, 104, 129, 149, 154, 179
  standardized 3, 4, 5, 7, 22, 88, 95, 96, 99, 103, 108, 119,
    131–132
  relation to RMI profiles 88
Text bound view 98, 99
  See also Text reproduction model
Text difficulty
  archaic vocabulary 82

complexity of ideas 17, 19
  in initial RMA session 41
  poor writing 17, 19
  and context for reading 104
  and graphophonic cues 68
  and predictability 65, 82
  See also Text selection
Text features 40, 158
  archaic vocabulary 82
  pattern 194
  redundancy 75
  unexpected syntax 160
  and illustration 194
  and predictability 65, 194
  See also Cohesion
  See also Miscues affected by analogies/idioms
  See also Miscues affected by foreign language/language variation
  See also Miscues affected by unfamiliar names and words
Text length 25, 117
  in CRMA 168
  effect on miscues 25, 43
  and strategy lessons 178
Text reproduction model 56, 110, 111, 141, 205
  See also Accuracy
  See also Word oriented model
Text selection
  See Selection of material
Textual authority
  and reader beliefs 96
Transactional sociopsycholinguistic model 1, 2, 11, 15, 22, 23, 39,
    104, 111, 112, 117, 203
Transcripts 42, 46, 90
Typescript preparation 25, 34–35, 90
Typescripts
  marking miscues 26
  use in CRMA 166–167
  use in RMA 43, 131

Vocabulary 57, 82, 113, 153, 164
Volume of reading 55
Vygotsky, L. 203

Watson, D. 9, 18, 21, 24, 26, 34, 40, 41, 42, 52, 89, 90, 109, 110,
    120, 143, 163, 178, 189
Weakness 11, 17, 52
Weatherill, David 189
Whole language 22, 180, 186, 199
Wilde, S. 192
Wong, B. 87
Word attack 16
Word identification 18, 59
Word oriented model 56–69, 98, 99, 110, 113, 139, 145, 149, 180,
    198, 204
Worsnop, C. 39, 44, 131, 149, 166, 189
Writing 19–20, 124, 198
Written language 16, 57